WRITING PROGRAM ADMINISTRATION AT SMALL LIBERAL ARTS COLLEGES

Writing Program Administration
Series Editors: Susan H. McLeod and Margot Soven

The Writing Program Administration series provides a venue for scholarly monographs and projects that are research- or theory-based and that provide insights into important issues in the field. We encourage submissions that examine the work of writing program administration, broadly defined (e.g., not just administration of first-year composition programs). Possible topics include but are not limited to 1) historical studies of writing program administration or administrators (archival work is particularly encouraged); 2) studies evaluating the relevance of theories developed in other fields (e.g., management, sustainability, organizational theory); 3) studies of particular personnel issues (e.g., unionization, use of adjunct faculty); 4) research on developing and articulating curricula; 5) studies of assessment and accountability issues for WPAs; and 6) examinations of the politics of writing program administration work at the community college.

BOOKS IN THE SERIES

The WPA Outcomes Statement—A Decade Later, edited by Nicholas Behm, Gregory Glau, Deborah Holdstein, Duane Roen, and Edward M. White (2012)

GenAdmin: Theorizing WPA Identities in the 21st Century by Colin Charlton, Jonikka Charlton, Tarez Samra Graban, Kathleen J. Ryan, and Amy Ferdinandt Stolley (2011)

WRITING PROGRAM ADMINISTRATION AT SMALL LIBERAL ARTS COLLEGES

Jill M. Gladstein and
Dara Rossman Regaignon

Parlor Press
Anderson, South Carolina
www.parlorpress.com

Parlor Press LLC, Anderson, South Carolina, USA

Printed in the United States of America

SAN: 254-8879

Library of Congress Cataloging-in-Publication Data

Gladstein, Jill M., 1968-
  Writing program administration at small liberal arts colleges / Jill M. Gladstein and Dara Rossman Regaignon.
     p. cm. -- (Writing Program Adminstration)
  Includes bibliographical references and index.
  ISBN 978-1-60235-304-6 (pbk. : alk. paper) -- ISBN 978-1-60235-305-3 (alk. paper) -- ISBN 978-1-60235-306-0 (adobe ebook) -- ISBN 978-1-60235-307-7 (epub)
  1. English language--Rhetoric--Study and teaching--United States. 2. Report writing--Study and teaching (Higher)--United States. 3. Writing centers--Administration. 4. Small colleges--United States. 5. Education, Humanistic--United States. I. Regaignon, Dara Rossman. II. Title.
  PE1405.U6G55 2012
  808'.042071173--dc23
                              2012005637

                    1 2 3 4 5

Cover background by Lisa-Blue, © 2010. Used by permission
Cover design by David Blakesley
Printed on acid-free paper.

Parlor Press, LLC is an independent publisher of scholarly and trade titles in print and multimedia formats. This book is available in paper, cloth and eBook formats from Parlor Press on the World Wide Web at http://www.parlorpress.com or through online and brick-and-mortar bookstores. For submission information or to find out about Parlor Press publications, write to Parlor Press, 3015 Brackenberry Drive, Anderson, South Carolina, 29621, or e-mail editor@parlorpress.com.

Contents

List of Figures and Tables   *vii*

Foreword: Writing Programs at Liberal Arts Colleges:
  Treasures in Small Packages   *ix*
    Carol Rutz

Acknowledgments   *xiii*

Introduction: Studying Writing Program
  Administration at Small Liberal Arts Colleges   *xv*

I A Grounded Theory of Writing Program Administration   *3*

  1 The Small Liberal Arts College Structure of Feeling   *5*

  2 Grounded Theory and Mixed Methods Research   *23*

  3 Mapping Small College Sites of Writing   *35*

  4 Configurations of Writing Program Leadership   *42*

  5 Positioning of Writing Program Administrators   *67*

II Curriculum-Centered Writing Instruction   *93*

  6 Writing Requirements   *95*

  7 Staffing First-Year Writing   *120*

  8 Redefining Small College Writing Programs: Leadership
    Configurations and Writing Requirements   *139*

III Student-Centered Writing Instruction   *155*

  9 Writing Centers   *157*

  10 Supporting Diversely Prepared Writers   *170*

IV Small College Writing Programs   *187*

  11 Assessment   *189*

  12 Conclusion   *203*

Appendix A: List of Schools Invited to Complete the Survey   *213*
Appendix B: Writing at SLACs Survey   *215*
Appendix C: Initial E-mail Invitation to Complete the Survey   *227*
Appendix D: Supplemental Tables   *229*
Appendix E: Assessment Materials from Occidental College   *231*
Appendix F: List of Questions for Schools to Consider when
    Investigating Writing Program Structures   *236*

Notes   *237*
Works Cited   *243*
Index   *261*
About the Authors   *271*

List of Figures and Tables

Figures

3.1 Writing Program Structures *37*

5.1abc Comparison of Responsibilities within Explicit
Leadership Positions *71–73*

5.2 Comparison of Responsibilities between *Solo WPA/WCD* and *WCD Only* Leadership Configurations *74*

5.3 Comparison of Responsibilities within Writing Center Leadership
Configurations *75*

7.1 Enrollment Caps for FYC and FYWS *122*

7.2 Comparison of First-Year Writing Faculty Status *125*

7.3 Comparison of Types of Courses Taught by FYC and FYWS Faculty *126*

8.1 Distribution of Writing Requirements over Leadership Configurations *141*

8.2 Comparison of Leadership Configurations in Relation to FYC and
FYWS *143*

Tables

4.1 Leadership Positions beyond the Primary WPA/WCD *48*

4.2 Leadership Configurations at 100 Small Liberal Arts Colleges *65*

5.1 Classification of the SLAC WPA/WCD Position in Comparison with
Other National Surveys *79*

5.2 Comparison of National Survey Data on the Degrees of WPAs and
WCDs *80*

5.3 Status of WPA and WCD Positions within Different Leadership
Configurations *86*

6.1 Writing Requirements at Small Colleges *97*

6.2 Verticality of Writing Requirements *118*

7.1 Faculty Development at Small Colleges *137*

8.1 Distribution of Leadership Configurations over
   Writing Requirements   *146*

9.1 Location of the Writing Center on Campus   *161*

9.2 Staffing of the Writing Center   *163*

9.3 Writing Center Staff Size (Schools with a 100% Undergraduate Staff) *165*

9.4 Writing Center Staff Size (Schools with a Mixed Staffing Model) *165*

9.5 Training Offered to Writing Center Tutors   *167*

10.1 Methods of Identification of Underprepared Students   *178*

10.2 Support Provided to Underprepared Students   *184*

11.1 Types of Writing Assessment at Small Colleges   *195*

D.1 Age of W Course Requirement   *229*

D.2 Length of Time as the WPA   *229*

D.3 Number of People Involved in Administering Writing "Program"   *229*

D.4 Number of Course Releases Assigned to WPA   *230*

E.1 Occidental College's Features Rubric   *234*

E.2 Occidental College's Research Rubric   *235*

Foreword

Writing Programs at Liberal Arts Colleges: Treasures in Small Packages

Carol Rutz

Question: Why write a book about the administration of writing programs in small liberal arts colleges (SLACs) that collectively account for only about five percent of the post-secondary options available to students in the U.S.? *Writing Program Administration at Small Liberal Arts Colleges* offers answers to that question based on top-notch research. By collecting and analyzing comparative data on writing programs, the authors demonstrate that SLACs exhibit a culture of long-standing commitments to writing and writing instruction; SLACs organize writing programs in creative ways; SLACs, though small in scale, can achieve institutional agility difficult for large universities; and SLACs have much to learn from one another—and much to teach colleagues at other, larger institutions.

Far from being negligible in the greater pantheon of higher education, the SLAC acts out a historical commitment to liberal education rooted in rhetoric, both written and spoken. Smaller institutional and class sizes allow for greater interaction between faculty and students, often resulting in focused attention on writing to learn, writing in the disciplines, and writing across the curriculum. The SLAC mission typically specifies citizenship and communication as institutional goals, and small schools take their missions seriously, actively working with alumni to update expectations of employers, graduate and professional schools, and service opportunities.

Much has been written about the tendency of graduate programs to replicate themselves by preparing graduate students for tenure-track teaching and administrative positions in research institutions. However, as study after study reports, graduate students in all fields are wise to broaden their job search strategies as they seek to put their graduate degrees to work. Toward that end, graduate programs are beginning to inform their faculty and graduate students about opportunities at regional universities, community colleges, proprietary institutions, the corporate world, non-profits, and yes, SLACs.

At SLACs, a writing program may consist of required courses, writing across the curriculum, writing in the major, or perhaps required or optional capstone projects with a thesis component. The program may be housed in a department (often English), and it may include a writing center staffed with professional tutors, undergraduate peer tutors, or professional staff responsible for training and supervising undergraduates. In some cases, the writing center is separate from the curricular components of the writing program, and an independent, non-departmental writing curriculum may be staffed with one or more professionals charged with faculty development, assessment, and outreach. As the authors observe, some of the organizational features of SLAC writing programs reveal long-standing practices based more in tradition than in function. Nevertheless, SLACs can adapt to changing expectations, often embracing a challenging new idea more easily than a larger institution.

However a SLAC writing program is configured, it serves a common institutional mandate: teaching and assessing writing skills as a learning outcome. Writing lends itself well to assessment, and assessment methods work best when tailored to local situations. SLACs teach and support writing in a variety of ways—carefully documented in this volume—that can support thoughtful assessment as well. However, the busy WPA at one SLAC may be unaware of assessment programs at similar institutions. The authors of this book show through multiple methods that good answers to common (and vexing!) questions reside in colleagues' experiences. A phone call between writing program administrators, writing center directors, deans, or program faculty may open up possibilities invisible to problem-solvers at a given site. In this sense, the authors promote collaboration across campuses and consortia in search of innovative ideas.

Readers from SLACs will find that their local writing program, whatever its design, is represented in the authors' exhaustive inventory, along with other models well worth consideration. Anyone who wants to know the likelihood that a SLAC has, say, a writing center separate from an academic department can find the answer here—as well as data on FTE, assessment methods, staff vs. faculty appointments, and much more. As a reference, readers will be impressed with the range and completeness of the research.

Most important, however, is the deep understanding of the SLAC world reflected by the authors, and theorized through data and experience. Those who prepare WPAs for jobs in all kinds of schools will find the insights here relevant as they teach and advise graduate students. Readers currently at SLACs will understand their own institutions better in the context of the larger SLAC universe—a universe of surprising variety, innovation, and commitment to writing instruction and administration.

Acknowledgments

Pomona and Swarthmore Colleges have been generous in their support for this project, providing funds that furthered this research in a variety of ways—including for the several face-to-face meetings that a bi-coastal collaborative writing project requires. Any endeavor such as this also owes much to the time, patience, wit, and insight of friends and colleagues. Lisa Lebduska collaborated with us on the design of the survey, helped with data collection, and contributed to the literature review. Mary Buchner, Katy Johnson, Yancy Liao, Stephanie Liu, Anna Lyczmanenko, Andrew Ragni, Chelcie Rowell, and Tiffany Tsai all served as research assistants, showing skill and care in the painstaking and at times burdensome tasks we gave them. We are grateful to Jeff Ludwig for his careful copy-editing of the manuscript. Our thanks to Gretchen Rossman and Melissa Nicholas for helpful feedback on early drafts of several chapters (and to the former for methodological reassurance, as well). Sue McLeod, Margot Soven, Dave Blakesley, and our anonymous reviewer from Parlor Press all provided crucial feedback; Dave has also been a gentle shepherd throughout the editing process. Carol Rutz and Brenda Boyle read drafts of the complete manuscript, helping us focus and refine it in the final stages. Finally, our audiences at the CWPA Conference in 2010; the SLAC-WPA Conferences in 2009 and 2010; Franklin and Marshall College; and Haverford College were essential early audiences and helped us to clarify our arguments. We would also like to thank Ann Jurecic, Barb Lutz, Deb Martinson, Kim McDonald, and Kerry Walk for the time they all spent listening to us talk about this project and its process.

Jill would also like to thank her colleagues at Swarthmore College for their support and guidance. I would like to thank Diane Anderson for providing perspective, Ken Sharpe for his practical wisdom, Peter Schmidt for his words of encouragement, and Ellen Magenheim for always listening. I also would like to thank the many writing associates who provided support and understanding as I attempted to balance the demands of the program with the desire to write this book. My friends and family deserve my gratitude for always being there when I needed a little bit of encouragement. To Barry and Amy Gladstein, who provided guidance on some of the visuals represented in the book, and to my parents, Joyce and Lee Gladstein, for hosting a writing retreat. Finally, I want to thank K'Ton Ton for our early morning walks that served both as a stress relief and also as a place where the writing process was given a space to flourish away from the confines of the computer.

Dara would also like to thank her colleagues in English and beyond at Pomona College; their support as this project developed has been invaluable. In particular, I've appreciated the sympathy and enthusiasm of Pam Bromley, Cecilia Conrad, Kevin Dettmar, Oona Eisenstadt, Kathleen Fitzpatrick, Katherine Hagedorn, Stephanie Harves, Nina Karnovsky, Kyla Tompkins, and Meg Worley. (While I cannot thank every faculty member who taught ID1 between 2005 and 2011, I am sorely tempted.) Anne Dwyer and Erin Runions are the best of writing groups, at once challenging and fun; David Menefee-Libey and Bob Gaines helped me better understand the norms of collaborative work and writing. Mariama and Anya Regaignon have provided perspective throughout, and Greg Tzeutschler Regaignon helps me stay balanced—and balancing.

This book is dedicated to the writing program administrators and writing center directors who work at small liberal arts colleges—our fellow SLACers. This book emerged from our only partly selfish desire to get them all into a single room to talk about writing programs at small schools. Their drive, determination, creativity, and generosity have never stopped surprising us, even as we grow to count on it as a feature of the SLAC community. We hope that this book helps them as much as they have helped us.

Introduction: Studying Writing Program Administration at Small Liberal Arts Colleges

We began this inquiry with a superficially simple question: "What, exactly, does writing program administration at private small liberal arts colleges look like?" In fact, as the many scholars mapping the field of writing program administration in the twenty-first century can attest, the sheer number of different programs makes any version of this question a daunting one. National studies of different types of writing programs—first-year composition, first-year English, writing across the curriculum, writing centers—and of corresponding writing administrator positions provide glimpses, but the researchers describe the difficulties inherent in simply gathering the data, not to mention those involved in understanding the similarities and differences across institutions when every program and position is necessarily oriented to serving its local context (see Charlton and Rose; Knight and Isaacs; Skeffington, Borrowman, and Enos; Thaiss and Porter; and the Writing Centers Research Project).

To date, there has been no empirical, national study of writing programs at private small liberal arts colleges. Recent studies by Melinda Knight and Emily Isaacs; Jillian Skeffington, Shane Borrowman, and Theresa Enos; and Chris Thaiss and Tara Porter have all included small colleges and private universities. These studies have broken their data down by institutional size, but they do not provide analysis of what impact size might have. Pamela Bromley, Kara Northway, and Eliana Schonberg provide a deeper analysis of how size may matter in their comparative study of writing centers at a small private college, a mid-size private university, and a large public university. Small liberal arts colleges also appear occasionally in representative essays in collections on other topics, but this is not a form that allows us to generalize about the range of programs and positions at this type of institution (see Cornell and Newton; Fremo; and Rutz). None of the studies we reviewed discuss the impact being a public (or private) institution has on the delivery of writing instruction. Indeed, while we might speculate that public institutions are characterized by greater bureaucratic complexity and find themselves under increased pressure to be accountable than their private counterparts, we have found no systematic analysis of this question.

Seeking to address the absence of small colleges of all types from the scholarly literature, Gretchen Flesher Moon, Patricia Donahue, Thomas Amorose, Paul Hanstedt, and others formed the Small College Special Interest Group affiliated with the Conference on College Composition and Communication (CCCC) in the late 1990s (see Hanstedt and Amorose), which in turn inspired two scholarly projects: "One would survey general pedagogical and administrative issues; the other would examine gaps in the historical record" (Donahue and Moon xiii). With the publication of a special issue of *Composition Studies* on the small college and the university in 2004, and of *Local Histories* in 2007, both of these projects saw the light of day, although neither collection includes an empirical study of multiple institutions.[1] *Writing Program Administration at Small Liberal Arts Colleges* extends these efforts by presenting data and analyses from one hundred private small liberal arts colleges in the United States. These analyses are the result of mixed methods, grounded theory research. The primary instrument was a ninety-seven-question survey sent to individuals at 137 schools in the summer of 2009. These schools were drawn from the Annapolis Group membership and from the baccalaureate, liberal arts schools participating in the Higher Education Data Sharing Consortium (see Appendix A for a complete list of the schools invited to participate). Of the initial 137 possible participants, 109 (80%) responded to the survey. We then followed up by email with respondents to gather supplemental data to clarify their responses; triangulated the survey data by analyzing site documents, such as institutional and program websites and college catalogs; and conducted both individual and focus group interviews. (We include the initial email request and the survey in Appendices B and C, respectively; see Chapter 2 for a full discussion of our methodology.)

Our most significant finding concerns the impetus for professionalizing writing programs and positions at small colleges. Perhaps surprisingly, it develops when institutions focus on and value writing across the curriculum (WAC)—not first-year composition. Therefore, professionalization often involves making WAC structures that have developed organically more explicit, intentional, and vertical. The deliberate ownership of an institution's culture of writing across the curriculum is strongly associated with greater verticality in the writing curriculum and more extensive and professionalized leadership for the writing program. Writing programs at small colleges are not typically contained within single departments, and their structures are rarely coextensive with the administrative positions that lead them.

It is our hope that this picture will bring these institutions into greater focus for the field of writing program administration and that, as a result, our understanding of WPA work as a whole will be complicated and enriched.[2] While any presentation of the "best" approaches to writing instruction at small colleges lies beyond the scope of this project, here we offer some of the most significant ways in which small college writing programs seem to differ from national expectations. First, the writing programs in the sample are informed by a notion of "program" that is more elastic and amorphous than that which appears in much of the WPA literature. These institutions are likely to have—and to need to be aware of—a variety of sites of writing instruction. Second, the logic, ethos, and structures of writing across the curriculum are more pervasive at these institutions than seems to be typical of larger universities. Third, and perhaps most strikingly, these are institutions that, in 2010, are in the midst of change—change that focuses not on introducing writing as a new value, but rather on surfacing and supporting a longstanding commitment to writing and writing instruction.

Writing Program Administration at Small Liberal Arts Colleges

I

A Grounded Theory of Writing Program Administration

1 The Small Liberal Arts College Structure of Feeling

It is, Sir, as I have said, a small college. And yet there are those who love it.

—Daniel Webster

In laying the foundation of a thorough education, it is necessary that all the important mental faculties be brought into exercise. It is not sufficient that one or two be cultivated, while others are neglected. A costly edifice ought not to be left to rest upon a single pillar. . . . The mind never attains its full perfection, unless its various powers are so trained as to give them the fair proportions which nature designed. . . . By frequent exercise on written composition, [the student] acquires copiousness and accuracy of expression. By extemporaneous discussion, he becomes prompt, and fluent, and animated. It is a point of high importance, that eloquence and solid learning should go together; that he who has accumulated the richest treasures of thought, should possess the highest powers of oratory. To what purpose has a man become deeply learned, if he has no faculty of communicating his knowledge? And of what use is a display of rhetorical elegance, from one who knows little or nothing which is worth communicating?

—Committee of the Corporation and the Academical Faculty, Yale College

In global terms, small liberal arts colleges are an unusual type of higher education institution. Distinctively American, their current missions and ethos tie them closely to the history of higher education in the

United States, and particularly to the many institutions founded before the Civil War. In this chapter, we outline that history, with a particular focus on the role of writing and rhetoric in it. In doing so, we describe how the culture and ethos of private small liberal arts colleges in the twenty-first century is tied to their material conditions—most notably, their size.

Before the late-nineteenth-century rise of the research university, *all* institutions of higher education in the United States were what we would now recognize as private small liberal arts colleges: They were small, they were residential, and they were more or less what we currently understand as private.[1] The education offered at *all* these institutions was primarily aimed at preparing young men to become sectarian ministers and missionaries. Our epigraphs recall this moment, and give a direct taste of antebellum rhetoric concerning higher education. In *Dartmouth v. Woodward*, Daniel Webster offered the argument that ultimately led to the Supreme Court's decision to protect Dartmouth College from direct governance by the New Hampshire state legislature. This decision is the first basis for the distinction between public and private institutions of higher education in the United States, and Webster's emotional invocation of Dartmouth's size in this context is striking. The reference is at once modest and proud. Dartmouth's size, it seems, would justify the Court disregarding the New Hampshire legislature's decision to administer the college directly; size also seems to have inspired passionate loyalty in alumni such as Webster himself. It is thus offered as one of the determinative features of the college, a material fact with a clear affective dimension.

Just over a decade later, the faculty at Yale College responded to a different sort of challenge to a liberal arts education. Responding to curricular reforms at institutions including Amherst and Harvard Colleges and the University of Vermont, the Yale faculty issued a report defending non-professional, residential, undergraduate education as the central mission of American institutions of higher education. Defending the study of Greek and Latin, the *Yale Report* also emphasizes the centrality of writing and rhetoric to undergraduate education. To this early nineteenth-century faculty, knowledge without the ability to communicate that knowledge is purposeless. Although no school in the current study still adheres to the curriculum the *Yale Report* elaborates and defends, written and spoken language instruction still pervade the education offered at the schools discussed here.[2] In their 2010 *CCC* article reporting on the WAC/WID Mapping Project, Chris Thaiss and Tara Porter note that 51% of the roughly 1,200 U.S. institutions in their sample have identifiable writing across the curriculum (WAC) programs (540); by contrast, 92 of the 100 schools in our sample have writing across the curriculum. Small colleges, it seems, are twice as likely to have writing across the curriculum as the national norm. That is a striking (if crude) statistic, one that resonates with something that historians have noted about the early years of the modern WAC movement: that it began, in the 1970s and 1980s, at small liberal arts colleges.[3]

The one hundred schools we discuss throughout this book are small, private, undergraduate, liberal arts colleges. Although each of these institutions is committed to the notion that it is unique, we found that their common size and shared genealogy have produced a common set of values, foci, and practices. We use Raymond Williams' concept of *structure of feeling* to describe the common ethos of these schools because Williams developed the concept in order to understand the relation between the personal and the social. In *Marxism and Literature*, Williams defines "structures of feeling" as "meanings and values as they are actively lived and felt, and the relations between these and formal or systematic beliefs" (132). A structure of feeling, he writes, designates "a social experience which is still in progress, often indeed not yet recognized as social but taken to be private, idiosyncratic, and even isolated" (132). Upon analysis, Williams continues, it nonetheless "has its emergent, connecting, and dominant characteristics" (132). A structure of feeling has form and is rooted in material and historical conditions. This concept therefore provides a way to understand, first, how the shared values and assumptions of small colleges are grounded in their material conditions and history. Second, because structures of feeling are always and continually "*in process*," as Williams puts it (132), this concept simultaneously illuminates the anti-bureaucratic, anti-formalist bias of these institutions *and* the ways in which, in fact, they have always and continue to formalize particular values. In our presentation here of the small college structure of feeling, we present their shared history in order to articulate the institutional culture of small liberal arts colleges—the central tendencies of this diverse and heterogeneous set of small schools.[4]

RESIDENTIAL AND LIBERAL ARTS

In *The Founding of American Colleges and Universities Before the Civil War*, Donald G. Tewksbury identifies twelve "permanent colleges"—that is, still in existence in 1932, when he was writing—as being founded in the 1820s, up from seven in the previous decade (16). The number nearly tripled in the 1830s, when Tewksbury identifies 35 new colleges. After a plateau in the 1840s, the number doubled again in the 1850s, to 66 (16). Throughout their early decades, all of these institutions struggled to stay open (Pfnister 147; Potts; Rudolph 177–201). Tewksbury provides a framework for understanding how U.S. higher education developed in direct and striking contrast to the form it had taken in European countries. In particular, he focuses on the early conditions that produced the U.S. as a "land of neighborhood colleges" (3). The early U.S. college, he contends, "was typically a frontier institution" (1). This was true from the earliest days of higher education in North America: when Harvard University was founded as "Newe College" in 1636, for example, its buildings were surrounded by a stockade, and Newe Towne (now Cambridge, MA) was considered the frontier (Tewksbury 1–2). This position on the "frontier" was one factor in the American importation of the custom of residential learning from England (Rudolph 26). In continental Europe, universities founded in well-established cities more often relied on residents of the town to provide lodgings for students. For ideological and practical reasons, the colleges built in part to shore up the identities of frontier towns had to provide places for their students to live.

If the U.S. was a land of neighborhood colleges during the first half of the nineteenth century, it was a land whose neighborhoods were defined in religious as well as geographic terms. As Tewksbury points out, "practically all the colleges founded between the Revolution and the Civil War were organized, supported, and in most cases controlled by religious interests" (55). The goal of these institutions was to prepare young men to become ministers or teachers; the dramatic expansion in numbers of colleges in the first half of the nineteenth century, then, was a product of the missionary fervor associated with the Second Great Awakening. Frontier communities—established ever-farther westward—were imagined by the various Protestant denominations as needing colleges to train local men to become ministers for those towns and their surrounding areas (on frontier colleges, see Pfnister). Eastern colleges tended to imbue their graduates with a sense of mission to reproduce their alma maters further west; the preponderance of originally Congregationalist and Presbyterian colleges west of the Mississippi can in fact be traced directly to the relatively high enrollments at Yale and Princeton during these decades (Tewksbury 70–74).

Starting in the 1870s, colleges in the U.S. began to increasingly model themselves on German research universities. While "colleges" had been primarily concerned with educating the next generation of civic and religious leaders, the new "universities" were primarily focused on the production and dissemination of new knowledge. This had myriad consequences. Instead of a place of general education, the university became a place of specialization. Faculty came to be scholars and researchers first and teachers second. Institutions of higher education had been growing larger and developing increasingly diverse objectives since the first of the Morrill Land Grant Acts was passed in 1862. The Morrill Act specifically called for universities to "teach such branches of learning as are related to agriculture and the mechanic arts" (7 U.S.C. Sec. 304). Whether it was educating future scholars or future professionals, the nineteenth-century university departed from the colonial and antebellum college in understanding its purpose as that of professionalizing students. Institutions that resisted the shift, even as they slowly embraced the university's organizational, curricular, and pedagogical innovations—as well as its mandate to contribute to the production of new knowledge—are, by and large, those we now identify as liberal arts colleges. (This too-brief historical sketch relies heavily on the work of Brereton, *Origins*; Crowley; Lucas; Oakley; Rudolph; Russell, *Writing*; and Tewksbury.)

Because small liberal arts colleges are institutions that resisted this massive reform, it is perhaps easy to imagine them as instances of an inherently conservative educational type. In certain ways, this view misunderstands that moment of differentiation (Pfnister 158–60). The historical record suggests that the late nineteenth century's expansion of higher education opportunities was a complex moment. Some liberal arts colleges pre-date the rise of the research university by decades; Amherst College, for example, was founded in 1821 on the classical model drawn from Oxford and Cambridge, and was the site of aborted curricular reform shortly thereafter (Rudolph 122–24). By the 1870s, however, Amherst was holding conservatively onto the classical curriculum and its mandate to train future missionaries. By contrast, many women's colleges (including Vassar, Wellesley, and Bryn

Mawr) and historically black colleges (such as Morehouse and Spelman) were founded during the second half of the nineteenth century. For these schools, adopting the classical curriculum associated not just with Oxford and Cambridge but also with Yale and Princeton was a daring act, suggesting that female students and students of color were capable and worthy of undertaking the course of study designed to produce public intellectuals and leaders.[5] Thus, while some individuals and institutions saw modernity as demanding a new type of higher education, others saw the liberal arts college as serving an important function for the new century.

The foundational curriculum for all these institutions was the so-called "classical curriculum" that had formed the basis of Oxford and Cambridge educations for centuries. This curriculum centered on the study of Latin and Greek languages and literatures, as well as philosophy, rhetoric and logic, history, and mathematics. It prescribed the course of study for all students for all four years. Designed originally to provide a preparatory grounding for young men with a religious avocation—who would become priests or ministers—it was closely associated with the education of the elite. Indeed, this difficult generalist educational program was imagined to form the moral and mental fiber of future leaders. But while U.S. institutions imported this curriculum and its structural relationship to class, they also adapted it to the demands of their particular local situations. As a result, an approach that Frederick Rudolph calls a "parallel course of study" was developed (111). In institutions with a parallel course, students could choose at the outset of their college careers to follow either the classical curriculum or an alternate course, which typically included modern languages, applied mathematics, and science or social science. Both courses prescribed the students' educations for the next four years, and students could not easily switch between the two. Lafayette College was founded in 1824 with a mandate to serve first-generation college students and specifically promising to include the study of modern languages in its regular curriculum (Rudolph 113). Union College, founded in 1828, from the outset offered two parallel courses of study: Students could pursue the traditional, classical curriculum *or* they could choose a course of study that focused on modern languages, mathematics, and science (Rudolph 114). Rudolph argues that this alternative course of study helped make Union one of the most popular pre-Civil War colleges: "By 1829 it stood third in enrollment among American colleges, and by 1839 it was second only to Yale" (114).

The 1820s saw the rise of such parallel courses and, at the same time, a number of even more radical educational and curricular experiments, including: faculties (rather than dormitories) as the organizing principle of the university; elective systems of study; and the possibility of concentrating on specific areas of study (Rudolph 115–124; Urofsky). In 1827, the faculty of Yale College was asked to review that institution's approach to education, specifically investigating the question of whether it should replace or supplement the study of classical languages with modern languages. The faculty's response—now commonly known as the *Yale Report of 1828*—was literally a reactionary and conservative document. It defends both the study of classical languages and the non-professionalizing nature of a liberal arts education. Published in *The American Journal of Science and Arts* in 1829, the *Report* had immediate and wide circulation.

The *Yale Report* is divided into two sections. The first challenges the trend toward both electives and student specialization, insisting on the importance of a prescribed curriculum. The second defends the focus of that prescribed curriculum on Latin and Ancient Greek, insisting that such study—by virtue of its very difficulty—provides the kind of mental discipline that prepares undergraduates to pursue any course of study deeply, or any profession successfully, thereafter. The Yale faculty insists that the very similarity of modern languages' grammar to English makes them unfit for this purpose (*Yale Report* 38). Throughout, the *Report* underscores the values of community and close colloquy between faculty and students, and among students themselves. Indeed, it remains a resonant articulation of the purpose and goals (the structure of feeling, if not the method) of a liberal arts education in the twenty-first century.

We can see this in the passage below, which articulates a vision of the undergraduate education as offering an invaluably preparatory education that "strengthen[s] and enlarge[s] the faculties of the mind" through the wide-ranging and disciplined study of the liberal arts (30). The Yale faculty insists that their object is not to

> *finish* [the undergraduate's] education; but to lay the foundation and to advance as far in rearing the superstructure, as the short period of his residence here will admit. . . . He has, at least, been taught *how* to learn. . . . Our object is not to teach

that which is peculiar to any one of the professions; but to lay
the foundation which is common to them all. (14)

In particular, the notion that the student is being taught "*how* to learn"
during the undergraduate years is imagined by the 1827 Yale faculty—
and the myriad institutions that were founded in the ensuing two decades on the so-called "Yale plan" (Rudolph 131)—as deriving directly
from both the curriculum and the pedagogy of the classical curriculum. The *Yale Report* emphasizes discipline not in the relatively recent
sense of a "department of learning or knowledge" ("Discipline," def.
2), but in the sense that Michel Foucault elaborates in *Discipline and
Punish*. The classical curriculum, through the very difficulty of the
study of Greek and Latin grammar as, well as through the students'
collective experience of their educations, was designed to produce a set
of graduates with shared values, experiences, and orientations.[6]

As Melvin Urofsky argues, "The influence of the [Yale] Report
cannot be overestimated"; it successfully quashed efforts to make the
classical curriculum less rigid, with more room for student choice and
specialization (Urofsky 61). It was not until Charles W. Eliot became
the President of Harvard in 1869 that higher education began to aban-
don that curriculum and some of its attendant structures and pedagogies. In two highly influential essays published in *The Atlantic Monthly*
in 1869, Eliot outlined his vision of the modern university. This vision
drew heavily on the continental European model. In it, the university was organized into discipline-based departments and students did
not all proceed through their educations in lock-step, taking identical
courses in an identical order. Instead, they chose their courses and
concentrated in particular areas of study. It was an education that built
expertise in particular areas, even if it did not fully forsake the *Yale
Report*'s desire for a more general education.

The rise of the research university in the latter half of the nineteenth century has been well rehearsed in composition history because of the close association of its development with the development
of the first-year composition course and hence our field (see Berlin,
Rhetoric and Reality and *Writing Instruction;* Brereton, *Origins;* Connors, *Composition-Rhetoric;* Crowley; Donahue; Gannett, Brereton,
and Tirabassi; and McLeod, *Writing Program Administration* 24–32;
Russell, *A Curricular History*). Briefly, as Harvard University rose to
national prominence in the 1870s, its creation of the first-year composition course was widely influential. We follow what Cynthia Gannett,

John C. Brereton, and Katherine E. Tirabassi call the "weak version of the [Harvard] narrative" (428). In other words, we accept the notion "that Harvard played an important role in the development of composition courses and programs, both in inventing new approaches and in the spreading of its graduates and textbooks to college programs throughout the nation" (Gannett, Brereton, and Tirabassi 428). This shift—from a standardized curriculum taught by a small group of faculty organized as a collective body with writing and rhetoric instruction diffused throughout the four years, to an elective curriculum taught by multiple groups of faculty organized into disciplinary entities with writing and rhetoric instruction organized into a course or set of courses—continues to structure conversations about the purpose and shape of higher education today (see Arum and Joksa; Bok; and Jaschik, "Rankings Frenzy").

David Russell argues that, starting with Harvard's placement exam and first-year course in the 1870s, "cross-curricular writing programs were almost always a response to a perceived need for greater access, greater equity" (*Writing* 271). This pattern holds true with broader general education requirements as well; in essence, they are rooted in a desire to perpetuate liberal arts ideals while adapting to changes in student demographics, the expansion of knowledge, and the demands of the economy.[7] This was one engine driving Harvard—and other institutions nationwide—in the 1870s and 80s to balance classical ideals with the increasing specialization made manifest through departmentalization. The first decades of the twentieth century saw the rapid spread of this model. For example, Lisa Mastrangelo's *Writing a Progressive Past: Women Teaching and Writing in the Progressive Era* charts the moments of departmentalization at both Mount Holyoke and Wellesley Colleges, noting their implications for curricular requirements. U.S. higher education was, in the first half of the twentieth century, in many ways, primarily focused on the consolidation of departmental entities and the massive shift toward more elective curricula.

Although relatively slow to embrace some of the philosophical underpinnings of this shift, small liberal arts colleges today are organized into discipline- and interdiscipline-based departments, and students do specialize in a particular field or fields. These institutions typically take a more collective approach to general education than is characteristic of larger institutions. Many requirements are embedded rather than designated; students can fulfill them by taking one of several courses rather than one specific course. This may be particularly true of writing requirements, which are residual not just of the first-year composition course inspired and disseminated by Harvard, but also of the ways the classical course of study diffused instruction in rhetorical practices throughout the curriculum. The much greater homogeneity of the nineteenth-century college may account for the apparent ease with which writing and rhetoric instruction, and rhetorical practices more generally, permeated the culture of the institution. We argue that this homogeneity was not simply that of the student body or its academic preparedness, although the former was certainly the case. Nor was it simply that of the community of faculty and students—although this was certainly the case, as well. Rather, it may be that one important kind of homogeneity that enabled curricular and extracurricular writing and oratory to interact and catalyze one another in the nineteenth-century liberal arts college was that of the curriculum itself. The very diversity of course offerings, courses of study, and ways of fulfilling distribution and other requirements at the modern university may make it difficult for student rhetorical activities to build on shared experiences in class. In the following section, we turn to some of the practices that developed in the nineteenth-century college under the classical curriculum in order to trace some of the ways small institutions have been able to develop and maintain diffused cultures of writing and rhetoric, even as they have moved into more various and heterogeneous curricular structures.

Educational Communities

Small liberal arts colleges are thus Janus-faced institutions, looking back toward the days when American higher education was only delivered in small, residential communities, while at the same time looking forward—innovating curricula and embracing new populations of students. The values of the nineteenth-century college, therefore, continue to shape the small college structure of feeling today. While no college in the sample is as small as a typical antebellum college (Harvard's enrollment in the 1830s hovered between 200 and 300), nevertheless, when we speak of these institutions as "small" we mean that literally. The average size of the student body of the schools in the sample is 1,883, and the faculties of these schools are consequently small as well. (The largest is 340.) Almost all of these campuses are compact, with academic and residential buildings in close proximity to one another. Leadership structures are lean at this type of institution, and administrative bureaucracy is typically minimal. Faculty committees do much of the work that is the province of career administrators at large institutions, and small college deans, associate deans, provosts, and even some writing administrators are often rotating positions held by tenured faculty for multi-year terms.

These material facts are transmuted into a value system that resonates with the emphasis on close colloquy emphasized by the *Yale Report*. Advocates for this type of institution repeatedly turn to notions of *intimacy* and *community* as the intertwined qualities that distinguish a small college education from others. In scholarship published in the early years of this century, the governing analogy is that of a small business versus a big chain. Small colleges are likened to "small, partner-owned business[es]" (Hebb 99) and "mom-and-pop grocery stores" (Seery 2). Byron Stay extends this logic, contending that "relationships built at small institutions resemble those in a family much more than a corporation" (151). The mission statements of schools in the sample overwhelmingly emphasize the residential and hence communal nature of the education they provide; they typically promise "close collaboration among peers, professors, and staff" (College 1) and that they will provide a "caring environment" (College 2), envisioning the institution as a "community of learning" (College 3).[8] As Hanstedt and Amorose emphasize, "the language used to refer to the institution inscribes community as an ethos of the institution" (22).

This rhetoric does important work. Faculty and students alike come to these schools believing (or soon coming to believe) that education is most effective when it happens through face-to-face interactions between individuals or in small groups. In addition to bragging about their small classes and low student-to-faculty ratios, small colleges promise that students will be taught almost exclusively by tenure-line faculty throughout their careers. This commitment arises not only from the notion of institution as community or family, but also from the historical mission of these schools to educate the next generation of civic (and, originally, religious) leaders. Students at small colleges are apprentice scholars and leaders; they are all assumed to have an intellectual interest in their own educations. This approach to pedagogy and curricula then informs not just major curricula, which send high percentages of students to graduate school every year, but also general education. These institutions are premised upon a liberal arts commitment to the non-professionalizing education of the whole student.

Their size makes this feasible. Similarly, the scale of these institutions collapses distances between faculty and administrators. Hanstedt and Amorose put this aptly:

> Whereas the sheer size of a larger university generally prohibits intimate professional relationships between faculty and administration, these barriers are removed at smaller institutions, creating a culture of transparency where almost everyone is known by name and reputation. (17)

The material scale—size of the student body, size of the campus, size of the faculty, and so on—means that even historically marginalized offices are closer to the center than they are at large schools. On a small campus, the margin is never that far away.

This proximity helps us understand why writing instruction seems to pervade education at small colleges. In "Kitchen Tables and Rented Rooms," Anne Ruggles Gere develops the notion of writing's "extra-curriculum" (79), a term she borrows from Rudolph. Rudolph discusses the extracurriculum in broader terms, including fraternities and athletic teams as well as literary and theosophic societies (136–56). Rudolph's narrative of the extracurriculum looks at participation in extra- or co-curricular activities, such as literary societies and "rhetoricals" (public oratorical performances that might include debates and orations). This participation, he contends, empowered students to critique and ultimately change college curricula. Extracurricular literary societies, for example, provided students with arenas in which to build up their knowledge of science, social science, and modern literature—a first step toward making a case for their inclusion in the curriculum itself (Rudolph 145–46). Gere focuses, by contrast, on the ways these organized, collective linguistic activities were not totally re-appropriated into the formalized structures of the curriculum itself. She celebrates entirely extracurricular writing practices such as independent writing groups, admonishing teachers of composition to learn from them. In fact, we can find a point of origin for the strongly diffused culture of writing at small colleges in the very co-curricular structures both Gere and Rudolph discuss. In particular, the nineteenth-century college's pedagogical apparatus surrounding rhetoricals seems to have had a lasting, residual effect. This pedagogy is fundamentally student-centered, which may well be part of its power.

As Sharon Crowley has pointed out, when U.S. higher education institutions adopted the European model, colleges and universities changed not just *what* but also *how* faculty taught. Most crucially, it seems to have entailed a shift away from a pedagogy that focused on the student as an active learner. Recitation was the dominant pedagogy associated with the classical curriculum; in it, "students demonstrate[d] their grasp of traditional wisdom" (Crowley 56). The new research university, by contrast, relied on lecture, in which "professors pass on the results of original research" (Crowley 56). In recitation pedagogy, students were called upon to read or scan passages in Latin or Greek, to translate them, and to answer questions about them (Russell, *Writing* 39). In essence, this was a catechistic method, in which students answered questions but did not ask them. While the mastery of traditional wisdom is hardly the sole or primary goal of education in the twenty-first century, it is worth noting that the focus from recitation to lecture was a shift from a student- to a faculty-centered classroom.

At the same time, the shift away from a curriculum that students undertook in lock-step with one another for four years resulted in the loss of rhetoricals, which students had traditionally performed in several times over the course of their careers. These took place outside of class time, but were woven into the fabric of the course of study in two ways. First and foremost, they were a "mandated part of the curriculum" (Russell, *Writing* 41), and the topics for them were drawn from course material. Second, there is evidence in the historical record that students' contributions were "ordinarily first written out and often critiqued beforehand by the professor in charge of these exercises, either in conference with the student or in written comments on the draft" (Russell, *Writing* 40; see also Wright and Halloran).

Russell argues that the nineteenth-century college taught "language across the whole curriculum" through its reliance on recitation pedagogy and regular rhetoricals (*Writing* 39). Sharon Crowley offers a similar insight, pointing out that while composition "was taught chiefly by professors of rhetoric, . . . exercises in composing were built into the entire curriculum [such that] the whole faculty took responsibility for seeing to the improvement of young men's composing skills" (49–50; Brereton, *Traditions* 9). While Russell, Crowley, and others have evaluated the pros and cons of both recitation and lecture pedagogy, our focus here is on how the practice of rhetoricals unified curricular and extracurricular language use in a way that was possible only in small and homogeneous communities. While this homogeneity may have in origin been social—a product of students and faculty of the same sex, race, socio-economic class, and religious denomination—it was also a product of the scale of the community and its internal relationships, as well as of the prescribed course of study, which meant that students went through intellectual and social hurdles as a cohort.

In his discussion of rhetoricals in *Writing in the Academic Disciplines*, on which we draw heavily, Russell describes how these exercises unified the institution (41). They are premised on a group small enough to gather and listen to its members in a reasonable amount of time. In addition, the topics for rhetoricals were tied to students' year, and hence to their position in the prescribed course of study. Russell offers Kansas University's structure for rhetoricals as a typical example. Freshmen and sophomores performed declamations; juniors presented "original essays and oration"; and seniors practiced their commencement exercises (Kansas U., qtd. in Russell, *Writing* 41). Further relying on students and faculty sharing a body of knowledge, topics for rhetoricals were typically closely allied with the whole course of study. These topics "were drawn from a common *public* store of knowledge and received ideas, a shared tradition" (Russell, *Writing* 42–43; see also Connors, *Composition-Rhetoric* 45).

In addition to bringing curricular topics into community discussion through the rhetoricals themselves, then, rhetoricals catalyzed the kind of conferences over drafts that have been enshrined at the heart of writing pedagogy (see Connors, *Composition-Rhetoric*; Varnum). This method is premised on the features and values of a small community—not least because of the time such conferencing takes. It may be unsurprising, then, that as small colleges adopted departmentalization and some of the curricular features of the modern university at the end of the nineteenth century, they retained and adapted some of the pedagogy that had developed in the preceding decades under the old curriculum.

One key instance of this lies in the development of the "laboratory method" or "laboratory approach" to writing instruction, a pedagogy that emphasized one-on-one conferences between faculty and students, and which historians of writing centers have identified as one origin for writing center pedagogy (see Boquet, "'Our Little Secret'" and *Writ-*

ing Centers; Carino, "Early Writing Centers"; Lerner, "Time Warp," "Punishment and Possibility," and *Idea*; and Shouse). It seems that the laboratory method, in turn, derives from the small college context. An essay John F. Genung wrote in 1895 on "English at Amherst College" for John Morton Payne's *English in American Universities* may well be the first published account of such an approach to teaching English composition at the college level. He calls it the "*laboratory method*" (112). English composition classrooms at Amherst, Genung claims, are "veritable workshop[s], wherein, by systematized daily drill, details are mastered one by one, and that unity of result is obtained which is more for practical use than for show" (112; see Lerner, "Punishment" 54–55). Genung and his influential textbooks have been held up as problematic examples of the current-traditional method of teaching composition (see Kitzhaber, *Rhetoric*; Berlin, *Writing Instruction*). It is worth noting, however, that here he emphasizes process and time. Indeed, writing an essay on "English at the University of Minnesota" for Payne's collection, Fred Newton Scott recalls Genung's point in order to argue for the laborious and time-intensive nature of teaching composition (122). By the time Frank Cady was writing of the laboratory method at Middlebury College in 1915, he could assume that his readers understood the approach. Cady's piece reveals a distinct focus on working with individual students, on writing processes, and on "posing complex rhetorical problems" (Carino 17).

One trajectory for the lab method of writing instruction has been writing centers which, like rhetoricals, exist in the overlapping space between the curriculum and the extracurriculum (see Lerner, "Punishment" and *Idea*; Shouse). But another is writing across the curriculum, at least as it is practiced at small colleges. The classical curriculum's pedagogy casts a long shadow. As a result, practices that rely on close student-teacher contact and close connections between curricular and extracurricular rhetorical practices provide fertile ground for cultures of writing as reliant on pedagogy as formal curricular mandates. Small colleges may be, in a sense, naturally hospitable to writing across the curriculum not just because they are relatively selective or have relatively homogeneous student bodies. These institutions have two long-standing pedagogical commitments: to close work between students and faculty, and to undergraduate education as a distinct mental discipline, undertaken and expressed through complex rhetorical performances. These residual practices of the nineteenth-century college may help us explain the prevalence of WAC at the institutions in our sample. They may further explain why these institutions in the twenty-first century seem to be interested not simply in committing further to writing across the curriculum, but also to a more explicit emphasis on writing and communication throughout students' educations.

VALUES IN TENSION

The mission of small colleges therefore seems strikingly coherent, and we do want to emphasize what unifies schools of this type. But Williams emphasizes the ways in which structures of feeling encompass relations that range "from formal assent with private dissent to the more nuanced interaction between selected and interpreted beliefs and acted and justified experiences" (132). Any structure of feeling encompasses tension and contradiction. Any particular small college will have its own structure of feeling, which will exhibit tendencies and habits that may pull against what we present here. Williams would remind us that even those tendencies and habits are not entirely random, that they are encompassed by the structure of feeling that is comprised of a dynamic but recognizable set of relations. The small college structure of feeling sketched above transmutes smallness into community, putting a premium on intimacy and personal interactions. But that system is also made up of elements and values that are in direct tension with one another. These, too, derive from the size and history of these schools.

One of the most basic of these tensions is between faculty leadership and faculty autonomy. Faculty at small schools play a large role in governance of the institution. As a result, they are expected to serve on committees and, conversely, abide by the decisions of those committees. Departments and faculty at small colleges also expect significant autonomy in their teaching and scholarly endeavors; as Bianca Falbo puts it in her title, "teaching is a private affair." While this tension is present at all institutions of higher education in the U.S., we argue that it is particularly pronounced at the schools in this study. As noted above, these faculties have strong roles in college governance. Many of the institutions in the sample do not have faculty senates; instead, votes are taken by the faculty as a whole. Senior administrative positions through the provost level are held by tenured faculty on rotating appointments. (As we discuss in Chapter 5, such rotating appointments are not uncommon in the leadership of writing programs on these campuses.) It is standard across institutional types for matters pertaining to curriculum and to tenure and promotion to be the province of the faculty; at small schools, faculty are involved in most aspects of the life of the college. As a result, service is both expected and valued at small schools, and faculty often become generalists in service, contributing to a wide range of endeavors over the course of their careers, and becoming knowledgeable about most aspects of the life of the institution (Marek 45; see also Hanstedt).[9] Small college faculty are simultaneously autonomous agents and expected to dedicate significant time and energy to the institution, its policies, and its future.

This type of autonomy is extended, in different ways, to students. The focus on education as occurring through individual relationships (between students as well as between faculty and students) leads to a notion that students can and must struggle with questions of direction and purpose in order to learn. This belief in autonomous individualism leads to a principled refusal at the institutional and the pedagogical levels to spell things out, a sense that the process of coming to understand is an essential and irreplaceable part of learning. This often manifests itself—as we discuss in Chapter 6—in a fairly minimal requirement structure. It has its roots in these schools' historical commitment to a non-professionalizing liberal arts education.

The tension between faculty governance and faculty autonomy leads to a philosophical preference for leadership over administration. As noted earlier, administrative bureaucracies at small schools tend to be flat. Even at schools whose respondents describe them as bureaucratized, academic affairs is led by a single Chief Academic Officer with only one or two associate provosts or deans reporting to her or him. In many ways, this preference is one of individual enterprise over bureaucratic structures. (In many cases, oversight for a variety of initiatives is maintained by faculty committees, as we discuss in more detail in Chapter 5.) Small colleges, then, prefer leaders to bureaucrats and committees to offices; they prefer collaborative rather than executive modes of decision-making. Some policy decisions at small schools (like large ones) are necessarily made by administrators while others are the province of the faculty. In both cases, in a small community, there is both a strong desire for consensus and a sense that the faculty ought to be consulted on most matters touching upon academic life writ large. A need for efficiency and formalized processes is often in tension with the ideal of personalized, face-to-face consensus. But the absence of such codified measures poses a danger. As these institutions grow in size and become more diverse, tacit policies and informal lines of communication can function in exclusionary rather than inclusive ways to new faculty and students. Implied expectations are in their very nature not transparent, but at the very same time, the steps an institution takes toward transparency can be read as a dangerous bureaucratization that devalues the individual and threatens the educational ethos of the liberal arts college.

In "Delivering Composition at a Liberal Arts College," Carol Rutz argues that small schools can initiate change quickly and easily, provided those changes are in line with the underlying historical mission of the institution. She describes small colleges as paradoxically able to "sustain long, dearly held traditions even as new ones are invented" (70). The structure of feeling of a particular small college, then, includes elements that have emerged slowly over the course of its history as well as the elements of the current moment, both of which can at once foster and hamper innovation.

As Williams explains, social experiences that are still in process can be taken to be "private, idiosyncratic, and even isolating" (132). Many of our survey respondents insisted on their programs' and schools' difference from the norm, and this perception can lead to a strong sense of exceptionality—a sense that may well contribute to the elision of small schools from some of the national conversations about higher education. The notion of a small college structure of feeling allows us to draw parallels where individuals—and institutions—are invested in seeing only differences. While conducting this research, we often found this to be the case for small college writing program administrators and writing center directors, many of whom understand their own professional narratives as unique and, in some cases, isolating. In reviewing these narratives, we have drawn connections and identified patterns across a large set of institutions. Smallness is likely to feel different on different campuses, and each institution has its own unique history and mission. But education and academic life at all the schools in the sample are significantly determined by the material and affective dimensions of size, dimensions weighted by their common history of being small schools.

2 Grounded Theory and Mixed Methods Research

> [I]f we continue to rely on belief in our pedagogies and administrative decisions, whether theorized or not, whether argued from logic or anecdote, experience or conviction, we do no better to support a case for those decisions than what most detractors do to support cases against them. Instead, we need a more robust plan for building on the strong base of existing research into our assumptions about how students best learn to write.
>
> —Chris M. Anson

The adage that process is as important as product holds unsurprisingly true for this study. We entered this project with the most general of research questions: "What do writing programs at small liberal arts colleges look like?" This led us to a methodological question: "How do you find out what writing programs at small colleges look like?" With limited resources (including time), we set out to learn all that we could about writing instruction at a set of small private colleges and to identify trends within that group. The methodological challenge was to find an approach that would allow us both to describe the role of writing at small colleges and to theorize what this description means for these colleges and the field of writing studies as a whole. The mixed methods approach of grounded theory (see Johnson and Onwuegbuzie; Strauss and Corbin) seems to suit those intertwined goals because it allows us to create, as Joyce Magnotto Neff puts it, "a dialogue between description and theory" (134). As practitioner researchers (Swarthmore and Pomona Colleges are included in the data set, and we are the WPAs on our campuses who completed the survey), we realized that our own work directing writing centers and writing programs, combined with narratives from colleagues at similar institutions, had not yet been described in any systematic way. Most of the published scholarship focuses on the narratives of individual schools; it has not yet described or theorized about a set of small colleges. We were confident that with a grounded theory approach, the data would lead us to more refined analytic questions—and, ultimately, to the concepts and categories that would help us and our audience understand our subject. This approach relies on more than surveys and interviews; triangulating such self-reported data with document analysis and other methods of data collection deepens the analysis and provides a fuller and more accurate picture of the subject than would otherwise be possible.

We discovered early on in the research process that this is a set of institutions in the midst of change. Serendipitously, this research tapped into current conversations at many of the participating schools about how writing should be addressed in and outside the curriculum. Our methodology allowed us to capture a bit of these conversations, enabling us not only to provide a picture of the programs in the sample at this point in time but also of the pressures for change those institutions currently face.[1] The ongoing nature of these conversations has also meant that this was an action research project (see Greenwood and Levin; Adler-Kassner). The analyses can be and have been used by participants to work for change at their home institutions. We hope others will also be able to use an action research process to both gather data and build consortia, and through those intertwined endeavors promote both local and national change.

PARTICIPANTS

In May of 2009, we invited 137 schools to participate in this study. (The list of invited schools is provided in Appendix A). These 137 schools were drawn from the Annapolis Group and the Higher Education Data Sharing Consortium's "Baccalaureate-Liberal Arts" participants (HEDS).[2] We wanted a sample large enough to allow us to document trends, but also wanted to limit those invited to a particular subset of small colleges in order to perform a comparative analysis and to allow the data to be used on the respective campuses. However, the term "small college" is necessarily relative and somewhat ambiguous (Hanstedt and Amorose 18–19; Gladstein, Lebduska, and Regaignon 15–16). To make more transparent our decisions for inclusion and exclusion, we relied upon these two consortia because they were already established, explicitly serve small, private colleges, and together form the largest group of institutions with which our colleges routinely share data and compare themselves. We assumed that these consortia would have a keen interest in both participating in the research and in learning about (and hopefully using) the analyses.

The Annapolis Group provides a forum for its roughly 130 member institutions—all private small liberal arts colleges—to "share best practices, seek higher levels of excellence, and advance the cause of liberal arts education on a national scale" ("About the Annapolis Group"). Through semi-annual meetings, the schools' vice-presidents for academic affairs (or other chief academic officers) and presidents work together to:

- increase their own professional effectiveness by discussing ideas, best practices, and questions of mutual concern;
- articulate, interrogate, and promote the values of liberal arts education;
- debate issues of institutional, regional, and national scope; and
- develop new ways for their institutions—both individually and collectively—to serve the public good. ("About the Annapolis Group")

The synergy between these goals and our own for both this research project and for the Small Liberal Arts College-Writing Program Administrators (SLAC-WPA) consortium led us to choose the Annapolis Group members as the first sample. We expanded this sample by seven schools that had been among SLAC-WPA's first member institutions, but had not participated in the Annapolis Group. These additional seven, however, contribute to the Higher Education Data Sharing Consortium (HEDS), "a not-for-profit organization of private colleges and universities that assists member institutions in planning, management, institutional research, decision-support, policy analysis, educational evaluation, and assessment" (Higher Education Data Sharing Consortium). The seven schools added were all classified as "Baccalaureate-Liberal Arts" institutions. We found that the combination of these two groups gave us a sample of diverse schools that held core missions and values in common. This sample includes some of the most selective schools in the country, as well as some that admit over three-quarters of the students who apply. Some of these schools have international profiles, while others are primarily known locally. While we discuss the details of survey administration below, we note here that out of the 137 schools invited to participate, 109 at least *began* the survey, yielding an initial response rate of 80%. After the survey response period ended and preliminary inspection and cleaning of the data took place, three schools were eliminated because their responses were incomplete. Over the course of the data analysis process, an additional six schools were excluded from further analysis because they were clear outliers: Three had no writing requirement and no writing program administrator, and the other three had such diffused cultures of writing that it was difficult to include them in the categories of analysis described later.

Thus, the final sample comprises one hundred schools, representing a diverse set of institutions under the umbrella designation of private small liberal arts college. Ten of the schools in the sample are single-sex (seven are women's colleges, and three are men's colleges); two are historically black colleges. Schools from the Midwest (25 schools) and the South (25 schools) each represent a fourth of the total data set; the West (11 schools) represents a little over 10%, and the combined Mid-Atlantic and Northeast represent over one third (39 schools). Current enrollment ranges from 592 to 3,966,[3] with an average of 1,883 students per institution.

These institutions are all small, private, mostly residential, four-year colleges, but their admissions acceptance rates range from 16% to 92%. While some of the most selective schools in the sample are also the most financially secure, those two characteristics do not correlate precisely. (In any case, a particular institution's wealth does not necessarily translate into generosity toward the writing program.) As of 2009, the endowment per student ranged from $7,813 to $876,400; the average is $165,240. Tuition covers a smaller yet significant range, from $25,500 to just over $50,000 for 2010–2011. Some of these institutions operate mostly from endowment, whereas others are more tuition-driven, a difference made manifest by the varying impact of the economic downturn on institutions' operating budgets. The percentage of students on financial aid, as reported by the institutions' websites, ranges from 18% to 95%, with an average of 56%.

DATA COLLECTION

A ninety-seven-question survey took the lead in the study, but the research design incorporated multiple methods of data collection (see Appendix B for the complete survey). As we processed the data from the survey, and as new questions emerged, we analyzed site documents such as institutional websites and catalogs for all the schools in the sample. We corresponded with our respondents, asking both clarifying and follow-up questions; when appropriate, we corresponded with a second respondent at the school in order to get (for example) perspectives from both the writing program administrator and the writing center director. We conducted individual and focus group interviews in order to gather more impressionistic data. And, in the case of three schools, we asked respondents for fuller descriptions of their assessment projects so that we could highlight those in Chapter 11.

SURVEY

The main data source for this project was the ninety-seven-question survey sent out to all respondents. This survey was a revision and an expansion of the initial survey created when establishing the SLAC-WPA consortium (see Gladstein, Lebduska, and Regaignon). After implementing that first survey, which contained forty-nine questions, we refined the questions to gather a clearer picture of the different writing programs. We also developed an additional set of questions.

Both surveys had limited choice and open-ended questions, covering six main areas:

1. administrative structure of the writing program,
2. writing requirements, including first-year writing and WAC,
3. writing centers and related programs,
4. faculty development,
5. assessment, and
6. identification of and support for diversely prepared learners.

These areas represent the general areas of responsibilities for writing program administrators and writing center directors; they are key potential sites for the delivery of writing instruction and the diffusion of a culture of writing on individual campuses (Yancey 1). In addition, the second survey also included questions about writing program changes that had occurred within the past ten years.

Prior to distribution of the survey, we received approval from the Institutional Research Board of Swarthmore College. We also piloted the survey with four individuals, representing different positions and programs. Using feedback from the pilot, we refined the survey before the final version was administered. As with the earlier survey, we found that some questions worked better than others, As a result, we do not include all ninety-seven questions in our analysis. The excluded questions did not produce clear responses because the respondents interpreted them very differently, which is not an uncommon problem (Skeffington, Borrowman, and Enos 10–11, 14–15). For some questions, we sent respondents follow-up or clarification questions by email, asking them to answer a different set of questions so we could extrapolate the information we needed. For example, question #12 asks respondents to report the percentage of their time spent teaching writing courses, teaching courses outside of the writing program, and administering the writing program. Some respondents gave us percentages, while others informed us of course releases, and some did not provide responses totaling 100%. We therefore sent a follow-up question to *all* respondents asking how many courses they taught each year compared to the regular course load of faculty members at their institutions. This allowed us to translate all responses into the same units which, in this case, gave us a much clearer sense of the percentage of time respondents spend teaching versus doing administrative work. (The chart of course release data is available in appendix D.)

We sent the survey via email to individuals at 137 schools in May, 2009. We first used names we had gathered when building the SLAC-WPA consortium. For those schools that were new to the group, we attempted to identify the writing program administrator or writing center director via each college's website. If we were unable to find someone, we sent the survey to the English department chair (if the writing program seemed to be a part of the English department), an academic dean, or a college's institutional researcher. In some cases, this person forwarded the survey to the WPA and/or WCD.

The first request (see Appendix C) referred to the initial SLAC survey and our desire to expand the findings, and explained our intentions for the collected data. As an incentive, we offered respondents an advance copy of "Consortia as Sites of Inquiry" (Gladstein, Lebduska, and Regaignon, then forthcoming). We hoped that this would allow potential respondents to see the action research component of the project, and therefore understand how participating in the study would not only further our research but also their work on their individual campuses. After the initial request, we sent out three email reminders and kept the survey open throughout the summer and fall in order to increase the response rate. In the end, 109 schools responded to the survey, yielding an 80% return rate.[4]

Once the survey was closed, we read through the responses and created an individual profile for each school based on both the survey data and clarification and follow-up questions. Before returning to the participants with those questions, however, we examined institutional websites in order to confirm descriptions of writing requirements and to better understand the administrative structures for writing programs. Remaining questions were forwarded to the respondent. In order to thank respondents for this further information—and to provide a preliminary view of our findings—we sent the PowerPoint slides from a presentation Gladstein gave on writing requirements at small colleges in January, 2010 ("Writing Requirements").

To triangulate and better support our emerging conclusions, when possible, we also sent follow-up questions to a second person in the writing program. For example, if the survey had been completed by the writing center director, we sent another set of questions to the writing program administrator in order to ask more specific questions about the latter position. Between the original and second respondents, eighty-nine of the one hundred schools in the final data set answered questions beyond the original survey via e-mail, over the phone, or in person.

We credit two factors in the high initial and follow-up response rates. For the initial survey responses, we maintained an ongoing effort to "pinpoint the most likely respondent" and to follow-up multiple times with those potential respondents (Thaiss and Porter 537). Second, this research project was tied directly to membership in a community, and we sought to involve our respondents in the research process by providing them with early access to data about similar types of institutions and programs. In this way, the small college WPAs' participation in the project offered the potential for information, collaboration, and community.

ADDITIONAL METHODS OF DATA COLLECTION

As noted above, the survey data took the lead in our analyses; however, we employed additional methods to triangulate the results and, in some cases, gather more detail.

Site Documents. One of these methods involved the examination of site documents, such as institutional websites and college catalogs. With research assistants, we examined institutions' websites to gather demographic information on founding dates, current enrollments, endowment size, and percentage of students on financial aid. We also conducted a thorough website search, which included reading the college catalogs of the one hundred respondents to clarify questions related to writing requirements and WPA positions.

Individual and Focus Group Interviews. Before both the 2009 Council of Writing Program Administrators (CWPA) Conference and the 2010 SLAC-WPA Conference, we invited any interested survey respondents to participate in a focus group or individual interview. The goal of the focus group interviews—three total—was to gather small groups of SLAC WPAs and WCDs together to discuss some of our initial findings. One focus group was held at the CWPA Conference with six participants; two took place at SLAC-WPA, and included three and four participants, respectively. Although we developed a list of questions for each focus group, we felt it important to leave the direction of the discussion up to the participants, so that we could see what issues were most pressing for small college writing program administrators. Each group discussion lasted fifty to sixty minutes and was audio-recorded. After each focus group session, participants signed a written consent and received a gift card as a token of our appreciation. These focus group discussions were transcribed and used during the data analysis stage. In addition to providing important clarification, details, and context for the trends our analysis identified in the survey data, these discussions also provided important insight into how these individuals and institutions are grappling with change and weighing the pros and cons of a wide variety of approaches to writing instruction.

We also conducted four, one-on-one interviews. During the July, 2009 CWPA Conference, four survey respondents (three of whom volunteered for both the focus group and individual interviews) were interviewed. Individual interviews used informal discussion and several open-ended questions designed to elicit more information about individuals' survey responses. Interviewees were also asked to identify an area or areas of concern, or interests related to their writing programs. Each interview lasted between twenty and forty minutes and, with the respondent's consent, was recorded. Interviews were transcribed and used during the data analysis stage to further deepen our understanding of the survey data. Like the focus group interviews, these provided valuable detail and context, augmenting our understanding of the dynamic nature of these institutions.

The final set of interviews involved the WPAs at the three schools showcased in our discussion of assessment. As we processed the data from the survey, the responses around assessment raised more questions than answers, so we decided to select three schools to highlight. These schools were chosen because of their diverse approaches to assessment and the nature of their writing programs. The WPA from each of these schools was sent a set of questions via e-mail. Afterward, phone conversations took place to address any additional questions. As we continued with data analysis for the rest of the book, more questions emerged for these participants. At the 2011 Conference on College Composition and Communication (CCCC), two of the three WPAs took part in a sixty-minute interview, and all three reviewed Chapter 11 in draft form and offered feedback. In these interviews, we asked open-ended questions about the origins of their respective approaches to writing assessment, their sense of the trade-offs involved in their particular approaches, and whether their goals had driven the establishment of those assessments or were derived from them.

Connecting to the Scholarly Discourse. Additionally, we performed extensive literature reviews designed to bring our analyses into national conversations. To that end, we reviewed the key debates and discussions on general education, writing requirements, WAC, first-year writing instruction, writing centers, support for developmental writers and English Language Learners, WPA and WCD positions, assessment, and new challenges and directions facing writing programs in the twenty-first century. In addition, we actively sought scholarly literature—including doctoral dissertations—that specifically focused on the schools in the sample, or that addressed questions central to rhetoric and composition from the vantage point of small colleges. Finally, in order to better understand the structure of feeling of small colleges, we examined the place of small liberal arts colleges in conversations about U.S. higher education in the nineteenth and twentieth centuries, and sought to understand the historical development of this particular type of institution.

DATA ANALYSIS

Once we closed the response period for the survey and realized the amount of data generated, we began to code the data. Through the triangulation of methods described above, we created categories of analysis that we fed back into the analysis in order to address new questions that emerged from this process. As Anselm Strauss and Juliet Corbin describe, coding

> involves interacting with data (analysis) using techniques such as asking questions about the data, making comparisons between data . . . deriving concepts to stand for those data, then developing those concepts in terms of their properties and dimensions. A researcher can think of coding as "mining" the data, digging beneath the surface to discover the hidden treasures contained within data. (66)

The processes of data collection, analysis, and theorization are intertwined and iterative in grounded theory. We therefore discuss the process by which we generated our analytic categories—especially the configurations of leadership—throughout the book. Small colleges like to believe that they are unique, and they often use language that makes it challenging to compare institutions. For this reason, it was important throughout the study to ask questions of both the data and the participants themselves to clarify our analytic constructs. Our goal has been to unearth data that could have been lost or embedded in campus jargon and therefore not in line with the terminology of the field.

As we processed the initial survey data, we raised three sets of additional questions:

1. What are the sites of writing at small colleges? What are the explicit and embedded writing requirements (if both exist)? Where else is writing taught or supported at small colleges? Who's doing the teaching of writing?

2. What are the positions charged with the administration of writing? Where are the writing program administrators and writing center directors located? Are those positions defined explicitly? If not, in what other positions are the responsibilities embedded? Which sites of writing are not administered by a WPA or WCD? How are they administered?

3. What is the relationship of WPAs and WCDs to the sites of writing identified in question #1? What kinds of power, authority, or influence do WPAs have over explicit sites? Embedded sites? How does the degree to which either position or site is embedded versus explicit determine the WPA's relationship to such sites?

Each set of questions informed the comparisons we made from the initial survey data, and then again with data gathered through other research methods. We discuss these different categories—and the processes of developing them—in more detail in the relevant chapters.

LIMITATIONS

There are, of course, limits to our findings. We have primarily relied on self-reported data provided by the WPA and/or the WCD from each school. While we triangulated those data with information from college websites and course catalogs, we could not conduct site visits or interview enough people on individual campuses to provide additional perspectives on some of these items. With such a large data set, we are unable to provide thick descriptions of the writing programs at individual schools. We were unable, for example, to look at syllabi or writing assignments. Our data do allow us, however, to present a broad stroke portrait of the role of writing and writing program administrators in a subset of small liberal arts colleges in the early twenty-first century. We offer these data in direct dialogue with both the historical situation of small colleges in the U.S. and ongoing debates in rhetoric and composition. Our intention is not simply to help current and future SLAC WPAs. Small college faculty and administrations will find here a snapshot of current practices, as well as a heuristic to apply to their own institutions' delivery of writing instruction. Scholars of rhetoric and composition will find not simply a lacuna filled with empirical data, but a new way of thinking about writing programs' administrative structures. It lies beyond the parameters of this project to make recommendations for what might be the most effective writing program. If we have learned anything, it is that writing program structures are tied organically and deeply to their local conditions, and that any accurate evaluation must begin with an understanding of these conditions. Our goal has been to uncover the different models and approaches for writing instruction that are practiced at SLACs today; we leave it to future research studies to tackle questions of effectiveness.

3 Mapping Small College Sites of Writing

[P]art of the effectiveness of a [writing] program is directly tied to the extent it is responsive to the cultural and social context. Only through the examination of larger contextual influences, which composition teachers and writing program directors often view as constraints, can one arrive at an adequate understanding of how and why the program operates as it does.

—Stephen P. Witte and Lester Faigley

In the small college context, *programs* in the traditional sense can be difficult to see. We therefore follow the lead of our respondents, and use the term elastically. In this, we are also building on the provocative definition Louise Wetherby Phelps offered to the WPA e-list on February 24, 2009. "A writing program," she begins, "is an administrative structure that implements a responsibility to facilitate the practice and learning of writing at an institution." After pointing out that we might well then apply the term to myriad entities—writing centers, first-year writing requirements, basic or developmental writing programs, WAC initiatives, and so on—she explains that "to experts in the field, these multiple, variable functions are not an arbitrary collection of separate little writing programs, but components of the greater whole that they call the college or university 'writing program.'" In other words, a "writing program" may not be explicitly labeled as such, but can productively be identified in and from the disparate entities charged with delivering different types of writing instruction.

In this analysis, a "writing program" is the material form of an institution's culture of writing. It is the courses, people (administrators, faculty, and students), offices, positions, centers, policies (written and tacit), and customs that make up how writing is taught, learned, and practiced on a particular campus. It is contained within the culture of the institution, a culture which is also shaped by its particular historical and material conditions. In WPA scholarship, these programs—these material cultures of writing—are typically divided for analysis into their component courses, positions, and offices. As a result, for example, the focus is on first-year composition versus basic writing as courses and therefore programmatic entities; WPA positions; and writing centers versus curriculum- or course-based writing programs.

These categories of analysis do not work as well for small college writing programs, although most of the schools in the sample do have many of these features. There are, as Paul Hanstedt and Tom Amorose point out, "volumes of research on . . . the work of the WPA," but we must also understand "how pedagogical practices and administrative roles so familiar to compositionists get altered, or even canceled, when they are enacted at the small college or university" (23). The elasticity of small college writing programs led us to develop a heuristic derived from three sets of relationships:

- the relationship between curriculum- and student-centered sites for the delivery of writing instruction;
- the relationship between explicit and embedded sites for the delivery of writing instruction; and
- the relationship between writing across the curriculum (WAC) and writing in the disciplines (WID).

As we combed through the data, looking for patterns and trying to understand how the various programs' vocabularies related to one another, we began to see that different schools emphasize different vectors for delivering writing instruction. As we sought to understand these vectors, we drew on the notion of "sites of writing" that Kathleen Blake Yancey develops in *Delivering College Composition: The Fifth Canon* (1). Thinking, as Yancey encourages us, of sites rather than programs opens up our view of where and how writing—and hence writing instruction—happens on any campus. Since different sites have different emphases, however, we adapted Martha A. Townsend's identification of student-, faculty-, and curriculum-centered approaches to writing across the curriculum to this broader context ("Writing Across the Curriculum" 443). What emerged was a Venn diagram in which each of the circles represents a domain of writing activity (see Figure

3.1). At some institutions, the primary site of delivery for writing.instruction (and hence its administration) is rooted in the work of supporting student writers; we call this the *student-centered domain*. These sites include writing centers, peer or professional tutoring programs, and specifically support struggling writers wherever they may be. The culture of writing of these institutions, by extension, is student-centered. At other schools, the culture of writing is *curriculum-centered*, where the primary delivery and administrative site is curricular, rooted in the work of staffing and teaching first-year and other writing requirements. A writing fellows program is situated in the overlapping space, since it is a student-centered approach to a curricular requirement. Although at first glance this mirrors the system of institutional organization that divides offices and areas of responsibility between Academic and Student Affairs, in our sample, the emphasis of the culture of writing did not consistently correspond to the writing director's reporting line.

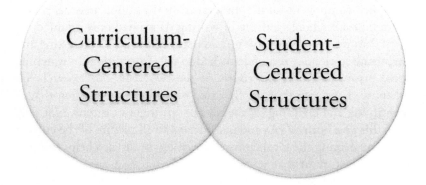

Figure 3.1 Writing Program Structures

We mapped institutions' cultures of writing on this Venn diagram. What seems at first to be a simple representation actually contains layers of complexity. These two overlapping spheres represent at the same time the institutional locations of the different sites of writing and the WPA/WCD responsibilities—as a result, it reveals the focus of a writing culture. As a result, identifying and mapping the different pieces on the Venn diagram raises nearly as many questions as it does answers. In seeking to understand a particular institution, it was important not to overlook aspects of the writing program that were embedded in other curricular or student-centered offices, programs, or requirements. We therefore distinguish between *explicit* and *embedded* entities. *Explicit* sites of writing are clearly named in college catalogs, websites, job titles, and other institutional documents. They include: "writing requirement," "Director of Writing," and "Writing Center." *Embedded* sites of writing are housed inside other institutional entities. For example, a first-year seminar requirement becomes an embedded writing requirement when it lists writing instruction as one of the program's goals but is not listed as students' "writing requirement." A department chair becomes an embedded WPA when she or he oversees the staffing for a department-based, first-year writing course if the chair isn't identified, and doesn't self-identify, as the Director of Writing. In other words, embedded sites of writing instruction and administration are evident and identifiable. They are not tacit, but they are also not primarily named in ways that label them first and foremost as vectors of writing instruction.

As researchers, we found that we had to identify embedded as well as explicit components of the "programs" in the sample in order to understand each school's culture of writing. If we had only counted explicit features, we would have missed many of the most interesting and surprising stories our respondents had to tell. In addition, in watching these institutions over the course of the two years our research has taken, we have seen that the first step toward change is often that of identifying and claiming *all* the sites of writing on campus. Not only does this give both WPAs and institutions a full picture of the current relations shaping the local culture of writing, but it also helps bring to light the history of that school's approach and how the current program fits into national conversations. (Carol Rutz's work is an excellent example of this approach. See her "Delivering" as well as Rutz, Hardy, and Condon.)

As we discussed, writing has always been a part of teaching at small private liberal arts colleges. It is, to quote one survey respondent, "in the water." Faculty at small colleges typically believe in and employ writing-to-learn pedagogies, and students are expected to learn how to write in and for their major disciplines by the time they graduate. But there is tension between these two goals, which are typically associated with writing across the curriculum (WAC) and writing in the disciplines (WID), respectively. In particular, the generalist orientation of many first-year writing requirements, combined with the specialist writing students do as seniors, has led many schools in the sample to be concerned about what one participant called "the murky middle." In this realm, there is what another called "a leadership and pedagogical vacuum," where writing instruction is expected, but not supported.

We present our findings in chapters that follow through the logic of the Venn diagram described above. In the next chapter, "Configurations of Writing Program Leadership," we describe the six configurations of writing program leadership identified in our sample. These descriptions focus on whether these leaders are centered in the curricular or student spheres, as well as on how embedded or explicit these positions are. In "Positioning of Writing Program Administrators" (Chapter 5), we build on these configurations in order to discuss the status and responsibilities of these various positions. In both chapters, we discuss the trends in the data set and the pros and cons inherent in these configurations. We therefore complicate some of the national conversations about writing programs and writing center administrator positions from the vantage point of the small college context. For example, in addressing the issue of professionalization, we underscore the ways in which the university preference for tenure lines may misunderstand a small college WPA position, and how that position is moving an institution toward a robust structure for its culture of writing. Attending to local context, after all, means working with institutional norms and histories in order to help that culture develop organically.

The next two sections focus on the curricular and student-centered realms, respectively. Section II focuses on the curricular delivery of writing instruction. In "Writing Requirements" (Chapter 6), we present the trends in writing requirements at small liberal arts colleges, arguing once again that to overlook embedded requirements is to misunderstand an institution's culture of writing. The requirement data show that these are largely WAC-based institutions. The next two chapters focus on how requirements are implemented. Chapter 7, "Staffing First-Year Writing," focuses on the dominant approaches to first-year writing, discussing how first-year composition and first-year writing seminar programs are configured, specifically in terms of the interrelated questions of class size, exemption, and staffing. National conversations about first-year writing typically elide the latter, WAC-based, approach. Small colleges trouble that elision, offering numerous examples of how this approach succeeds. In particular, this chapter explores how WAC-based approaches make first-year writing a vehicle for college-wide dissemination of writing pedagogy, while FYC-based approaches promise greater consistency in how those courses are taught. Chapter 8, "Small College Writing Programs: Leadership Configurations and Requirements," returns to leadership configurations. By putting leadership configurations in relation to requirements, this chapter presents the trends in program structure at the schools in the sample. This allows us to more fully understand the complexity of curriculum-centered sites of writing.

Section III turns to the student-centered realm. Here, questions of how to materialize a culture of writing focus on the support of individual students rather than on curricular innovations. At small colleges grappling with supporting students with diverse types of preparedness, changes begin to be made both to particular student-centered structures and the administrative oversight of these structures. As we discuss in Chapter 9, "Writing Centers," writing centers at small liberal arts colleges share the contours, goals, and challenges of most writing centers nationwide, although they exhibit an overwhelming reliance on peer tutors. We discuss why this might be, building on the findings of the Peer Writing Tutor Alumni Research Project to show how the lessons of peer tutoring are consonant with the historic and current missions of liberal arts colleges. Chapter 10, "Supporting Diversely Prepared Writers," addresses the question of diversely prepared writers. Academic support is a vexing topic for small colleges. As student populations change, these institutions need to rethink some aspects of their approach to writing instruction. Crude placement mechanisms that rely on quantitative data are anathema to small colleges, but as numbers of English Language Learners (ELL) increase at these schools, new conversations are starting to generate change. In some cases, the influx of new student populations seems to be driving the creation of new administrative positions on the student-centered side. In other cases, new initiatives in the field, such as directed self-placement, provide small colleges with useful ways to understand the tasks they face.

Section IV concludes the book. First, in Chapter 11, "Assessment," we argue that assessment at small colleges brings student- and curriculum-centered concerns together. Assessment has come belatedly to small colleges, in part because much of the language of the assessment movement is antithetical to the small college structure of feeling and its emphasis on unquantifiable learning. But the assessment models we uncovered reveal the nature of small college writing programs as inter-related and complex, since they bring together curricular assessment, student support, and faculty development. In this chapter, we describe three programs in detail, showing how the scale of these institutions makes assessment feedback loops possible and necessary in order to sustain a strong culture of writing. In the conclusion (Chapter 12), we describe what writing programs typically look like at small colleges at the beginning of the twenty-first century. We put the trends and patterns uncovered by our analyses in the context of questions for future research.

Small liberal arts colleges offer writing-rich environments in many ways. Writing may be highly visible, in the form of explicit requirements, established committees, and other formal structures; or it may be visible but embedded in other entities. Most challenging of all, it may be diffused throughout the institution in the pedagogical practices of the faculty and the habits of the students. Most small college faculty believe in the importance of writing and, at the very least, assign it regularly. The goal of this book is to provide the fullest possible picture of the field of writing program administration from the vantage point of a particular type of institution. In doing so, we have also sought to offer *all* writing program administrators some tools and considerations for analyzing and understanding their local contexts. There is no one perfect design for a writing program at a small liberal arts college. But in our encounters with our fellow SLACers—the writing program administrators and writing center directors involved in this study—we have been constantly struck at their abiding commitment to getting it right, to maximizing the educational opportunities for students and faculty alike. While one aspect of this work is bringing their particular institutions into conversation with the trends and discussions in the field, another aspect is shedding light on local structures as they exist. We hope that this book helps both endeavors.

4 Configurations of Writing Program Leadership

The hybridization of our location offers the means to break out of insularity and into a non-hierarchical, dynamic professional space, one that can accommodate the diverse identifications evident in our membership base and our multiple locations, as scholars and teachers engaged in, and by, WPA-work.

—Jeanne Gunner

In order to better understand the variety of reporting lines a director of a . . . writing program might see, let's begin by looking at what the "normal" reporting line would be if the program were housed within a traditional English department. In this situation, the director would have some kind of administrative or quasi-administrative title and report to the department chair or head. This structure is clean, straightforward, and easily understood . . . Once outside of departmental structures, however, the program director might report to a dean, an associate dean, a provost, an associate provost, or perhaps some other administrative entity. Part of the determination of the reporting line will depend on the nature of the program itself.

—Barry M. Maid

Barry Maid and Jeanne Gunner provide us with different ways to think about the constraints and possibilities contained in any writing program's structure. While Gunner celebrates hybridity, Maid offers a more pragmatic view of the difficulties that complex reporting lines can produce. Together, they direct our attention to what the positioning of the writing director reveals about the place and mission of writing instruction. How a writing program is configured has wide-ranging implications for its place and purpose. Institutions have philosophical, ideological, and historical reasons for developing their particular leadership configurations—as well as for reassessing them periodically. At small colleges, "hybrid" locations abound, and the reporting lines for writing program administrators are rarely "clean, straightforward, and easily understood." This complexity reflects the diffused nature of writing instruction at these institutions, and may require the WPA to create a "program" out of pieces that are not officially related. To do this—to use the position to create positive change—a WPA needs to understand how his or her position and its responsibilities fit into the institution's larger leadership structure.

The historical affinity of small colleges for writing across the curriculum leaves traces in these diffused structures and their complex leadership configurations. As Catherine Blair points out, WAC's grounding in a theory of knowledge that any community's "language is imbedded in its context . . . leads to a social theory of the university that holds that each of the disciplines is a separate culture, a context created through a separate language" ("Only One" 384). Many of our respondents described institutions that subscribe to this theory, and explained that in their contexts it would be inappropriate and ultimately counter-productive to have a single department be the primary site of writing instruction or, indeed, of administrative responsibility for writing. At some institutions, however, this principled resistance has resulted in a leadership configuration so diffuse as to be nearly impossible to locate. While in some cases this may be the result of poor website design or the tendency toward the insularity already discussed, in others it may indicate a culture of writing so deeply embedded that the institution cannot fully articulate its place or value.

In her 1999 essay, "Identity and Location: A Study of WPA Models, Memberships, and Agendas," Gunner examines "how we have formed and are forming our professional and organizational identity via WPA scholarship and its implicit and explicit models of the WPA position" (31). Challenging the self-reproducing insularity of conversations about WPA work, Gunner reviews the literature published in *WPA: Writing Program Administration* and other writing studies journals in order to show how WPA positions were theorized between 1979 and 1999. Critiquing the normalization of a "WPA identity" as professional, managerial, and research-driven in the face of a much more diverse membership, Gunner invokes Marcia Dickson's call "for local conditions as the guideline to program structure, with the issue of control decentered, replaced by collaborative enactments of WPA work" (Gunner 43). In delineating the common local conditions for a set of similar institutions, it is our hope to provide a heuristic for understanding the contours of programs that do not fit the norm, or that are not coextensive with their respective administrators (on the latter assumption, see Gunner, "Identity" 33).

The schools in this sample have programs that are, in a sense, difficult to recognize. As we sought to understand the programs at these institutions, we started by identifying their writing requirements. To describe trends in the sample most clearly, however, we begin here with the different configurations for leadership of writing. "Leadership" is a perhaps less bureaucratic notion than "administration"; this focus therefore reflects the anti-bureaucratic nature of the small college structure of feeling, a paradoxical system of values that resists formalization. Far from collapsing "program" into "WPA," these configurations uncover the variety of relationships between different writing administrative positions by bringing the curriculum-centered and student-centered pieces into conversation with one another. How an institution assigns human resources to the task of leading its culture of writing reveals which aspects of that culture it emphasizes.

Identifying and naming configurations allows us as researchers to document trends in the sample. In theorizing trends in light of the small college structure of feeling, we are seeking to understand how the trends uncovered compare to what may or may not be described in the WPA literature. This analysis provides us with terminology to discuss the complexity of small college writing programs in ways that, to date, the field has not. Our categories of leadership configuration enable comparative analysis between similar units in our data sample, units that pride themselves on their uniqueness. This analysis also leads us to name those things that were embedded, or that were left unnamed by the survey respondents, but which nevertheless seem to play a role in the leadership configuration of an institution. As a result, we rethink how "program" and "administration" are defined at small colleges.

In the remainder of the chapter, we turn to configurations of leadership positions within the different writing programs. We begin by describing the process of analysis that led to the different configurations. We then define and analyze the configurations we have uncovered, introducing a rich description of each. In describing the pros and cons of these various leadership configurations, we ask why particular institutions subscribe to particular configurations. After describing the individual configurations, we then discuss the trends within them. We conclude with a series of more general considerations for any institution or WPA attempting to map and refine their leadership configurations.

CONFIGURATIONS OF LEADERSHIP

As discussed earlier, it is common for writing programs at small colleges to be made up of a variety of entities that may be more or less well-coordinated with one another. This is why we have used the term "program"—following Phelps—in the broadest sense possible. Survey respondents reflected our own difficulty in identifying the various pieces of their programs. For example, in response to question 36, "Are these different pieces [items such as WAC and first-year writing, checked off in question 35] part of a formal writing program?" forty-three respondents answered "no," and one responded "sort of." Of the fifty-four who responded that they *do* have a formal program, we noticed when analyzing the data that some respondents had omitted a site of delivery for writing instruction and, with it, a part of their leadership configuration. For example, one institution has a first-year composition requirement that is embedded in the English department, administered by a WPA, and a well-established writing center with a writing fellows program overseen by a writing center director. In completing the survey, the writing center director (WCD) did not include first-year composition as part of the writing program. From conversations with the WPA and WCD, we do not believe this was necessarily an issue of personalities failing to get along, but rather that the institution has chosen to understand its endeavors with writing instruction as independent units rather than unified components of a formal program. What is labeled as the writing program includes the activities of the writing center, whereas first-year composition constitutes a requirement facilitated through the English department. The fact that the explicit writing program leadership rests in the student support structure implies that the culture of writing relies more on addressing student deficits with writing. Upon a closer look, however, with a broader notion of program, we are able to uncover two parallel narratives for this institution's culture of writing—one that supports developing writers as individuals, and one that develops writers through the curriculum.

Other respondents signaled that their institutions have a similar resistance to compartmentalizing or centralizing activities around the culture of writing: "Not many faculty at this college would call what we do a 'formal writing program'; they are more like separate component parts," wrote one respondent. Another mused, "They are different, and we work to make them complimentary [sic], but I wouldn't describe what we do as 'formal.' It has developed somewhat anarchically." And a third confesses, "the teaching/learning of writing is dispersed, with no coherent oversight or cohesive plan bridging the various pieces." No matter what explicit components of a writing program are in place at an institution, we also identified the embedded components of an institution's leadership configurations in order to fully understand the material aspects of the school's culture of writing. We find that explicit structures do not necessarily correlate with more value or resources for writing. In other words, an embedded structure does not *necessarily* indicate a lack of respect for, or attention to, writing instruction. While it is true that aspects of a program can be so embedded as to provide little value to the institution, in other cases, the embeddedness exists to promote a faculty-owned, diffused culture of writing. According to Martha Townsend, John Bean reported such a rationale for Seattle University's decision *not* to adopt a writing intensive requirement in order to facilitate writing across the curriculum ("Writing Intensive" 237).

Small colleges' comfort with embedded elements may also derive from their historical preference for both faculty governance and faculty autonomy. In order to articulate the implications of this for WPA work, Thomas Amorose builds on David V. J. Bell's distinction between power, authority, and influence (Amorose, "WPA Work" 89). While power operates through the prospect of explicit sanctions (both positive and negative), authority "relies . . . on tradition and social institutions" (89), and influence "uses persuasion, in this case persuading people of the benefits that could accrue from their own acts" (90). Responding to "a body of literature . . . advis[ing] the writing administrator on how to claim and use power to offset threats and dangers to her program" (94), Amorose insists that this emphasis is not useful in the small college context: "[I]nfluence is easily the most necessary to the small-school WPA, while authority may be the most available" (93). "The solo exertion of power," he warns, "can prove problematic and even dangerous" (93). In our discussions of the configurations of leadership in our sample, we draw on the three types of WPA agency Amorose elaborates. We are, however, reluctant to insist that one form of agency trumps the others in every case.

By mapping the institutional cultures of writing on the Venn diagram presented in the previous chapter, we categorized all the writing programs in the sample into one of six leadership configurations. The Venn diagram is an apparently simple heuristic for complex structures. Our analysis explores the complexities of each of the leadership configurations. We developed the configurations by looking at several types of data: survey responses and follow-up questions; website and catalog analysis; and self-classification. Subscribing to grounded theory practice, in some cases we asked respondents to identify their institution's configuration. As we looked over the profiles of the different schools, it became clear that schools typically provided leadership positions for both the curricular and the student side. We first categorized the different requirements (see Chapter 6), and then looked to see if a person or committee oversaw each requirement. This process was repeated when looking at student support. The first one-third of the survey asked questions about the respondent's position within the writing program and the institution, and also for a description of additional leadership positions within the writing program. As we began to cull through the data, our goal was to uncover trends or patterns in how writing programs are defined and administered at small colleges. In some cases, respondents' answers on the survey identified all positions, but (as mentioned earlier) in some cases they did not. As we further analyzed the various data for each school, we formed a hypothesis about that institution—often to then find additional components in other locations or embedded within different entities. In some cases we uncovered a leadership vacuum.

In articulating these configurations, we refer only to the primary writing program administrator and writing center director. Sixty-seven of the respondent schools do not have leadership positions within the writing program beyond those two, but other schools have at least one other person who assists in the leadership of the writing program.

Table 4.1 shows the presence and contours of these additional positions.

Table 4.1 Leadership Positions beyond the Primary WPA/WCD.

Type of position	Number of schools
No additional administrative positions*	67
At least one additional full-time position	20
At least one part-time position	6
Dean or Chair (embedded)	3
Intern	1
Post docs	1
Data Unavailable	2

* This does not include administrative assistants or clerical assistance.

The sections that follow are organized according to the two-position configurations we identified, including: *Explicit WPA + Explicit WCD*; *Solo WPA/WCD*; *Explicit WCD Only*; *Embedded WPA + Explicit WCD*; *Explicit WPA Only*; and *No WPA or WCD*.

Explicit WPA + Explicit WCD

The most common leadership configuration at small liberal arts colleges, represented by thirty-eight of the schools in our data set, includes an explicit writing program administrator (WPA) with curricular responsibilities and an explicit writing center director (WCD) with student-centered responsibilities. As explained in Chapter 3, the "explicit" designation for these positions derives from either the inclusion of this work in the job title or the survey respondent's self-identification. The WPA may oversee the first-year writing program, a suite of academic writing courses, WAC, or a combination of the three, depending on the individual school's writing requirement and culture—there is no overwhelming pattern. Twenty-five of these WPAs represent permanent positions in which the individual was either hired or appointed to that position for an indefinite amount of time; thirteen of these WPA positions rotate amongst the standing faculty. (The latter category is more typical for WAC directorships, although in five cases the position of director of FYC rotates amongst English department members.)

These thirty-eight schools also employ an explicit WCD, whose responsibilities rest within the student-centered domain. In four cases, the WCD also serves as the director of academic or learning resources. It is typical in the field to consider such positions as writing center directors (see, for example, Balester and McDonald 62; Healy, "Writing Center Directors" 28–9). We found that some of our respondents self-identified as writing center directors even though their appointments and titles were in learning or academic resource centers.

The *Explicit WPA + Explicit WCD* leadership configuration sends a clear signal that the institution has committed to both the curriculum and student-centered modes of delivery for their culture of writing. Ideally, the two individuals have their own responsibilities, but they collaborate and work together to present a shared vision of writing. For example, the WPA and WCD may collaborate on faculty development sessions, in which the WCD shares his or her insights from working in the writing center, and combines them with the WPA's insights from his or her oversight of first-year writing. Together, the two individuals work to foster a culture of writing across the curriculum. When such collaboration takes place, the WPA and WCD promote a shared vision of the writing program, even though they may have different institutional homes.[1]

The explicit nature of the commitment to writing that this configuration indicates, however, does not guarantee that the two positions in this configuration are part of a formal writing program, or even that they have a shared vision for such a program. The institution may feel that the separation of these identities bolsters the diffused culture of writing it wishes to foster in its faculty and students: If no one person or department oversees all the sites of writing, then the college as a whole owns writing. The danger of this configuration, we learned as we spoke to our respondents, is that it's possible for explicit WPAs and WCDs to operate in parallel universes—they rarely work together and, in some cases, do not even define themselves as belonging to the same writing program. Eight of the thirty-eight respondents in this category reported that they did not think the different sites of writing as part of a formal program. Six of the thirty who said they had a formal writing program failed to account for another site of writing delivery or another WPA (for example, the WCD) when describing that program, which suggests that there are few opportunities—or perhaps little inclination—for collaboration at those institutions. Certain factors seem to contribute to this. For example, if the WPA position is defined as a rotating position, the individuals who assume it may not invest in the responsibilities long enough to make significant changes or to develop collaborative projects with the writing center director. (It is important to note, however, that this kind of rotation may have no effect on the degree of coordination or collaboration between the two spheres. In some cases, the rotating WAC director works closely with the writing center director to provide faculty development and to work on different assessment projects.) This kind of fractured writing program can derive from competing cultures of writing on a single campus, and can, as a result, send contradictory messages to students and faculty about the role of writing in undergraduate education. For example, a composite institution that we'll call "Mixed Signals College" has an explicit writing center director (located in a larger academic support center) and an explicit writing program administrator (a rotating position held by tenure-line faculty for two-year terms). At Mixed Signals, the academic support center is perceived on campus as a deficit-model support center for struggling students. The WPA is charged with chairing the writing committee, which oversees a WAC-based requirement that no student can place out of. As a result, Mixed Signals has both deficit and developmental models for writing instruction competing for its attention and time. The culture of writing is, at best, murky.

Another complication we cannot see in the basic map of *Explicit WPA + Explicit WCD* is that, in some cases, there may be an aspect of the writing requirement, program, or culture that does not fall under the jurisdiction of either the WPA or the WCD, creating a leadership vacuum. In a school that requires both first-year composition taught within the English department and a first-year writing seminar taught by faculty across the college, for example, the "explicit WPA" may be the WAC director overseeing the seminar program, while the composition program is overseen by the chair of the English department (who serves as an additional, embedded WPA—a category we discuss shortly), whose responsibility for first-year composition is comparable to that of any other course staffed by her department. The reverse may also be true, where the WPA oversees first-year composition, but a faculty committee or academic dean oversees the WAC aspects of the curriculum. In both cases, the existence of a third entity with administrative responsibility for a site of writing may reinforce the notion that this structure is one of separate and distinct—rather than coordinated—domains.

Ultimately, the *Explicit WPA + Explicit WCD* configuration promotes autonomy for both positions, with each able to assume responsibility and authority over her or his respective sphere. On the other hand, it leaves open the possibility of the two administrators working at cross-purposes and, as a result, failing to articulate a unified vision for the place of writing at the institution.

Solo WPA/WCD

The next category may be the most unique to the small college context. These WPAs oversee aspects of the curriculum-centered writing program, such as first-year writing and/or WAC, while also supervising the logistics of the writing center and, in some cases, a writing fellows program. Twenty-nine schools utilize this configuration. At two schools where this position is shared, the individuals collaborate on all aspects of the writing program in a fashion similar to two individuals serving as co-directors of a writing center. Because these leadership configurations are focused on *positions* rather than *individuals*, we have classified these schools under this category rather than in the *Explicit WPA + Explicit WCD* category.

The *Solo WPA/WCD* configuration conjures up the image of the WPA who serves as "all things writing" on her or his campus, serving as the locus of questions, concerns, initiatives, and programs that range widely and amorphously. As Rebecca G. Taylor puts it, in these cases, "there is no 'us'" for the writing program; "[t]here's only me" (67). The nature and extent of the responsibilities assigned to any solo WPA/WCD depend on both the individual person and the institution's expectations, assumptions, and desires for its culture of writing. It is possible that the culture of writing on a particular solo WPA/WCD's campus may be one that sees the writing program comprised of a service course designed to reverse the writing deficits of incoming students, and a writing center created to work with remedial students. The solo WPA/WCD is the person who will then singlehandedly "fix" the writing "problem." At other institutions, the solo WPA/WCD is clearly valued for his or her expertise in rhetoric and composition; she or he is therefore able to bring the institution's values and the best practices identified in the field into conversation and collaboration to improve the culture of writing on campus. As with any leadership configuration, then, the range of schools employing it presents a complicated picture.

Schools may stumble into this configuration. The solo WPA/WCD's portfolio of responsibilities may have expanded as the writing "program" grew slowly and organically. Schools may also elect this type of position because it reflects a culture of writing that intertwines student-focused and curriculum-centered approaches to writing instruction. (This would be the case at an institution where the WAC-based writing requirement is primarily supported through a writing fellows program.) One of the challenges of this configuration is that there can easily be multiple and simultaneous understandings of it. For some, the solo WPA/WCD supports student writers; the position exists to work with diversely prepared students in the writing center and through academic writing courses. Others on the same campus may believe that the primary responsibility of the solo WPA/WCD is to support the WAC program by (1) training, mentoring, and providing writing fellows to courses, and (2) conducting faculty development sessions and overseeing assessment projects. But this challenge is also an opportunity. The solo WPA/WCD position allows writing program leadership to address both goals with one person. By unifying these responsibilities, the school's culture of writing can celebrate the development of *all* students as writers.

It is possible to see this position as necessarily overburdened and isolated, but it is important to also recognize that solo administrators have enormous leeway to design and implement initiatives in the hybrid space between the curriculum- and student-centered domains. Every leadership configuration comes with both pros and cons. The scale of a small college means that the solo WPA/WCD—like any small college WPA or WCD—is likely to find him or herself highly visible and necessarily less marginalized than at larger institutions (Hebb 98). As Libby Falk Jones points out, however, "[v]isibility is a two-edged sword; . . . it brings recognition and can thus lead to accomplishments . . . [but] a highly-visible WPA, especially one expected to be a change-agent, can serve as an easy target for a variety of institutional complaints" (80). While this is true of all SLAC WPAs, these pressures and opportunities are particularly vivid in the case of the *Solo WPA/WCD* configuration.

WPAs work with others on campus to mold and lead the institution to a stronger culture of writing. Fifteen of the twenty-nine solo WPA/WCDs work with a faculty advisory committee and another four have an assistant director to help with the leadership of the program. Even though the person may feel as if he or she is the only writing person on campus, there may be embedded opportunities for collaboration. The institution may choose to have a committee in addition to the solo WPA in order to maintain shared ownership of the writing values, but without expertise, this committee may not be able to provide faculty development or assessment. It would be a rare small college to be comfortable with a single individual overseeing a crucial part of the curriculum alone; faculty governance diffuses such responsibility onto committees at nearly every turn. As a result, solo WPA/WCDs can sometimes look like caretakers with little actual authority. But by leading from within—by exerting influence, rather than looking for power—solo WPA/WCDs can transform writing instruction at their institutions.

In an attempt to show shared ownership of the culture of writing, however, the college may inadvertently create a leadership vacuum. For example, at the hypothetical Tipping Point College, the writing requirement mandates that students take a set of writing-intensive courses, which fulfill certain guidelines and typically have attached writing fellows. This college also has a strong writing center. The solo WPA/WCD oversees the writing center, the writing fellows program, and a set of academic writing courses. He or she also provides faculty development for those interested. Approval, oversight, and assessment of the writing-intensive courses, however, fall under the purview not of the solo WPA/WCD, but of a faculty committee—the membership of which rotates, and to which the WPA/WCD is not appointed *ex officio*. The institution may intend to promote faculty ownership of the writing requirement, but this approach creates a leadership vacuum in the curricular domain. No one with both expert and institutional knowledge is poised to respond to questions or concerns about the writing-intensive courses or the requirement. To address this vacuum, there needs to be a formalized relationship between the solo WPA/WCD and the faculty writing committee so that they can work together in providing ongoing, informed leadership for the hybrid, curricular- and student-centered writing program. At some institutions, this is done by having the solo WPA/WCD serve *ex officio* on the curriculum or writing committee. In such cases, the solo WPA/WCD could in some cases take the lead, but could also rely on the support and backing of the faculty committee.

Most of the solo WPA/WCDs' curricular responsibilities are WAC-centered rather than focused on a departmentally-based, first-year composition requirement. As a result, we saw few patterns for where these positions were housed, and it seems that this can be a central challenge for these positions. This is exacerbated when, for example, an institution moves from first-year composition to a WAC-based first-year writing seminar. While a solo WPA/WCD housed in English makes sense for a first-year composition requirement, this institutional home does not always translate easily when a college adopts first-year writing seminars. Some solo WPA/WCDs may find themselves in two reporting lines: to the English or writing department chair for their work with the first-year writing course, but to the provost or academic dean for their writing center or WAC work. (No solo WPA/WCDs report to deans of students.)

Perhaps the most signal challenge of the *Solo WPA/WCD*, however, is juggling.[2] As far as we know, this leadership configuration is particular to the small college context; it may well be that at larger institutions with more students, and hence bigger programs, it is impossible to imagine one person serving as "all things writing" on campus. The small college context may well also make it simultaneously easier and more tempting for individual WPAs and WCDs to expand the scope of their positions. As Thomas Amorose, Judith Hebb, Libby Falk Jones, and Erika Spohrer have variously noted, writing program administrators at small schools often find themselves at significant decision-making junctures—invited to serve on major committees or task forces, with easy and regular access to the upper administration. Taking advantage of such opportunities, however, means that solo program administrators will have to let go of other projects and initiatives. This calculation becomes even more complicated when the line between assumed and expected responsibilities is blurred. When only one person oversees the writing program, these responsibilities can become overwhelming. The solo WPA/WCD needs to be aware of how she or he spends time, how this division of time benefits the institution, and what may be lost if some responsibilities are prioritized over others.

More than almost every other leadership configuration we found, the *Solo WPA/WCD* structure is dynamic, both resulting from and furthering change. In fact, without understanding the recent histories of the schools with this configuration, it can be difficult to understand its complexities. Twelve of the twenty-nine solo WPA/WCD positions evolved out of a change within a preexisting configuration. Some solo WPA/WCDs started as writing center directors, firmly rooted in student-centered responsibilities. When their institutions shifted toward a more WAC-focused curriculum, those positions assumed additional responsibilities for faculty development and assessment (and, in some cases, became campus leaders on a variety of fronts as a result). Other solo WPA/WCDs were originally hired into English departments from other fields and, because of their secondary expertise in rhetoric and composition, were asked to create a writing center, writing fellows program, or WAC initiative. There is no clear pattern to how these shifts were initiated. In some cases, the change began at the initiative of the individual in question, while in other cases it came at the behest of the institution. In almost every instance, these positions were not originally designed to encompass all the responsibilities of the current incumbents, nor were they originally rooted in the overlap between curriculum- and student-centered domains. Over time, the institution and individual will need to decide when a second position needs to be added to the leadership of the writing program; at that time, they will also need to determine whether the configuration should be split into explicit WPA and explicit WCD or if the blended configuration should be maintained by hiring an assistant director.

Explicit WCD Only

The leadership configuration for sixteen of our respondent schools seems to rest in the student-centered domain. These schools lack a single person on campus who has explicit or embedded responsibility attached to the curriculum side of the writing program. The distinction between the *Solo WPA/WCD* configuration and the *Explicit WCD Only* is subtle. In the case of *WCD Only* schools, the institution—or sometimes the individual him- or herself—defines this position as primarily responsible for supporting the culture of writing attached to students rather than the curriculum. This can mean that these positions at first seem marginalized; however, we found that these writing center directors often had considerable stature and respect on their campuses.

Interestingly, all sixteen of these *Explicit WCD Only* schools take a WAC-based approach to the delivery of writing instruction, a more consistent pattern than we see in either *Explicit WPA + Explicit WCD* or *Solo WPA/WCD* institutions. Six require writing-intensive courses beyond the first year. None have first-year composition housed within a single department, but only one does not have first-year writing. This WAC philosophy means that there are typically sites of writing instruction peppered throughout these institutions, although most of these schools have elected to locate rhetoric and composition expertise in the student-centered domain. The diffused nature of curriculum-centered support for writing may help to explain why the respondents from this set of schools saw the least formality in their institutions' writing programs. Twelve out of sixteen (75%) do not see the various pieces they identified as part of a coherent or formal program. More than any other configuration discussed thus far, the *Explicit WCD Only* writing center directors seem to operate through the kinds of indirect measures and moral influence that Amorose describes.

When we asked these respondents to tell us whether they are the writing center director or writing program administrator (in an attempt to distinguish between *Solo WPA/WCD* and *Explicit WCD Only*), these individuals identified themselves as the writing center director, and then explained that the WPA position does not exist on their campuses. As the writing center director at College 5 explained,

> I'm the writing center director. There is no one WPA here. To the extent that we could carve out a definition of that position, I'd say it's a role shared by several people, including the chair of the Ad Hoc Writing Course Committee, the chair of the Curriculum Committee, the chair of the [interdisciplinary humanities and social science] department, the [FYWS] coordinator, the Core Division Director, and me.

When it works well, as Gunner points out, this hybridity of location can foster exciting collaborative efforts across the institution, pulling many stakeholders into the project of understanding and developing the institution's culture of writing ("Decentering" 9). As with this example, in the *Explicit WCD Only* configuration, the writing center director rarely works in isolation; half of these schools maintain some version of a writing committee. In one case, the writing center director in fact has two co-assistant directors. In another, the director has assistance from the associate director of the learning and teaching center. Three people in this category are the directors of writing, teaching, and learning centers, but as discussed earlier, they self-identify as writing center directors. These writing center directors may have more power than implied by their status or position (something we'll pick up in the next chapter). They may have the autonomy and leeway to influence the curricular side of the culture of writing without having official responsibilities attached to it. Indeed, this can be a kind of ideal position from which to influence pedagogy throughout the college. A well-respected writing center director can make writing-centered pedagogy attractive and effective in part because he or she has no formal power over the curriculum.

On the downside, the configuration of *Explicit WCD Only* can send the message to the college community that writing instruction is not a matter of curricular concern, but rather a skill that students must master, albeit with institutional support. This, in turn, can imply a deficit model in which the writing program exists only to help those students who come to the institution underprepared for its academic rigor. These assumptions about the nature of writing instruction in turn shape the status of and pressures on the program's leaders. When a program is understood to exist solely in order to address gaps in student skills—to "fix" their writing problems—the writing center director will find it difficult to influence pedagogy in any meaningful way.

The lack of curriculum-centered leadership (such as an explicit WPA position) may also create a vacuum in that realm. For example, a school we might call "Rudderless College" has a first-year writing seminar requirement overseen by a faculty committee. The charge of this committee is to approve which courses are labeled FYWS based on guidelines adopted a decade ago. The writing center director serves on this committee and remains the only constant, as committee membership changes each year. The committee may facilitate an occasional faculty development session, but basically, once a course receives the FYWS designation, it is up to individual departments to oversee the success of these courses. No one person—or stable group of people—has responsibility for the success of the first-year writing seminar or is available to respond to any challenges that may arise with it. The requirement survives due to faculty commitment to the program, but the program has stagnated. As students increasingly complain about the uneven quality and requirements of the seminars, and departments resent allocating faculty resources to a program they do not understand, Rudderless may find itself doubting the utility of the program and of a first-year writing requirement entirely—rather than realizing that it has not provided the program with adequate leadership. One possibility to save the writing requirement at Rudderless would be for the writing center director to step in. At some of the *Explicit WCD Only* schools in our sample, we have seen a WCD facilitate faculty development sessions or an assessment project, hoping that such efforts will revitalize the first-year writing program by helping the institution realize what that program could become.

If the writing center director has success filling this gap, his or her responsibilities may grow beyond the initial portfolio. Due to the strong writing across the curriculum approach of the schools in the sample, we anticipate that, over time, at least some of these writing center directors will be pulled closer to the space where student- and curriculum-centered domains overlap and that, concomitantly, the institutions' configurations will morph from *Explicit WCD Only* to *Solo WPA/WCD*. The adoption or development of an *Explicit WCD Only* configuration can be a crucial first step toward a more integrated culture of writing. That said, it is important to fully understand how the writing center and its director are positioned on any particular campus and to identify the responsibilities attached to this position.

Embedded WPA + Explicit WCD

In *Explicit WCD Only*, we saw how aspects of the writing program could be diffused across positions and aspects of the institution. In the description from the writing center director at College 5, for example, it was clear that while the student-centered structures were centralized under her leadership, oversight of the curriculum-centered structures had many different locations. In *Embedded WPA + Explicit WCD*, by contrast, an explicit writing center director position exists alongside a single position which is not labeled "WPA," but whose portfolio of responsibilities includes the work of administering some aspects of the curriculum-centered writing program. Thirteen of the institutions in our sample fall into this category. Most often, these positions are those of directors of general education or chairs of English departments. In both cases, the administrative work falls under their purview because the courses in question do so. All of these programs have a first-year writing requirement; eight have a first-year composition course housed in a single department, and five have a WAC-based first-year writing requirement situated in a formal general education program, sometimes with its own name. For example, one school may have a program entitled *The "Open Book College" Critical Thinking Core Program*, in which the first-year writing seminar stands as one of a suite of courses students are required to take.

Embedded WPAs can be difficult to spot. In fact, a writing center director hired into an institution with this configuration may discover only belatedly and with surprise that there is, indeed, an embedded site for the administration of the curriculum-centered aspects of the program. It is perhaps evident that a self-identified writing program administrator is highly unlikely to be hired into an embedded position unless the institution wants to shift the position from embedded to explicit leadership. These positions tend to rotate amongst the institution's tenure-line faculty, and the WPA work they do is typically defined—to use David Schwalm's distinction—as tasks rather than as a position (9; see also McLeod, *Writing Program Administration* 8–9). Embedded WPAs do not self-identify as campus leaders regarding writing—even if they are leaders in other regards.

In contrast to the *Explicit WPA + Explicit WCD* configuration, primary leadership in this configuration seems to lie in the student-centered realm. Our lead respondents from schools with this configuration were predominantly writing center directors, and these WCDs are more likely to have tenure and/or faculty status than do those in the *Explicit WPA + Explicit WCD* and *WCD Only* configurations. This may be because the WCDs at *Explicit WPA + Explicit WCD* schools are junior to the WPAs, while at *WCD Only* schools they are more often staff positions. (We discuss issues of status for all writing administrative positions in Chapter 5.) This difference underscores the ways in which the WCDs in this configuration seem to have significant respect and influence on their campuses, which we might otherwise overlook. On the other hand, their influence may be limited by an embedded WPA's presence; without providing leadership for the culture of writing, the embedded WPA may have a strong sense of ownership over his or her piece of the writing program. The writing center director may have to work carefully around the embedded WPA's turf in order to find ways to further support and influence the teaching of writing across the institution.

Typically, such opportunities develop when a college wants to expand its writing across the curriculum initiatives (as is the case in *WCD Only* schools). For example, hypothetical Stealth College has an embedded WPA who is the chair of the English department. This English chair oversees the writing requirement because it is a first-year composition course staffed entirely by English faculty. This chair is primarily concerned with staffing and scheduling the thirty-five sections needed each year. Most of these sections are taught by full-time, non tenure-line faculty, one of whom is also charged with overseeing the daily operations of the writing center. After some time directing the writing center and seeing students from across the entire college, this WCD realizes that there is a leadership vacuum around writing across the curriculum (which no one at Stealth is thinking about consistently), and proposes that his or her responsibilities shift slightly to encompass those initiatives. We heard a story much like this from our respondent from College 24, a tenure-line writing center director:

> WAC is not very robust at [College 24] in any kind of programmatic way; rather, individual faculty continue to integrate writing in their courses in meaningful ways but without the support and stimulation of ongoing faculty development. Our WAC committee, that is to say, has become an administrative body for the certification and recertification of WI courses but really doesn't have a pedagogical presence. Thus, my proposal to use the WC and its student/tutor based operations is a way of generating a "bottom up" rather than "top down" approach to WAC and to revitalize that program.

The sequence of writing requirements at College 24 is more complex and vertical than that we imagined for Stealth College. At College 24, there is a two-semester first-year composition sequence (administered by the English department chair), plus two additional writing-intensive courses (administered by the WAC committee). In his response to the survey, the writing center director identifies a lacuna in the school's leadership configuration: "individual faculty . . . integrate writing in their courses in meaningful ways but without the support and stimulation of ongoing faculty development." Using writing center resources to take the lead in providing faculty development, this director is likely to move into the overlapping space between curriculum- and student-centered domains and shift the culture of writing in significant ways.

While keeping first-year writing the domain of a single department, the *Embedded WPA + Explicit WCD* configuration allows WAC to be "owned" by the faculty as a whole—a democratization important to the small college structure of feeling. On the other hand, this configuration may foster separation between various components of the writing program. If, as at College 24, the WCD focuses faculty development efforts on WAC, first-year writing faculty may miss out on those opportunities. In particular, if first-year composition is led and taught entirely by literature faculty, and unsupported by the writing center or WAC, the course and curriculum may suffer from that disconnection from the field of rhetoric and composition.

Explicit WPA Only and No WPA or WCD

The last two configurations we analyzed from the data are by far the smallest. While the $n=2$ in each case makes it difficult to generalize, we nevertheless want to describe these two structures because they pose important considerations. Two schools' structures were *Explicit WPA Only*. Analogous to the *Explicit WCD Only* configuration, these schools have a writing program administrator who oversees a part of the institution's writing requirement (one oversees first-year composition and the other oversees WAC initiatives), but no single position whose responsibilities include those of a writing center director (even embedded). At first, we considered describing these institutions as *Explicit WPA + Embedded WCD*—a possible configuration that we did not actually find in our sample. In fact, these institutions have embedded writing tutoring in a learning or academic resources center. In both cases, however, the director of that center is not solely responsible for training, oversight, and support of the writing tutors. Instead, those responsibilities are dispersed, with, for example, administrative oversight coming from the director but training in writing center pedagogy coming from another position.

It is difficult to generalize with only two schools in the sample exhibiting this configuration. In both cases, the limited or overlapping nature of the WPA's responsibilities poses particular challenges. At one, the writing requirement is solely a first-year composition course housed in English. Here, the WPA simply carries out a set of largely managerial tasks to make sure that the first-year composition course runs smoothly. Student-centered writing support is provided to students by a small group of peer tutors and one professional tutor, all housed in an academic resource center. We were unable to determine how much training these tutors receive and who provides it. There seems to be no formal WAC program at this institution. Writing instruction here is the province of a single department, and the WPA's work is so little distinguished from that of the chair of English that he or she is without either the status or the platform necessary to provide real leadership.

The other institution with this configuration presents a much more positive picture. It has a first-year composition requirement and a WID approach to writing beyond the first year; its writing tutors (both peer and professional) are housed in a larger, academic tutoring center. There is no clear writing center director; while the tutoring center has a staff coordinator who oversees scheduling and day-to-day operations, tutor development for the peer tutors is provided by one of the professional tutors. On the curricular side, the English department chair functions as an embedded WPA, overseeing the composition course. In addition, there is an explicit WPA charged with assessment, faculty development for composition faculty, and development of individual majors' disciplinary writing plans. (We might have designated this as a seventh configuration, *Embedded WPA + Explicit WPA*, but true to our approach throughout, we respected our respondent's identification.) While this configuration laudably unifies faculty development and assessment in the hands of a writing specialist, the overlapping and perhaps competing areas of responsibility for writing at the curricular level make this configuration a political challenge. While both of these institutions have a diffused approach to writing program leadership, the second seems to support a stronger culture of writing.

The last category—*No WPA or WCD*—represents the two schools in our sample that have a writing requirement, but for which the respondent identified the school as not having a writing program administrator, a writing center director, or even a writing program. (As we discussed in Chapter 2, three schools were dropped from the sample because they had no WPA, WCD, and writing requirement. Three schools were dropped because each had a completely diffused leadership configuration.) In both of these cases, an academic dean completed the survey. Both of these schools require a first-year seminar that is not writing intensive. One of the schools also requires a first-year writing seminar, while the other requires a writing-intensive course beyond the first year. One of the two schools has a faculty committee overseeing aspects of the writing requirement. In both cases, the tutoring of writing is, as we describe above, deeply embedded within a learning center.

This category provides no focused and expert leadership for writing. Given that such collaborative and dispersed ownership of the writing requirement is in some ways a logical expression of the small college structure of feeling, an institution might well ask not just when, but why it should create a formal position to administer any part of its culture of writing. Institutions with this configuration are isolated from national conversations in rhetoric and composition and are, as a result, missing out on many of the best practices developed in the field. A writing program administrator, as we have discussed throughout, is crucial in bringing those developments to his or her campus, and helping local colleagues adapt and refine to foster a particular culture of writing. More research is needed to understand the particular cultures of schools with writing requirements but no formal writing program administrators.

COMMITTEES

Committees provide a way to share leadership and governance of writing while also capitalizing on the kinds of expertise we believe are needed and best embodied in a professional writing administrator. The centrality of committee governance at small colleges provides a mechanism through which oversight of writing is simultaneously centralized and shared. Forty-nine of the schools in the sample have a faculty writing committee, although the goals of these committees vary. The make-up of these committees also reflects the cross-disciplinary nature of writing instruction at these institutions, since they typically draw on faculty from several disciplines, often with an aim of achieving a balance among the three academic divisions. Some committees also include students. In some cases, the committee has a direct role in administering the requirement: educating faculty, with or through the WPA, about writing across the curriculum; developing or disseminating the local definition of what constitutes a "writing-intensive" or "writing-rich" course; or determining which proposed courses meet the criteria. When the WPA is either a standing member of such a committee or has a close working relationship with it, this committee can provide a crucial platform for launching and maintaining conversations about the teaching of writing.

Committees that do not have direct oversight of requirements are often charged with faculty development around it. The committee may advise the writing program administrator and writing center director on the challenges faculty have in teaching writing and make suggestions for workshops or speakers. Several of our respondents commented on how the writing committees on their campuses had initiated small assessment projects. In these cases, such efforts helped other faculty embrace assessment as a way to gather data with an eye toward improving pedagogy and student learning, rather than simply justifying existing practices. While we discuss writing assessment at small colleges in more detail in Chapter 11, it is worth noting here that our respondents emphasized how writing committees could initiate projects particularly effectively because they were not perceived as advancing specific agendas. For example, the writing committee might invite a sub-set of faculty teaching in a first-year seminar program to read a set of student papers together in order to assess the impact of the seminar on student learning. In some cases, the writing program administrator is consulted and asked to provide a rubric for such sessions, while in other cases, the committee—which often includes the WPA—works with the assembled group to create guidelines for assessment based on the papers they have gathered for the exercise.

TRENDS AND FURTHER CONSIDERATIONS

Identifying the leadership configuration of an institution's writing program is a key step in understanding not just the local culture of writing but also the material conditions that shape it. In this chapter, we have sought to elaborate the complexities inherent in each of the six configurations identified. Naming and analyzing these configurations allows us to go beyond Marcia Dickson's call for understanding writing programs as organic entities, growing out of and attuned to their local conditions. Local context matters, but understanding how one institution resembles and differs from another is the key to evaluating and ultimately improving them. Leadership configurations have long been the field's entry point into understanding writing programs (Gunner, "Identity" 31–32). While a program is not synonymous with its director, these configurations help us begin to identify groups of schools within our sample. Table 4.2 presents the number of each configuration represented in the sample. Much like the norm assumed in WPA literature, the predominant leadership configuration at small colleges is the *Explicit WPA + Explicit WCD* configuration. Indeed, at this point, it seems almost natural that both curriculum- and student-centered spheres should benefit from explicit leadership. However, small colleges' history of embedded writing instruction throughout the curriculum makes it somewhat surprising that so many schools have allocated human resources to the curricular side.

Table 4.2 Leadership Configurations at 100 Small Liberal Arts Colleges.

Name of Category	Number of Schools
Explicit WPA+ Explicit WCD	38
Solo WPA/WCD	29
Explicit WCD only	16
Embedded WPA+ Explicit WCD	13
Explicit WPA only	2
No WPA or WCD	2

Currently, small colleges are creating and making more explicit leadership positions within their writing programs. In the last decade, forty-two of the schools in the sample expanded their configurations of leadership with full-time positions: twenty-five hired a new full-time writing program administrator or writing center director, and eight of these same schools hired more than one full-time position. Schools may have shifted from an *Explicit WCD Only* to an *Explicit WPA + Explicit WCD* configuration by hiring a new writing director to focus on the curricular side. Others, however, may have not had any systematic leadership historically but, over the course of the last decade, have added both a WPA and a WCD. The most significant trend we identified overall is that leadership configurations are changing and expanding as institutions realize that the very diffusion they value can produce a leadership vacuum and unrealized goals. One engine of this realization seems to be writing assessment, driven in some cases by external forces (see Chapter 11). Through assessment activities, small colleges revisit the question of why writing exists in the curriculum and begin to identify and measure goals around writing instruction.

At any college or university, understanding the culture of writing requires understanding the configuration of leadership of the writing program. This seems obvious, but fully understanding the relationship between the culture of writing and the leadership configuration is essential to supporting, developing, or changing that culture. Jeanne Gunner's resistance to a facile equation of administrator and program is well taken here. Understanding a leadership configuration in full encompasses comprehending how all the various pieces work together within the institution's particular and idiosyncratic culture. There is no perfect configuration, and no single structure guarantees a particular culture of writing. In addition, there is no single, ideal culture of writing across institutions—even institutions that share a structure of feeling.

5 Positioning of Writing Program Administrators

[T]he WPA has no uniform defined role. Each operates differently, depending on his or her individual context.

—Diane Boehm

The leadership configurations presented in the previous chapter help us better understand the material form of small college writing programs, but they do not help us understand what writing administrators at these institutions do on a daily or yearly basis—nor do they help us understand how those positions are understood in an institutional context. In this chapter, we move deeper into the leadership configurations, looking at the responsibilities and status associated with the writing program administrator and writing center director positions across our sample. Throughout our analysis, we tease out differences in this realm by considering the difference leadership configurations make to the WPA or WCD's status and set of responsibilities. We explore how these three factors—job responsibilities, position status, and leadership configuration—affect a position's degree of authority and influence on a given campus. The responsibilities of all types of writing administrators give us a glimpse into what a program does that isn't simply encapsulated in formal structures like requirements and writing centers. Our sample challenges assumptions in the field about what kinds of status (e.g., tenure lines, faculty status, PhDs in rhet/comp) are required for WPA authority. By examining the range of responsibilities undertaken by small college WPAs, the different levels of status, and the variety of ways writing program leadership positions are defined institutionally through different leadership configurations, we can begin to understand the work and place of writing program administration at small liberal arts colleges.

Most of the schools in the sample reported diffuse and at times amorphous cultures of writing. The writing administrators who were our primary respondents were at times rueful about this, at times proud. While this diffusion can make a program difficult to identify and lead, it's a residue of the nineteenth-century college's focus on language instruction across the curriculum. At small institutions today, most faculty still teach with writing, and many of them think of themselves as teaching students how to write. Only rarely is there a notion that teaching writing belongs to a small set of faculty or a particular corner of the institution. As a result, writing administrators of all types must persuade their colleagues across the college to evaluate the way they teach and, periodically, the way they structure writing curricula. Power—with its connotation of compulsion—is a misleading metric in this structure of feeling; small college writing administrators lead most effectively by quietly demonstrating their expertise.

In April 2010, Barbara L'Eplattenier began a thread on the WPA electronic list asking for the members' anecdotal sense of the extent to which the status of WPA positions had (or had not) improved since Gary A. Olson and Joseph M. Moxley's 1989 study found that "many freshman English directors possess little administrative power" (51) and were, in fact, considered "supervisor[s], not . . . director[s] in the full sense of the word" by the chairs of the English departments they surveyed (52; see also L'Eplattenier, "WPA's authority/Chair's attitudes"). In response, Edward White wrote that his 2005 survey of fifteen "large, public flagship institutions" found mostly "serious composition programs, with reasonable TA loads, WPA-led training programs, and other signs of modern WPA authority and recognition." "Professional program direction," he concluded, "seemed to be the rule, not the exception in those institutions." "At the same time," he continued, "my visits to campuses, particularly small ones, show that the old pattern is alive and well: the WPA is still a high level clerk for the English chair at plenty of schools" (White, "Re: WPA's authority/Chair's attitudes").

The question of the responsibilities that accompany these positions more directly addresses White's email to the WPA list. There, his concern with WPA positions at small schools was not so much with the individuals' status (in terms of faculty or tenure lines) so much as it was with the responsibilities that distinguish "professional program direction" from the work of "high level clerks." Susan H. McLeod registers the same concern—and similarly maps it onto differences in institutional size—in opening the chapter on "Distinctions and Definitions" in *Writing Program Administration.* McLeod offers two hypothetical job advertisements, one from "St. Clarence University," "an independent Catholic institution in the liberal arts tradition, with 1,200 students and 70 faculty," and one from "the University of Euphoric State," a PhD-granting institution with an English department numbering thirty faculty (7–8). In contrasting these two ads, McLeod (following David Schwalm) argues that the position at St. Clarence defines the work of writing program administration as "a *task* rather than a *position*" (Schwalm 9, qtd. in McLeod 8). This WPA works with other faculty in the department, most of whom teach composition, and has administrative work counted as service (McLeod 8). By contrast, the WPA at Euphoric State "is in effect the head of a department within a department . . . There is usually a place in the departmental organizational chart for this person," and there are clear guidelines for the position (and its evaluation) outlined in departmental bylaws (McLeod 8–9). In concluding her discussion of these hypothetical examples, McLeod explains that "although there are common administrative tasks and assignments among all WPA positions, the definition of a writing program administrator is very much site-specific, dependent on local history . . . and the size and complexity of the institution" (9).

We argue, first, that Schwalm's distinction between "task" and "position" does not map as neatly onto institutional size or type as McLeod implies. Second, and more importantly, we argue that the reality of all WPA positions is more intricate and nuanced than this tidy opposition suggests. Most institutions within the data sample do not define WPA work as exclusively belonging to a series of tasks, belonging solely to a codified position, or belonging to a particular academic status. Instead, most positions at small colleges are defined dialectically, moving between the different categories. In addition, many positions may look like a static collection of tasks from the vantage point of a job advertisement, but might carry an internal and institutional coherence and force that such a document cannot capture. The status of WPA positions and the responsibilities they encompass are tied together in messy and complex ways. In order to better understand these positions, we first turn to the work they do and then to the status to which they are accorded.

SLAC WPA RESPONSIBILITIES

In their 2007 study of WPA positions, Jonikka Charlton and Shirley Rose asked respondents to classify their responsibilities in programmatic terms (for first-year composition, WAC, or the writing center) (126–27). In the 2007 SLAC survey (see Gladstein, Lebduska, and Regaignon), we uncovered conflicting definitions of such essential terms as "administration," "program," and even "writing"; in addition, we found that being "responsible" for first-year composition constituted radically different work on different campuses.[1] In the 2009 survey, we therefore asked more focused questions about job responsibilities, inquiring as to respondents' oversight of such work as assessment, faculty development, tutoring, scheduling writing courses, and the like. Figure 5.1abc presents the various reported job responsibilities of the survey respondents in explicit administrative positions, broken down by position type (explicit WPA, solo WPA/WCD, and explicit WCD). Question #13 on the survey asked respondents to check off which items on a list were included in their job responsibilities. There also was a space where respondents could add responsibilities not included on the list.[2] Percentages represent the number of people within each category who reported having a particular responsibility as part of their position. (We do not have information about the relative importance of these areas of responsibility for each of the respondents.)

"The Portland Resolution" suggests that a WPA's responsibilities should include: scholarship of administration, faculty development, writing program development, writing assessment, registration and scheduling, office management, counseling and advising, and articulation of the writing program's goals and mission. As we see from the data presented in Figure 5.1abc, over 70% of the WPAs are involved with assessment, faculty development, curriculum development, and planning program events (which is one method for articulating the goals of the writing program). The same percentage of writing center directors hire, train, and supervise tutors, and advertise and plan events for the program. In fact, over 90% of the writing center directors who responded to the survey listed training, supervising, and hiring tutors in their area of direct responsibility. This meshes with the IWCA "Position Statement on Professional Concerns for Writing Center Directors" (see Simpson) and the predominance of teaching in these positions reported by the survey respondents. The majority of SLAC WPAs and WCDs thus report a set of responsibilities that are in line with the position statements of their national organizations. (We provide additional data about writing program positions—teaching load and length of time in position—in Appendix D.)

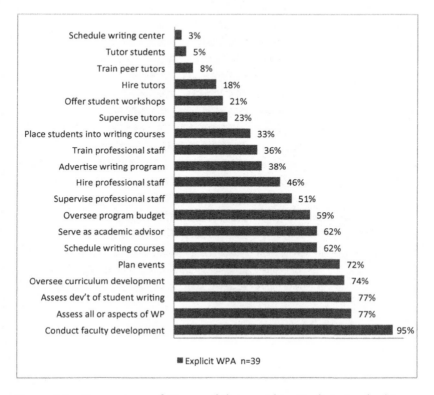

Figure 5.1a Comparison of Responsibilities within Explicit Leadership Positions

One striking finding is that over 90% of explicit writing program administrators and solo WPA/WCDs, as well as 70% of writing center directors, conduct faculty development. Although we have no comparative data for larger institutions, we speculate that this tendency in the sample might emerge from the widespread WAC culture of these schools. Because of their comparatively heavy reliance on WAC-based requirements such as first-year writing seminars, small college writing programs are taught by faculty from across the institution. (See Chapters 6 and 7 for full discussions of the different writing requirements in the sample and how they are staffed.) In this context, a large portion of the WPA's work becomes that of faculty development. Faculty

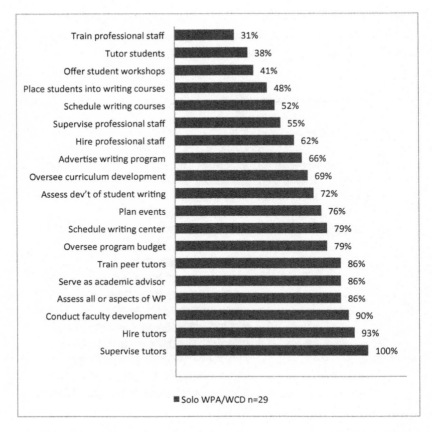

Figure 5.1b Comparison of Responsibilities within Explicit Leadership Positions

development on a small college campus is a way to: share expertise in rhetoric and composition; foster some level of programmatic consistency; and provide program-wide leadership and oversight. The emphasis on faculty development also highlights the autonomy of the individual faculty teaching these courses. The writing director's leadership is therefore that of one among equals rather than that of a manager or supervisor. Indeed, this close involvement with faculty may also be a reason why curricular reform—a new writing requirement, for example—can pull the writing center director towards the overlap between student- and curriculum-centered structures.[3]

Although placement of students into writing courses has historically been at the center of WPA work, only 33% of explicit WPAs

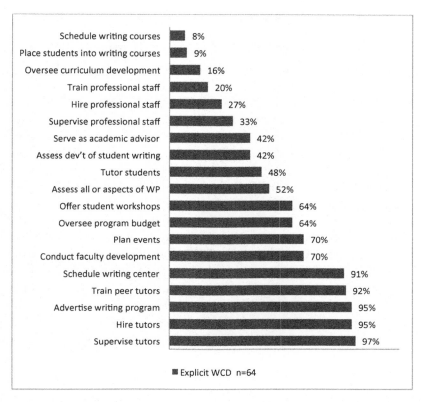

Figure 5.1c Comparison of Responsibilities within Explicit Leadership Positions

and 48% of solo WPA/WCD place students into writing courses (see Connors, *Composition-Rhetoric* 128–29; Royer and Gilles, "Placement Issues"). As we'll discuss in Chapter 10, few small colleges do much to formally identify the diverse degrees of preparedness of their students. Only twenty-one out of the one hundred schools use a placement exam, with almost an equal number of schools (20) not using any method for identifying these students. In addition, only thirty-two schools allow students an exemption from a required first-year writing course, where such exemption is typically based on AP test scores. This lack of formal placement mechanisms at small colleges emerges from their focus on students as individual learners, each of whom can and should develop as a writer over the course of her or his education. In addition, small colleges resist labeling underprepared students; in a small, residential community, such labels can easily become stigmatizing.

As we discussed in Chapter 4, the lack of a WPA in a particular leadership configuration may lead to an increase in responsibilities and authority for the writing center director. It is therefore important to look more closely at the explicit WCD category to see if differences exist between those institutions with only a writing center director and no WPA on campus, those with an embedded WPA, and those who have an explicit WPA. As discussed in the previous chapter, there are subtle differences between writing center director positions in the *Solo WPA/WCD* and *WCD Only* configurations; however, when their responsibilities are compared side-by-side in Figure 5.2, we see that the *Solo WPA/WCD* undertakes more of the responsibilities on the curricular side, such as curriculum development (69% vs. 16%) and placement (48% vs. 9%) than the *WCD Only*. This may be because the *Solo WPA/WCD* operates within the overlap of curricular and student structures. Interestingly, the only area where the *WCD Only* position seems to be more involved by a large difference is in advertising the writing program (95% vs. 66%). This may just be an issue of time; it may be that the *Solo WPA/WCD* has a greater number of different

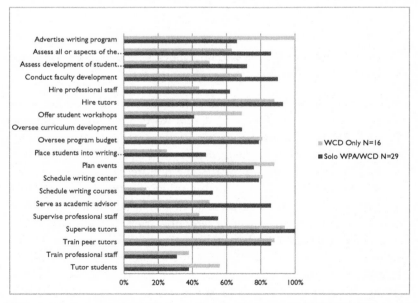

Figure 5.2 Comparison of Responsibilities between *Solo WPA/WCD* and *WCD Only* Leadership Configurations.

responsibilities and that, as a result, advertising the writing center or program is a lower priority.

In addition to revealing the curricular responsibilities of administrators at *Solo WPA/WCD* institutions, Figure 5.3 shows how writing center directors on campuses without explicit writing program administrators lead their institutions' cultures of writing. While 52% of all explicit writing center directors (not including Solo WPA/WCDs) are involved in program assessment, this percentage increases when we look only at leadership configurations without explicit writing program administrators: 47 of the 62 (76%) of the writing center directors who are involved in assessment come from a configuration without an explicit WPA. Writing center directors without an explicit WPA as a colleague are also more likely to oversee the writing program budget (*WCD Only* = 81% and *Em+Ex* = 77%) than their counterparts (51%) who work alongside an explicit WPA. The *WCD Only* director is the

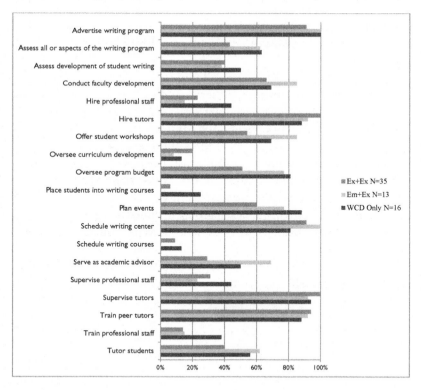

Figure 5.3 Comparison of Responsibilities within Writing Center Leadership Configurations.

individual most likely to be responsible for hiring (44%) and training (38%) professional staff, and also for placing students into writing courses (25%). (The precise contours of this work are not clear from the data. Professional staff may be either professional tutors or adjunct faculty, and we do not know the nature of these writing courses.) Finally, the writing center director who shares a leadership configuration with an embedded WPA is more likely to conduct faculty development (85%) and serve as an academic advisor (69%), which is typically a responsibility of faculty at small colleges.

We can therefore see, at the level of job responsibilities, that small college writing center directors function as campus leaders in leadership configurations without an explicit WPA. This may derive from how "program" is defined at those institutions. It may be that at institutions without an explicit WPA, the "writing program" refers to the writing center and excludes other sites of writing. In such cases, funding and leadership resources are allocated accordingly. It also may mean that these writing center directors have assumed responsibilities in order to fill a leadership vacuum created by a diffused curricular structure.

In individual and focus group interviews, respondents further revealed the level of their local authority and influence. It emerged that a significant factor in determining this level was in some cases how the WPA him- or herself understood the parameters and responsibilities of the position, rather than how the institution defined it. Some respondents clearly saw themselves as administrators who taught and sometimes conducted program research; others saw themselves as scholars and teachers, whose administrative work was part and parcel of other intellectual activities. The latter group included what we might call lifetime WPAs—scholars in rhetoric and composition, writing program administration, and writing centers—but we also found cases where faculty from other fields rotated into WPA positions, and nevertheless had an intellectual commitment to that work, to the field, and to the possible impact on the campus's culture of writing.

SLAC WPAs' Status

What we have shown of small college writing administrators' abilities to shape the teaching of writing on their campuses complicates earlier assumptions. Rather than deriving from the position *per se*, the authority of these positions stems from their place in the institutions' leadership configurations, from the portfolios of responsibilities associated with them, and from the perceptions individual WPAs have of their positions and agency. Questions of status—faculty or staff, tenure-line or non tenure-line—complicate this picture further. This is a pressing issue of professionalization for the field as a whole (see Gunner, "Professional Advancement"; Hult et al.; Roen, "Writing Administration"; Stygall; and essays in Enos and Borrowman by Isaacs; Langston; Reid; and Roen, Yancey, and Schwalm). We therefore begin by contextualizing our findings in three recent national studies: Jonnikka Charlton and Shirley Rose's 2007 replication of Linda Peterson's 1986 survey of the Council of Writing Program Administrators (CWPA) membership (see Charlton and Rose 2009); the 2009 Conference of College Composition and Communication (CCCC) initial report on its membership (Gere, "Initial Report"); and the Writing Centers Research Project (WCRP). Even though each study employs a different research design, the quantitative data show that small college writing program and writing center administrative positions are in line with national trends.

In replicating Peterson's survey, Charlton and Rose set out "to pursue our common questions about WPA identity and how it emerges, how it develops, and what it might become" (115). Their project entailed sending a 57-question survey exploring "[d]emographics, WPA experience, job responsibilities, status, and preparation" to 413 members of CWPA (116). They had a 55% response rate (226 respondents). In the fall of 2008, CCCC sent a survey to 1,036 of its members (Gere, "Initial Report"). Anne Ruggles Gere reports that 643 members responded to the survey, for a 62% response rate. The report does not describe the goals of the survey, but the questions revolved around the demographics of required writing courses, including their staffing and administration. Finally, WCRP "conducts and supports research on writing center theory and practice and maintains a research repository of historical, empirical, and scholarly materials related to Writing Center Studies" (WCRP). Bi-annually, the project sends a request to national electronic lists (such as WCenter) asking writing center directors to complete the survey in order to "provide the writing center community with much-needed comparable data regarding operational and administrative matters." Because the survey has an open call, response rates are impossible to gather. The survey asks for information on "writing center contact information, operations, tutor/consultant information, student usage, and administrative information," which includes information on the WCD position. (For the report on the 2003–2004 survey, see Griffin et al.)

Like all three of these surveys, the SLAC survey aimed to gather details about the writing programs within the potential membership of SLAC-WPA. Both the 2007 survey and the one administered in 2009 sought to create a portrait of writing programs and writing positions within a membership that differed—or perhaps was more specific than—those of the larger surveys (see Gladstein, Lebduska, and Regaignon). However, the various specific goals and questions of each survey project, as well as the fact that our research relies on mixed methods rather than survey data alone, makes direct comparison challenging. Charlton and Rose focus on the WPA identity and position; the surveys from CCCC, WCRP, and SLAC, by contrast, focus on both programs and positions. The methodology for each survey also varies, with different sets of researchers making different distinctions between types of positions. For example, we distinguish between *Solo WPA/WCDs* and *Explicit WPA or WCD* positions because these positions have significance to the SLAC context. The other studies do not make this distinction. Because Charlton and Rose are focused on academic rank, they combine "not yet tenured" and "non-tenure track" positions (123–24). We, however, found the difference between faculty and staff position more relevant both to the schools in our data set and to the national conversations we wished to engage. We therefore counted all positions with tenure or the possibility of tenure in one category.

Taking these differences in survey design into consideration, Table 5.1 shows academic status as represented in all of these studies. We include the data about *Solo WPA/WCDs* in both the SLAC WPA and SLAC WCD categories, as well as listing them separately, since we cannot directly compare those data. Looking first at WPA positions, we can see that the academic status of SLAC WPAs is comparable to that of CCCC members nationally: 73% versus 74% of the WPAs are on tenure lines (either tenurable or already tenured); 20% versus 14% are in faculty positions that do not carry the possibility of tenure; and while 6% of our respondents were in hybrid faculty-staff positions, 3% of the CCCC respondents were staff only. Similarly, the proportion of SLAC WCDs in faculty positions with the possibility of tenure is the same as the proportion of those reported by the WCRP (41%), and is slightly less than WCRP's proportion of WCD faculty positions without the possibility of tenure (18% vs. 21%). Since neither the CCCC nor the WCRP surveys includes the category of hybrid faculty-staff positions, we do not know what difference the presence of that category in our survey makes, or how those respondents would have classified themselves if required to choose between the two. Therefore, while it at first seems that SLACs have fewer staff positions than the WCRP respondents (20% vs. 34%), we cannot determine how these numbers might change, and whether some of the 34% in the WCRP are indeed hybrid positions.

Table 5.1 Classification of the SLAC WPA/WCD Position in Comparison with Other National Surveys.

	Tenure-Track Faculty position	Non-Tenure Faculty position	Hybrid between faculty and staff position	Staff position
SLAC WPA (n=79)	73%	20%	6%	0%
SLAC Solo WPA/WCD (n=29)	62%	28%	10%	0%
4C survey (n=601)	74%	14%	UA	3%
SLAC WCD (n=96)	41%	18%	22%	20%
WCRP (2004) (n=165)	41%	21%	UA	34%

Table 5.2 examines another important category of status—highest degree received—across these studies. Here we see that SLAC WPAs are typically as credentialed as their counterparts in national studies that do not control for institutional type. We found that some positions are configured based on the degree of the current incumbent rather than by the position itself and how it fits within the program's leadership configuration. For example, one institution—a composite that we call "Status Quo College"—classifies the writing center director position as a staff position because the current incumbent has only

a Master's degree, and only positions occupied by someone with a PhD are granted faculty status.

Table 5.2 Comparison of National Survey Data on the Degrees of WPAs and WCDs.

Type of Degree	Cs survey	Charlton and Rose	SLAC WPA	WCRP (2003)	SLAC WCD
PhD	83%	85%	89%	49%	64%
Masters	11%	8%	11%	47%	30%
Other	6%	6.5%	0%	UA	6%

We hypothesize that if this person were to leave and be replaced by someone with a PhD, the position would be re-classified to be at least a hybrid position. Small colleges define themselves in part through the fact that most courses are taught by faculty with terminal degrees. Only five writing center directors in the sample do not teach courses, and the prevalence of teaching in this position's typical portfolio helps explain the preponderance of some level of faculty status.

In their 1999 survey of writing center directors at small colleges, Shireen Carroll, Bruce Pegg, and Stephen Newmann found that the number of "small college writing center directors who are faculty appointments [was] almost half that of the national average" (3) as defined by Dave Healy's 1993 study, "Writing Center Directors." Nevertheless, they argue that individuals' survey responses indicate "overall satisfaction with their professional lives" (Carroll, Pegg, and Newmann 3). They report that when they presented this analysis to an audience at the 1999 National Writing Centers Association conference, session attendees suggested "that the size of small colleges may . . . foster collegiality and render distinctions between faculty and staff less pressing" (4). Our research corroborates their claims. Although our survey did not ask affective questions, we did not find a parallel between the status of a position and any particular level or type of authority. In fact, we found that the particular leadership configuration was more foretelling of a position's authority than the status accorded the position.

We addressed the question of how status and authority intersect in all three of our focus group interviews, asking participants how their positions were understood locally. The following excerpts are transcribed from a focus group with four participants. The excerpt below is from a discussion between Speaker 1 (a full-time, non-tenure-track faculty WPA at an *Explicit WPA + Explicit WCD* school) and Speaker 2 (a full-time, faculty-staff hybrid WCD at a *WCD Only* school). The excerpt illustrates the complex ways academic status interacts with institutional influence and authority. Both speakers describe themselves as leaders, and each uses his or her specific positioning to work within the institution's structure of feeling:

> *Speaker 1*: I see myself as a change agent. The faculty generally see me, I think and administrators, as a problem-solver. There's a way in which, [College 22] did an external review of their writing offering and came up short. It was clear that things were not very coherent; students didn't have very consistently useful things to say. It wasn't a wash, but it was clear that there wasn't a really kind of consistency or any sort of system holding together of the project, so in some ways I think when you begin a writing program, the site that never had one, and so they turned to a WPA. There was a tendency to say, "We have a problem, and you're going to solve it."

Even though Speaker 1 and his institution have different perspectives on the position—"change agent" versus "problem-solver"—both interpretations can be said to emphasize leadership. The WPA sees himself as changing the culture of writing in dramatic ways, while the institution hopes that its problem-solver WPA will more simply help it improve how faculty teach writing. Although Speaker 1 does not here seem to realize it, the end result of these different understandings of the position may be the same. Since the administration and faculty of College 22 look to their WPA to develop a writing program that is both more "consistent" and more "innovative" than what they had, he may well find himself able to change the culture of writing by focusing on the "problems" the institution has itself identified.

We would argue, in fact, that Speaker 1 and the institution have compatible visions. Speaker 1 will need to understand, though, how to best connect the two roles and activities within the context of College 22's particular culture and history. One crucial piece of this is whether or not his position has the authority and agency it will need to actually launch new initiatives. He describes College 22's context in a bit more detail here:

> *Speaker 1*: Writing courses were all owned by departments, as it were, so you had philosophy had one, political theory and so forth, and so I just changed them all to become Writing 101 courses. Even that kind of change causes unanticipated sort of anxieties.

On the surface, a change in course titles may not seem far-reaching. However, bringing writing courses together as an identifiable group makes writing instruction more explicit. This may lead to a sense that the set of courses requires a single, expert leader without compromising the institution's sense of collective ownership of writing instruction. Small colleges rely heavily on departmental structures. As a result, charging a single position or program with responsibility for a curricular requirement is a significant move. The challenge to this shift is that it could produce a sense that writing is now perpetually "someone else's" problem. The status of the WPA and the institution's leadership structure only tell us so much; the WPA's understanding of his local agency contributes to a fuller understanding of the scope of the position's authority.

College 22 hired someone without tenure status to take on these responsibilities. Due to his reporting line, the lack of academic status does not seem to be an issue:

> *Speaker 1*: It's only my second year. I've had pretty good results with this collaborative program and so forth, but it's sort of early to have that much to say. I think they respect me, I mean I, so that's not been a problem, so it isn't a status thing, so you know with seeing us as somehow lesser faculty . . . One thing I have noticed is that because I work so closely with the VPAA [Vice-President for Academic Affairs], you know I'm working right directly under him, and I have noticed a sort of envy of that relationship. You know, you've got his ear.

Even when an institution deliberately hires a problem-solver, change may not be easy. Speaker 1 saw this as he uncovered "unanticipated sort of anxieties" when he changed the course numbers. On the one hand, the institution asked him to bring consistency to the college, but for some, the change may have been seen as a bureaucratic usurpation of departmental or faculty autonomy. In this case, it may have been a band-aid that needed to be ripped off to move the culture of writing forward. This WPA points out that he has a direct line to the vice-president for academic affairs; in addition (although not mentioned in the quoted exchange), he is the director of a separate writing program that is not part of a department. College 22 has a new first-year writing seminar that Speaker 1 directs; and he supervises a tenure-track writing center director, a position that predates the WPA position. When this institution crafted the WPA position, then, they deliberately gave it considerable authority even without a tenure line. (As Speaker 1 notes, this "isn't a status thing.") It is also important that College 22 hired, in Speaker 1, a WPA with considerable expertise in the field; that expertise clearly garners him local respect and high academic rank, even without the security of tenure.

This situation contrasts with that of Speaker 2, who works at College 5, a school with a *WCD Only* leadership configuration. She describes her position as follows:

> *Speaker 2*: So I was hired as, I'm professional staff—I don't have a PhD. I was hired to be the caretaker for the writing center and another sort of teaching and learning tutoring program that was on the skids. And I had no idea what I was doing actually. And it's been ten years now, and I still function and am seen primarily as professional staff. I teach as an adjunct assistant. I am both the go-to person. On my campus there really aren't any writing specialists, so I am the person, and I have tried hard to point out to the faculty areas that are ripe for full faculty conversations and discussions and decision-making processes. It's been, it's a mostly congenial faculty that mostly apt to take those kinds of cues and has for the most part.

It would be easy to dismiss the position of Speaker 2, hired as she was to be "caretaker for the writing center" and without any faculty status. This designation can suggest that the institution places little value on writing, since they hired someone with a Master's degree in an unrelated field (in this case, social work) into a hybrid faculty-staff position that is primarily defined as "professional staff." It also may suggest that the culture of writing functions on a deficit model, where resources for writing are allocated to help those who need it rather than developing all students as writers. This position and the individual could easily be cast aside and left on the margins of the college, simply supporting the efforts of student writers but making no significant impact on the broader culture of teaching writing.

Instead, Speaker 2 has become a leader on her campus by uncovering the hidden agency within her position, and has worked with College 5's structure of feeling to broaden her position's authority and influence: "So my position," she explains,

> is mostly one where I answer any questions people have, I have really sort of created a WAC program through an initiative I sent through the curriculum committee and the dean that was funded. That was me, and I think everyone understands that it was me, and when there are questions it comes to me. But I also am shielded from some of the backlash. Some of the deflection, I am shielded from. Someone else owns this. So I actually have, it's actually a pretty wonderful job, and I think that my security in some ways, certainly my job security is less than yours [refers to Speaker 1] obviously. But in some ways, my job security is almost a sure cinch here, at least in the near future, and in part because I'm cheap, but also because I do a pretty good job. So I think a lot of the initiatives that have come out of my office and in sort of consultation with the curriculum committee, with the dean, I don't get blamed for, but I get to spearhead and I get to shape in many ways, and that's not a bad place to be.

As Speaker 2 learned how to work with campus partners to push her own initiatives, she extended her influence while feeling secure that she would be heard and respected. She did this by educating herself in the field of writing center scholarship—through attending conferences and the International Writing Centers Association summer institute—and adapting what she learned to her own context. As the writing center director at a *WCD Only* institution, she is a representative of the kind of writing center director Carroll, Pegg, and Newmann discuss, whose status as staff—somewhat paradoxically—gives her the freedom to work across and for the institution without having to focus on publication or gaining tenure. Because these individuals are apparently unthreatening—they do not have much instrumental power—they can work with the diffuse leadership structures of these institutions in order to effect change. When these individuals emerge as leaders (like

Speaker 2), it is typically because their faculty colleagues recognize their expertise and feel free to learn from it.

Neither Speaker 1 nor Speaker 2 has the security of tenure, but both are nonetheless leaders on their respective campuses. Speaker 1 was hired as College 22's first WPA to be a leader and to resolve some of the existing problems in its writing program, and then, through these solutions, serve as a change agent by suggesting innovations. Speaker 2 has become a leader by learning the field, her institution, and by working carefully with the currents of both. Their untenurable status does not seem to limit either of these WPAs.

We would certainly not advocate keeping positions off the tenure track when a new writing requirement or another shift in the leadership configuration initiates a structure best served by a tenurable WPA. In fact, we would argue that in many cases, creating tenure-line positions or converting existing positions to tenure lines is precisely what some small colleges need to do in order to maximize the potential and stability of their existing cultures of writing. On many campuses, a staff or hybrid position may paradoxically put the WPA in a box that works at cross purposes to the goals of the college's writing program. If an institution limits committee membership to tenured faculty, for example, the institution may not gain as much as it could from a non-faculty WPA's expertise and leadership. On the other hand, both Speaker 1 and Speaker 2 feel "shielded" in some way from "backlash" due to the configurations of their positions. As we discuss in Chapter 8, an institution has to decide which leadership configuration works best with its writing requirement and its broader structure of feeling. The academic status and location of the WPA and WCD positions within these configurations are key, interrelated elements.

THE STATUS OF SMALL COLLEGE WRITING LEADERS

As small colleges evaluate and re-evaluate how to structure programs that further their goals for writing, they examine their leadership configurations and the status of the positions that comprise them. Status designations can send significant messages about the institution's commitment to writing. Table 5.3 shows the academic status of writing program administrators and writing center directors within the different configurations. This comparison challenges how the field has defined commitment. In the wake of "The Portland Resolution" and

"Evaluating the Intellectual Work of Writing Administration," there has seemed to be widespread and outspoken consensus that WPA positions that are not tenured or tenure-track are marginalized, dangerous to assume, and generally—in Enos and Borrowman's term from their title—filled with "peril" (see also the essays collected in Dew and Horning).

Table 5.3 Status of WPA and WCD Positions within Different Leadership Configurations.

	Tenure Track	Non-Tenure Track	Hybrid	Staff	Data unavailable
WPA					
Ex+Ex (n=38)	68%	21%	5%	0%	5%
Solo WPA/WCD (n=29)	62%	28%	10%	0%	0%
Emb+Ex (n=13)	92%	0%	0%	0%	8%
WPA only (n=2)	100%	0%	0%	0%	0%
WCD					
Ex + Ex (n=38)	29%	18%	21%	32%	0%
WCD only (n=16)	19%	12%	44%	25%	0%
Emb + Ex (n=13)	54%	0%	23%	23%	0%

We have discussed some ways in which the small college context troubles that consensus, suggesting—for example—that staff or hybrid writing center directors can enjoy considerable institutional influence and no small degree of authority when their expertise commands respect.

Table 5.3 shows that 92% of embedded WPAs are tenured or tenure-track, and this same configuration has the largest percentage of tenure-track writing center directors. The embedded WPA, however, often functions as the clerk White describes; the chair of the English department serving as an embedded WPA *manages* the writing requirement, but doesn't serve as its leader. This creates a dilemma for any institution: Is it better to have a tenured faculty member manage a writing requirement or the writing center, or to have a non-tenured faculty member serve as a leader? If the field insists that the WPA must be in a tenure-line position, the *Embedded WPA + Explicit WCD* configuration may be the most feasible for many small colleges. The decision should not be that crude, and depending on the history of a specific institution, that kind of decision may not be necessary.

Take the hypothetical Poker Face College. It does not have an explicit writing requirement; instead, writing is embedded in other requirements, including a first-year seminar and a senior thesis requirement. The faculty at Poker Face believe in the idea of writing to learn, and they hope that all of their students will develop as writers throughout their time at the college. Currently, Poker Face has a *WCD Only* leadership configuration, and the writing center director is a staff position. The writing center is housed within a learning commons. The writing center director offers faculty development sessions when asked, but mostly the WCD is charged with overseeing a staff of peer tutors. The WCD and the writing center have a lot of respect on campus. In addition, there is a faculty writing committee that oversees the designation of courses as writing intensive. Students are strongly encouraged to take at least one of these courses, but they are not required to do so. After a recent internal review conducted by a committee of faculty, it has become clear that: first, many faculty would like more support in the teaching of writing and, second, both students and alumni are not sure that student writing develops over the course of a Poker Face education. It is acknowledged that students write a lot while at Poker Face, but it is unclear how much *writing instruction* occurs. The committee members are hesitant to change requirements without also ensuring that there is adequate leadership for those new requirements; they realize that they need to find new ways to support faculty and to assess what students learn.

It might at first seem that Poker Face should create a new, tenured faculty position to direct the writing program. But this is an institution that—like many small colleges—almost never hires at the senior level. If Poker Face makes the tenure of the writing director the driving factor, then it would need to appoint a standing member of the faculty to that position. It would then sacrifice expertise in rhetoric and composition, since no one currently on the faculty works in the field. While the writing committee might provide more ongoing and robust leadership, it similarly lacks expertise, and with a rotating membership, it is unlikely to provide the kind of continuity that Poker Face needs. A new tenure-track position poses different problems. Without existing rhetoric and composition lines to help the institution understand how to review a WPA, and in the complicated position of implementing new writing initiatives, a junior WPA would immediately be in a complicated, and even dicey, political position.

We would recommend instead that Poker Face College hire an explicit WPA in an ongoing, full-time, non-tenure track position to work closely with the WCD, who is ideally an individual with some administrative experience. Poker Face needs to learn from the expertise of an experienced WPA, but they are not ready to tenure a WPA. In making this hire, they should expect to scaffold into a tenured WPA position once the writing program is better established. (For a relevant narrative, see Townsend, "Negotiating.")

This hypothetical situation illustrates the challenges that small colleges encounter when they think about creating a new, explicit WPA position. Even schools with the best of intentions may run into trouble when they try to negotiate the status of the position. In replying to a follow-up question about her institution's leadership positions, one respondent explained that the WPA position at College 29 had previously been a tenure-line in rhetoric and composition housed in English: "Twice we hired new rhet/comp faculty to fill this position," she wrote, but

> both left before a tenure decision would occur . . . Our English Department generally has felt that the Writing Program should hire a rhet/comp person in English in a tenure-track position. [But b]ecause of the teaching/administrative load, the departmental practices, the complexities of leadership for a new faculty member—our hires left before a decision, with questions about how their evaluations worked. There is great need for interdisciplinary evaluations that work!

The challenge for the pre-tenure WPA at College 29 does not seem to have been departmental respect for the field of rhetoric and composition, since our respondent points out that there is consensus in the department that they need such expertise. Instead, the issue is the complex array of factors that shape the workload: balancing teaching and administration, departmental culture, and "the complexities of leadership." Our respondent's concluding exclamation—"There is great need for interdisciplinary evaluations that work!"—while crucial, in fact glosses over some of these other fundamental questions. A focus on questions of *evaluating* the work of writing program administration points us primarily toward questions of scholarship and teaching. The challenges of pre-tenure and non-tenure-line positions in the field, however, lie beyond such a narrowed rubric. They might instead be cast around questions involving the complexities of leadership and what it means to truly inhabit a position rather than simply holding it.

College 29 ultimately steered away from hiring any more junior WPAs. Rather than continuing to try to fill what appears to be an untenable (and untenurable) position, they have temporarily embedded those responsibilities in the position of English chair while they wait for their most recent hire in rhetoric and composition to gain tenure before taking over that work. They have consulted with local and regional scholars in rhetoric and composition so that they still benefit from new work in the field, but they have realized that the complexities of leading their writing program are too embedded in their particular structure of feeling for it to be feasible—or fair—for someone new to immediately do that work. While this realization came through the departure of two pre-tenure WPAs, their solution emphasizes the difficulty of leading a writing program while new to an institution more generally. Their solution has not been to hire a senior-level WPA with tenure. As mentioned, hiring with tenure is rare at SLACs—perhaps even rarer than it is at larger institutions—and, as with College 29, can seem particularly dangerous in the case of a WPA position, where authority and influence impact the individual's ultimate success or failure.

College 29's solution would not work in the case of College 3. The faculty first initiated a new writing-intensive requirement and then, much later, authorized an explicit writing center director position on a staff line to foster and develop the culture of writing. This change has been slow, taking more than ten years. The faculty and upper administration at College 3 have only gradually come to see that their desire to help their students develop as writers—and themselves as teachers of and with writing—is best fostered through the creation of a WPA position. While *all* institutions creating such positions should attend to the guidelines in "The Portland Resolution" and "Evaluating the Intellectual Work of Writing Administration," we worry that if a consultant told College 3 that such a position had to be on a tenure line, they would be likely to lose this momentum for another decade. At times, institutional change—like student learning—needs careful scaffolding.

Such positions, whether staff lines, hybrid faculty-staff positions, or full-time, non-tenure-track faculty lines, need the same careful design and planning as tenure-line positions. The CWPA guidelines are useful here. We would add that institutions creating such positions in order to foster the dramatic growth of a writing program should build in possible mechanisms for these positions to be converted to tenured or tenure-line positions in the future. There are models for this approach in the scholarly literature (see, for example, Townsend, "Negotiating"). Such scaffolding allows the institution and the individual to build the program and the expectations for the position, working collaboratively to ensure that both are achieved in ethical and sustainable ways—aimed at the success of the position, the program, and the individuals that inhabit and build them.

Numerous publications offer guidance on evaluating the work of writing program administration. The Council of Writing Program Administrators' "Guidelines for Evaluating the Intellectual Work of Writing Program Administration" and "The Portland Resolution" provide essential frameworks for designing positions and review guidelines. Any institution creating or filling a position in writing program or writing center administration needs to engage with those documents. Although, as Alice Horning puts it, "WPA guidelines advise against junior hires . . . few institutions recruit tenured faculty for the work" ("Introduction" 4).[4] While we are aware of the pitfalls of non-tenured (and non-tenure-line) administrative positions, we would argue that if carefully and responsibly designed, such positions attract candidates who are able to help their institutions develop in exciting ways. The crucial question is what sort of configuration is best for the institution's hopes for its culture of writing. While we do not wish to contest the argument that at most institutions the most secure position for a WPA is that of a full tenured professor in a powerful department, we would argue that both institutions and the field as a whole need to think with nuance and complexity about the best scenario if that ideal is not feasible.

Discussions of writing administrative positions for both program and center directors range widely. While some studies focus on specific types of responsibilities, offering new approaches and pragmatic advice, others have taken a more theoretical approach, offering new ways to understand such work at a meta-level. Any position is an institutionally-defined portfolio of tasks. Institutions position those portfolios differently, according them various types of status and putting them into systems of relations. Ultimately, we cannot praise or dismiss any position based simply on its status, its position, or its responsibilities. To best evaluate a particular position on a particular campus, we have to understand the local authority associated with its responsibilities and how it is positioned within the local leadership configuration. By looking beyond programmatic features and job titles, we complicate our understanding of what writing administrator positions are, can, and should be.

II

Curriculum-Centered Writing Instruction

6 Writing Requirements

There are curricular requirements that require writing, but it's not a "writing requirement."

—Survey respondent

One thing that we haven't mentioned that I think everybody shares is when I was at a huge research institution, writing centers, writing programs are almost all about frosh, and at a liberal arts college, at least in my context, it's the entire group, from frosh to seniors applying to fellowships and grad schools and even alums sometimes enter in, so we get writers everywhere, and that's the writing program. It's never just frosh, which is a—it's a good thing; it's just different.

—Focus group participant

On the whole, faculty at small liberal arts colleges assign large amounts of writing. This is unsurprising, given the typically small classes and the ways education at these schools has long been understood as developing students' mental discipline in preparation for later professional and specialist studies. Such writing occurs tacitly, operating as a component of the structure of feeling but without a formalized role in the writing program. If an institution wants to be able to demonstrate that it has helped students develop as writers over the course of their educations, it is important to—at the very least—embed this goal into curricular requirements where it can be identified, supported, and assessed. Even if the curricular requirement is embedded, the goals for student writing and role of writing in the curriculum can then be clearly articulated to students, faculty, and other stakeholders.

Thus far, we have distinguished between managing a requirement—as many embedded WPAs do—and providing leadership for it, as we assume is the ambition of the explicit, curriculum-centered, scholarly, professionalized WPA. In order to lead the writing culture of a campus, such WPAs cannot and should not limit their purview to those sites formally designated as *writing requirements*. To do justice to the writing program of a small college, WPAs must identify the full diversity of sites of curriculum-based writing instruction—the full diversity of writing requirements.

Approximately one-third of the survey questions related to writing requirements and curricula. In coding the data, we found—perhaps unsurprisingly—that the apparently simple question, "Does your institution have a writing requirement?" was sometimes difficult to answer with a one-word response. Ten respondents reported that their institutions had no writing requirements, but nine of those answered affirmatively to a subsequent question, "Are there other curricular requirements that do not require writing but encourage it?" This showed us that the picture was more nuanced than the initial yes/no question permitted. Triangulation of the survey data with content analysis of the institutional websites and catalogs of all one hundred participating schools clarified these types of responses. Through this analysis, we developed the distinction between *explicit* and *embedded* writing requirements—a distinction that is particularly important to understanding writing instruction at small colleges.

Explicit requirements appear in college catalogs and websites as formally designated "writing requirements." These documents articulate directly what students need to do—take courses, pass exams, submit portfolios, demonstrate competency, etc.—in order to meet the institution's goals for their writing educations. *Embedded* requirements are, in a sense, hidden in plain sight. Rather than appearing, clearly labeled, as the *writing* requirement, these are other kinds of curricular requirements—including first-year seminars and capstone exercises—that articulate writing as one of their goals. Instead of being announced in the title, the writing instruction appears in the program goals or in departmental statements about writing in the major or in capstone experiences. Explicit requirements are easier for students and faculty to identify and for researchers to tabulate. They mark a distinct and formalized commitment to the role of writing in the curriculum and at the institution. But embedded requirements may indicate that an institution is more saturated with writing and sites of writing instruction than it at first seems.

Table 6.1 presents an overview of the different writing requirements in the sample. It presents separately those that are explicit and those that are embedded. Most schools have more than one writing requirement. In this chapter, we present the types of writing requirements that exist in the sample. One significant trend is the presence of embedded requirements. Over the course of the research period, we observed a number of schools go from embedded to explicit requirements or begin discussions of how to bring embedded aspects of their culture of writing into greater focus. The distribution of types of writing requirements also reflects the strong writing across the curriculum culture of these schools: forty-four have W (writing-intensive) requirements and forty-five take a WAC-based approach to first-year writing with first-year writing seminars (FYWS). A number of schools are in the process of converting their explicit first-year writing requirements from composition-based to WAC-based. Finally, nearly all of the schools in the sample are currently interested in ways to build verticality into their cultures of writing, identifying ways and places between first-year requirements and senior capstones to deliver writing instruction.

Table 6.1 Writing Requirements at Small Colleges.

Explicit Requirements	Number of Schools
First-Year Composition (FYC)	38
First-Year Writing Seminar (FYWS)	45
Writing Intensive Courses (W)	44
Embedded Requirements	
First-Year Seminar (FYS)	19
Core Curriculum	10
Mid-level courses	4*
Department Statements	5
Theses and Capstones	95*
No Writing Requirement	1

* Can be both explicit and embedded.

In discussing the various requirements in more detail, we focus on the forms they take in the data sample and the trade-offs involved in any approach. We present our analyses starting with first-year requirements, which are both the most common and were the easiest to code. We then discuss the writing requirements that occur at the capstone level, and in what we call the "murky middle," reflecting the difficulty of locating it precisely. Within each section, we proceed from explicit to embedded requirements. Throughout, the analysis focuses on not just *what* requirements occur in the sample, but also *why* schools might choose these particular approaches. In the next two chapters, we turn to questions of implementation. Chapter 7, "Staffing First-Year Writing," discusses class size, exemption policies, and staffing; Chapter 8, "Small College Writing Programs: Leadership Configurations and Requirements," presents how different writing requirements are led at the schools in the sample and the kinds of pressures that seem to be leading these schools to make changes in their writing curricula and/or their leadership configurations.

Writing Requirements in the First Year

Ninety-six schools have some kind of first-year writing requirement. This is the most consistent moment in the writing curricula of these schools. It is also the clearest; the first-year writing requirements were the easiest to code, largely because these programs are the most formalized and unified. Capstone and murky middle requirements, by contrast, are typically owned by departments rather than the writing program.

Thirty-eight of the sampled schools have first-year composition (FYC). This means that it is not the most common form of first-year writing in the sample, although it is the course and requirement that have, in many ways, defined the history, shape, and fundamental debates of the field of rhetoric and composition. (See Berlin, *Rhetoric* and *Writing Instruction*; Brereton, *Origins*; Connors, "Abolition" 47–48 and *Composition-Rhetoric*; Crowley; Donahue and Falbo; Gannett, Brereton, and Tirabassi; and Kitzhaber, *Rhetoric* and *Themes*). This category includes courses with a variety of names—"Composition," "First-Year Composition," "English 101," and so forth—that are required of most or all first-year students, and that fall under the purview of a single department (most often English). For thirteen (34%)

schools in the sample, the first-year composition requirement is the only writing requirement of any kind.

Our focus here is the goals and purposes of these programs, writ large. As a result, our analysis addresses the tradeoffs inherent in different programmatic structures rather than those of different pedagogical approaches. There are therefore several significant debates about composition that we do not engage. Because the schools in the sample are not considering getting rid of first-year writing requirements, we do not enter into the abolition debate (see Connors, "Abolition Debate"; Smit). Several schools are, however, considering converting from first-year composition to the WAC-based first-year writing seminar—which we consider a viable alternative (see discussion below). Because our data include program or course goals, but not specific syllabi, we do not discuss how many schools take a writing-about-literature (see Vandenberg), writing-about-writing (see Downs and Wardle), or another approach to first-year composition. Nor do we enter into the current conversation about transfer (see Bergmann and Zepernik; Jarrett et al.; Nelms and Dively; Wardle, "'Mutt genres'" and "Understanding"). There are many ongoing debates about staffing first-year writing programs, which we discuss in Chapter 7.

We conducted an analysis of the goals and/or course descriptions for first-year composition at a randomly selected subset of nine of these schools, evaluating them in light of the CWPA "Outcomes Statement for First-Year Composition."[1] These analyses are unlikely to reflect the full complexity of these courses, because the most detailed statement of goals we received or found was a series of eleven bullet points. Most were a couple of paragraphs or a few sentences. The residential and insular nature of these colleges may well mean that such documents are not available to the general public, but primarily serve internal audiences. Of the nine schools we analyzed, there was only one school for which we could find no statement of goals or significant course description. For two schools, we extrapolated the goals from program or course descriptions—although, of course, course descriptions and outcomes statements are distinct genres.

The "Outcomes Statement" identifies five significant areas: "Rhetorical Knowledge"; "Critical Thinking, Reading, and Writing"; "Processes"; "Knowledge of Conventions"; and "Composing in Electronic Environments." While only one of the FYC institutions we examined acknowledged the "Outcomes Statement" directly, the priorities of these courses were, for the most part, in line with it. None of the institutions focused on composing in electronic environments as a priority, and three of the institutions emphasized all four of the other CWPA outcomes. There were no patterns to the outcomes omitted by the other institutions. Six schools indicate that by the end of their composition courses, students should have a sense of writing as a process requiring multiple drafts, "later re-thinking," and "flexible strategies for generating, revising, editing, and proof-reading" (CWPA, "Outcomes"). One institution simply promises that "writing involves drafting, discussing, and re-drafting" (College 31), and another prepares students to revise "in consultation with your instructor and peers" (College 32). A third institution elaborates more fully: "students must develop an awareness of the strengths and weaknesses in their writing and must acquire the necessary skill to revise and rewrite what they thought were final drafts of essays. They must, in other words, become editors of their own writing" (College 33). Four emphasize the rhetorical aspects of writing (see "Rhetorical Knowledge," CWPA, "Outcomes"): for example, students will learn to "fram[e] arguments for different audiences" (College 27) and will "[i]ncrease their rhetorical knowledge, considering audience needs and expectations" (College 34). Five programs identify mastery of conventions as a goal: using "clear and appropriate English prose" (College 33); developing "clarity of style" (College 36); and reviewing "grammar and . . . research skills" (College 35). Four institutions emphasize researched writing.

The most striking finding in this analysis is that all but one of these eight institutions explicitly present "critical thinking" as a goal for first-year composition. Like the second CWPA outcome, these courses focus on the intersections between critical reading, thinking, and writing. They encourage students to "use writing and reading for inquiry, learning, thinking, and communicating" (CWPA, "Outcomes") and strive to "teach college level thinking through college level writing" (College 36). While one institution emphasized that this requires "developing [the] habits of writing, reading, and critical thinking needed for composing effectively within the academic community" (College 35), another emphasized that students must learn "how to ask effective and productive questions of themselves and others" (College 34), and a third focused specifically on "critical reading" (College 27).

This emphasis on critical thinking and researched writing draws attention to the ways in which small colleges focus on developing students as scholars and intellectuals from the outset of their undergraduate careers. Patricia Linton, Robert Madigan, and Susan Johnson argue that first-year composition courses can be particularly effective at this because they help students understand and acquire the genres of disciplinary writing: "English faculty," they contend, "can prepare the ground for acquisition of disciplinary style" (64; see also Wardle, "'Mutt genres'"). This type of program can also become a vector through which to bring the latest research in writing studies to campus. But when first-year composition is the primary or sole writing requirement, it can also subtly work against a pervasive culture of writing. It may suggest to both faculty and students that writing instruction needs to occur once and only once—an inoculation against bad writing. In addition, it can suggest that only one discipline "really" cares about writing—and hence, perhaps, that when other disciplines communicate their research it isn't "really" writing in some important way.

Perhaps surprisingly, the more common first-year writing requirement among small colleges is the first-year writing seminar (FYWS): a program of writing-intensive, topic-based seminars that are explicitly labeled as the institution's writing requirement (or one of its writing requirements). Forty-five schools in the sample take this writing across the curriculum approach to first-year writing, an approach long associated with small colleges (see Bamberg; Moon; Runciman; Skipper). We follow Gretchen Flesher Moon's lead in thinking of this as a viable approach to first-year writing, "a third alternative to the FYC-or-no-FYC debate" (105; see Connors, "Abolition"). These programs are typically staffed by faculty from across the college and "introduc[e] students to the research community in the context of an interdisciplinary theme, generally coupled more or less tightly to the instructor's own area of research" (Brent 261). They thus allow students to develop the kinds of rhetorical and topical expertise many compositionists have noted are essential to students' development as writers (see Downs and Wardle; Joseph Harris, "Undisciplined Writing"; Russell, "Rethinking Genre"; Sommers, "The Call of Research"; Sommers and Saltz).

Using the same process as with FYC, we examined the program goals for ten first-year seminar programs. Of the ten schools we selected, we could find no goals information for two. The eight goals statements we found were, interestingly enough, typically more detailed and comprehensive than those for the first-year composition programs we analyzed. As with the goals statements for first-year composition, only one FYWS document specifically referenced the CWPA "Outcomes Statement" (that same document also referenced the outcomes statements of WAC-based writing programs at a number of large universities). Of the eight statements we have, only one references composing in electronic environments, and that in a minimal way, that students should "[g]ain experience in using technology for research and writing" (College 37). All eight emphasize critical thinking, writing as process, and the importance of learning conventions and attention to rhetorical concerns of audience and genre. These statements emphasize the social as well as the iterative nature of the writing process. For example, College 38 emphasizes that by the end of the semester, students should "know" that "writing is an iterative process" and "that pre-writing, composing, and revising are distinct intellectual activities," as well as understand "some useful roles readers can play in the revising process." In some cases, these statements make connections between categories, as when College 30 connects audience, genre, disciplinary conventions, and critical reading and writing:

> Academic writers develop an awareness of the intellectual concerns and conventions of their fields. These include assumptions about what make interesting intellectual questions and what counts as effective support for an argument, as well as conventions of acknowledgement, citation, document design, and so forth.

This connection between rhetorical concerns ("what make interesting intellectual questions") and "conventions of acknowledgement, citation, document design, and so forth" may well result from these programs' multidisciplinary natures. In addition, it may be that FYWS programs have to be more explicit about outcomes and course guidelines because they draw on faculty from widely divergent fields—some of whom come uneasily to the task of teaching writing. We speculate that the WAC-rich context of these programs has pushed their faculty to make their values more explicit as they came to consensus across (rather than within) disciplines.

Interestingly, there is more consistency across these programs than there was across the composition programs in the sample. One manifestation of this is the clear commitment to a WAC-centered education throughout these statements. (It may be that because FYWS is a common model across small colleges, there are ongoing conversations between these institutions about this type of program. We know that one such gathering occurred in February, 2011, as a Mellon 23 Workshop on "Teaching and Sustaining Multidisciplinary First-Year Seminar Programs.") When analyzed in broad terms for their alignment with the CWPA "Outcomes Statement," the goals statements in the sample—for both first-year composition and first-year writing seminars—did well, with the lacuna of composing in electronic environments. The FYWS program goals, however, tended to be more specific.

Proponents of this approach to first-year writing emphasize the ability of this type of program to change faculty attitudes about teaching (and teaching with) writing. Drawing on her experiences at two different small colleges, Moon underscores the way in which such programs not only "generate . . . considerable enthusiasm for faculty development programs on campus" (115) but also change institutional cultures of writing: "Faculty discourse about writing changes," she contends; "slowly perhaps, but it changes" (115). In addition, such programs seem to have a radiating effect: "Writing across the curriculum, both with and without formal recognition, flourishes at colleges with a first-year seminar program" (115; Runciman 50–51 makes a similar argument). Doug Brent's study of such seminars at the University of Calgary confirms Moon's claim at a larger institution with, he notes, "a record of low-grade hostility to WAC" (273). One area of concern with this approach to the delivery of first-year writing instruction is that it relies on non-experts to teach writing. FYWS programs therefore need strong, professionalized leaders to provide faculty development and also consistent, long-range administrative support to maintain faculty and departmental buy-in. Without the former, the quality of writing instruction suffers, and without the latter, participating faculty may gravitate toward a greater focus on the course topic than is consonant with the mission of the program. The next chapter explores these issues in more detail.

The least common explicit writing requirement is the portfolio requirement, with only three schools taking this approach. (Two require the portfolio at the end of the first year and one at the end of the sophomore year.) This designation does not refer to institutions that use portfolios as culminating assignments for first-year writing courses, but rather that have a formal portfolio requirement of all students at the end of the first or second year. We coded these as competency requirements, since students must demonstrate mastery of college-level writing before they can proceed into more specialized study. At College 16, for example,

> Competency in writing is a degree requirement. To meet this requirement, students must submit a portfolio of their own compositions to be evaluated by members of the general faculty and the Writing Excellence Program. Students whose portfolios are judged "inadequate" must take a composition course before resubmitting their portfolios for evaluation.

The other two institutions do not make this connection as clearly, but the function of the portfolio seems to be the same. Carol Rutz has written extensively about the sophomore-level portfolio requirement at Carleton College (see Rutz; Rutz, Hardy, and Condon; Rutz and Lauer-Glebov). We discuss Spelman College's portfolio requirement as an approach to assessment in Chapter 11.

Portfolio requirements, at their best, provide signal opportunities for students to reflect on their own progress as writers and learners, and also to understand the variety of genres of writing characteristic of the university. In addition, they allow faculty to gather and discuss student writing in concrete rather than impressionistic terms. In both of these ways, this type of requirement is comfortable for small colleges, which value student ownership of their own learning and which typically seek out opportunities for faculty to reflect on pedagogy. On the other hand, portfolio requirements require a centralized vision of the curriculum that is at odds with the value small colleges typically place on departmental and faculty autonomy. A portfolio requirement can suggest that all students must be developmentally ready to go through a single hurdle at the same time.

Nineteen schools in the sample embed a writing requirement in a first-year seminar requirement, but do not designate the first-year seminar the "writing requirement." This, in essence, is the difference between our FYWS and FYS categories. First-year seminar programs in the sample are required courses taught by faculty from across the college and designed, in different ways, to acculturate students to college. These programs may focus on introducing students to the principles of academic critical inquiry, including library research; they may introduce students to support services and focus on study skills; they may engage students in conversations on issues related to their social lives at college. Some institutions see first-year seminars as an opportunity for first-year students to experience the academic learning environment and to gain confidence in discovering and expressing their ideas and in having them challenged by others. (We distinguished between first-year seminar programs that embed writing as a goal and those that do not; the latter are not included in the count.) At six schools, the first-year seminar is their only first-year writing requirement; thirteen schools require FYS in conjunction with an explicit requirement (either FYWS or FYC).

We can see the specific types of goals of the first-year seminar programs in the sample more clearly by examining the catalog descriptions from Colleges 10 and 11:

> The purpose of the first-year seminar program is to introduce college-level disciplines and to contribute to students' understanding of the ways in which a specific discipline may relate to other areas in the humanities, social sciences, and sciences. A major emphasis of each seminar is placed upon the improvement of students' skills—their ability to read texts effectively and to write prose that is carefully organized, concise, and firmly based upon evidence. (College 10)

> All first year students are required to take, in their first semester at [College 11], one course with the following characteristics: 1) enrollment of no more than 16 first year students, 2) the instructor will normally be assigned as the students' academic advisor, 3) instruction in writing will normally be offered, and 4) the course is offered for regular departmental credit. . . . [T]ypically each department sets aside one section of an introductory course and tailors it to fit the characteristics listed previously. . . . In addition, some departments offer courses specifically developed to be part of the offerings for this requirement.

We can see here that writing is *one* of the goals of these programs, but not the foremost one; in most cases, there is little elaboration on what it means to provide writing instruction. This can mean that there is an institutional mandate to *assign* writing, but little faculty development on how to *teach* it. As a result, WPAs at schools with FYS programs may find that they have to seek out opportunities to work with the faculty teaching these courses. These are not explicit writing requirements, and so such opportunities may not be built in. Because of the shared mission of the faculty teaching in these programs, however, this can be a significant vector for the delivery of such writing-focused faculty development. Converting a first-year seminar program to a first-year-*writing*-seminar program is one clear way for an institution to surface, support, and augment the way it provides writing instruction. If there is no other writing requirement, this is a way for a school to focus its attention on writing instruction. While this will necessarily shift slightly the mission of such a program, the benefits to the institution's culture of writing may well outweigh the challenges of making that transition.

Ten schools embed first-year writing instruction in a required core curriculum ("Core"). We found two different approaches to core curricula in the sample. In the first case, "Core" designates a general humanities course or sequence of courses, typically focused around a "Great Books" inspired syllabus. (Institutions whose core curricula do not embed writing as a program goal are excluded from this category.) For the most part, these courses teach with writing but do not teach writing; their primary interest is in developing students' knowledge of canonical literature and philosophy through group discussion, the formal presentation of ideas, creative engagement with artistic processes, and written analysis of specific works. College 12, for example, describes the role of writing in its Core course, "Humanities," as follows: "all students can expect to be invited to treat Humanities as an opportunity for development of their ability to write effective analytical prose." The rhetoric of this description emphasizes students' agency; they "can expect to be invited" to consider the course "as an opportunity for development." As a result, it implies considerable faculty autonomy in determining how much to emphasize writing instruction. The programmatic consistency in this approach lies in the readings, not the writing instruction.

The other approach to a Core curriculum is more multidisciplinary, typically extending over multiple semesters and, in some cases, beyond the first year. Some of these curricula are focused on themes that reflect the historic emphases and missions of the individual schools; others focus on the Western intellectual tradition. In these programs, writing instruction is a goal for the sequence of courses but not for any individual course within the sequence. College 13's Core is one of the most extensive sequences in the sample, comprising fifteen courses from five different disciplines (English, history, philosophy, economics, and politics). This curriculum "is based on the supposition that truth and virtue exist and are the proper objects of search in an education" best undertaken through the "acquisition of philosophical and theological principles." The institution's website explains further that

> [d]iscovering and transmitting the wisdom of the Western tradition is an undertaking inseparable from the task of preserving language. [College 13] acknowledges an obligation, at once professional, civic, and spiritual, to encourage in its students a respect for language, and to train young men and women to write and speak with directness, precision, vigor, and color.

The alliance of written and spoken language in the context of an interdisciplinary curriculum centered on the Western intellectual tradition recalls the Classical curriculum of the *Yale Report* and nineteenth-century colleges in intriguing ways. But while reading and writing appear as inseparable processes here, education primarily involves apprehending the past—"discovering," "transmitting," and "preserving" the Western tradition.

The signal challenge of a Core curriculum with an embedded writing requirement is identifying how to shift the focus of these courses from reception to production, from students as empty vessels to students as novice scholars working toward expertise (see Sommers and Saltz). This is a significant epistemological shift to make, but without it, the pragmatic constraints on these courses make it difficult to shift their emphasis. Core curricula are often signature features of the institutions that have them, a fact which makes changing such programs difficult. As with first-year seminar programs, core curriculum programs can provide key entry points for faculty development around writing for a WPA. Both types of programs gather faculty who are committed to the education of first-year students and who are ready and even eager to think about the particular intellectual and developmental challenges those students face. But core programs are defined in terms of their emphasis on reading, which can make a shift toward writing instruction a greater challenge than it is in first-year seminar programs, which are already focused on critical inquiry.

WRITING REQUIREMENTS IN THE MURKY MIDDLE

Once requirements move out of the first year, even the most explicit of requirements are department-based and are often therefore more difficult to locate, support, and assess. The goal of this type of writing requirement is to create a space within the respective school or major curriculum to extend the development of writing beyond the first year. While these requirements do begin to address how students progress from the generalist writing instruction of the first-year to the highly specialized writing they will do in capstone exercises, there is a great range in how the role of writing instruction in these courses is described. While some schools develop verticality in their writing curricula through a required writing course that all students take during their sophomore year, the majority of schools with an explicit, mid-level course require students to take a number of writing-intensive or "W" courses. Other schools have embedded their mid-level writing requirement in another requirement, such as foundation courses or required courses within a major. Most of these latter approaches are departmentally driven and can create a "murky middle," in which it is difficult to ascertain the goals and outcomes of these features of the writing curriculum. As a result, it can be difficult for institutions to realize that they need leadership and faculty development for this part of their "program."

The most explicit mid-level writing course exists at two schools in the sample. At these institutions, all students are required to take a specific course during their sophomore year in addition to a first-year writing seminar. In both cases, these courses emphasize researched writing, and provide more explicit guidance about the place of these courses as part of the writing curriculum. College 39's description defines the goal "of Sophomore Research Seminars" as being to "help students learn research and writing skills":

> The S[ophomore] R[esearch] S[eminar] is intended to be a course focusing on learning research methods, as well as a WAC foundational course following the Preceptorial. As a result, faculty teaching the seminars will need to integrate the teaching of content with instruction and guidance in research and writing. . . . Instructors must provide instruction and guidance in planning and writing the research paper. Students in the Seminars should learn basic research skills, in-

cluding, but not limited to, how to frame a research question, construct an argument, create a thesis, identify and analyze secondary and (depending on the discipline) primary sources, use online and other resources in the library, and draw conclusions.

The goals for writing and writing instruction are clear to both students and faculty. This model assumes that all disciplines can appropriately craft a research- and writing-intensive, sophomore-level course (which may not be possible at all schools), and provides clear support for how this type of course can move students from the general writing lessons of the first year to the specialist skills of their capstone work. This approach will suffer if it loses institutional support, in the form of guaranteed smaller class sizes, for example. It will also suffer if faculty become dissatisfied with the results or the perceived costs of offering this course instead of other courses for the major. Nonetheless, this type of mid-level requirement is a promising avenue for small colleges, one that builds verticality into the writing curriculum.

A requirement that students take some number of writing-intensive courses is the second most common requirement in the sample overall, appearing at forty-four schools (often in combination with some sort of first-year requirement). This reflects the strong and historic affinity of small colleges for writing across the curriculum. These courses go by many names; while "writing-intensive" is most common in the WAC literature, "writing-rich," "writing-attentive," and "writing-enhanced" also appear in the sample. As shorthand, we refer to these all as "W" courses. Drawing on the work of Christine Farris and Raymond Smith, Townsend outlines the common features of such requirements. The "W" designation is attached to a departmental course number, indicating that the course meets locally defined standards for writing instruction. These typically specify numbers of formal papers, opportunities for revision, pedagogical techniques, and so on (Townsend, "Writing Intensive" 234–35).

Schools in the sample require anywhere from one to seven of these courses; 25 schools specify when in their careers students are expected to take them, while at 19 schools, W courses are simply a graduation requirement. For the two schools that specify that the courses be taken in the first year, there seems to be a more generalist approach to writing instruction, as is the case for College 14, which promises that "[w]riting intensive courses will devote a significant amount of class time to teaching students to write with precision, clarity, economy and some degree of elegance." The faculty guidelines build on this directly, elaborating the following goals for student writing: clear argument and purpose; focused paragraphs with appropriate evidence and analysis; appropriate engagement with sources; and stylistic correctness. They also mandate shared process-oriented pedagogical strategies, including drafting, in-class workshops, and peer review.

Although College 14 points out that these courses "follow paths and draw on techniques in accordance with instructors' interests and expertise," the program's writing goals are distinctly non-disciplinary. This contrasts directly with the approach taken by College 15, which specifies that students must take three W courses from two different departments before they graduate, distinguishing between "Writing Intensive (WRITI)" courses and "Writing in the Disciplines (WRITD)" courses. The "central goal" for both types of courses is rhetorical: "to ensure that students learn to become good choice-makers as writers, considering issues of purpose, audience, context, style, and form." Nonetheless, the College 15 faculty guidelines for WRITI courses emphasize writing-to-learn techniques, and specify that all courses should spend time weekly discussing writing; "model and foster a process-based approach to writing"; teach students to consider rhetorical issues when writing; and "encourage students to use writing as a means of self-expression, critical inquiry, creative expression, argumentation, communication, and exploration." While WRITD courses also emphasize process (they mandate revision with feedback, for example), their focus is on writing as a way to participate in disciplinary discourse communities: they "draw upon students' existing writing skills and focus their attention on disciplinary conventions and research methods, as well as the forms and genres valued most within the disciplines."

The umbrella description of the shared goals of all College 15's W courses emphasizes the rhetorical nature of writing:

> Liberally educated students should write well and use writing both to discover and construct new knowledge and to communicate their ideas to others. Writing is a complex activity; it is a form of creative expression and critical engagement that serves practical and intellectual purposes. Since writing shapes the views of others, courses that focus on writing should help students understand the effects of their own written language.

Although neither College 14 nor College 15's W course guidelines reference the CWPA "Outcomes Statement" directly, both clearly draw from similar vocabularies from the field of writing studies to articulate their goals for these courses. (For a discussion of the "Outcomes Statement" and WAC, see Townsend, "What the Outcomes Statement Could Mean.") This apparently easy resonance may in turn come from the long-standing commitment to writing that is part of the small college structure of feeling. College 15 introduces its requirement with this frame, admirably providing students and faculty with a sense of the largest purpose and rationale for the writing requirement at the same time it provides specific information about it. College 14's description of the requirement is, by contrast, much more pragmatic, focusing on when students must take these courses and what they should expect of them.

In *Teaching and Assessing Writing*, Edward M. White warns that while a "'W' program usually begins with a strong vote of confidence from the faculty and the administration," it is an approach that is "filled with traps for the unwary and usually leads to an unimagined fiasco" (161). Specifically, he warns that strong, ongoing faculty development programs, writing centers, administrative support (for smaller classes), and formative and summative assessment are essential (162). Townsend provides further detail about how to implement these initiatives; in her discussion of the University of Missouri program (see "Writing Intensive Courses and WAC"). But Townsend also points out in a message to WPA-L that, "theoretically at least, you shouldn't need W designators" at a small liberal arts college: "a WAC program at [that] type of institution should be able to reach all faculty, and the work of writing should be able to be distributed more or less evenly across courses" ("WAC SOS").[2] A W requirement at a small college, we argue, can formalize the diffuse culture of writing that is part of the structure of feeling, and can therefore ensure the kinds of support White and Townsend identify as essential to WAC's long-term success.

A small group of schools in the sample—five—took a less course-based approach to developing verticality in their writing curricula. (Three of these schools have a FYC requirement. and two have a FYWS requirement.) These schools have departmental statements about the goals for writing in the majors, which are published and available to students and the public.[3] These statements typically include information about *how* each department or program helps students achieve those goals. While these are explicit declarations of how writing operates in the different departments and their curricula, the actual requirements are embedded within departmental major requirements. We can see how this operates in the two examples below, both from College 40:

> **HISTORY WRITING IN THE MAJOR REQUIRE-MENT**: History requires clear analytical prose that can convey complicated ideas, present evidence, and walk readers through an argument. The discipline has its roots in the humanities and thus values elegant, polished writing. Writing in history is also a key part of the learning process. It is through writing that students take disparate facts and events and turn them into historical interpretation. All History courses contribute to the development of students' writing skills and are designed to prepare students for a final research project. **Therefore, History and interdepartmental majors will fulfill the College 40 writing-in-the-major requirement as they complete the requirements for the History (or interdepartmental) major.**

> **WRITING REQUIREMENT IN THE MAJOR**: Students fulfill the writing requirement in the Psychology major by completing a minimum of two (2) writing enhanced (WE) courses and one writing intensive (WI) course within the major.

> Upon completion of the major, psychology students should be able to:

> • Demonstrate competency in the various forms of writing within psychology ranging from lab-based empirical reports to more conceptual papers and reviews.
> • Appreciate the differences between scientific writing and other forms of writing.
> • Demonstrate an ability to write in an effective and persuasive manner. Effectiveness includes the ability to: (a) develop and present clear and logical arguments, (b) use correct grammar, (c) sufficiently elaborate and defend points, including backing up assertions with appropri-

ate evidence, (d) appropriately evaluate the audience and point of view from which a paper should be written (including providing sufficient context and definitions of content-specific terminology), (e) justify conclusions, and (f) integrate information from multiple sources.

- Differentiate between types of source materials (e.g., original research, academic summaries, popular press) and the role that each can/should play in different types of writing assignments.
- Demonstrate competency in writing in the style of the American Psychological Association, which includes technical, grammatical, and stylistic conventions.

A set of "WE" and "WI" courses follow the second description. We can see from these two different approaches to the same mandate at a single institution that this approach provides significant departmental autonomy while also engaging all faculty and departments in reflection about writing and writing pedagogy. The history department diffuses writing instruction throughout the major, presenting writing as both a value of the field and crucial to the intellectual processes of all historians, who "take disparate facts and turn them into historical interpretation." By contrast, the Department of Psychology designates specific courses and types of courses that pay particular attention to the task of writing about data in the field. Each major, therefore, has the luxury of articulating to itself, its students, and the institution as a whole how written discourse operates in its discipline or interdisciplinary field. In addition, this approach sidesteps the danger of course-based, mid-level requirements like W and mid-level courses, which can suggest that writing instruction only happens in courses that formally announce it as their province.

On the other hand, this kind of highly individualized approach to writing curricula suggests that the discourses of the university are entirely different from one another. Furthermore, a WPA seeking to provide faculty development for more than one department at a time may uncover resistance to the notion that any aspect of writing or writing instruction could be shared between, say, biology and religious studies. A similar problem may arise as the WPA seeks ways to assess student writing at his or her institution. The WPA may have to develop and implement a seemingly endless number of writing assessments.

(Anson and Dannels address this concern specifically.) The diversity of approaches this requirement enshrines may, furthermore, make the development of a shared, college-wide vocabulary difficult.

Finally, two institutions have a completely embedded mid-level writing requirement, in which writing is one of several stated goals for another general education requirement. There is little guidance as to how writing will be taught in these courses. For example, College 41 presents its mid-level courses as part of a vertical writing curriculum, but does little to specify the role of writing instruction. The school's catalog describes a three-part writing requirement that combines explicit and embedded elements with the goal of producing "capable and confident writers." Students can place out of the first-year writing requirement, or fulfill it by taking either a first-year writing seminar (explicit) or a first-year seminar (embedded). They then "continue their development as writers" through an embedded, mid-level requirement before concluding with a capstone course or courses designated by the major department, defined as the "final phase of the writing requirement." The mid-level "Foundation Courses" are taken during students' first two years and are interdisciplinary:

> These courses incorporate a variety of strategies, such as the presentation of conflicting and complementary viewpoints, cross-cultural investigation, laboratory experimentation, problem-solving and artistic performance. Through Foundations courses, students learn about different approaches taught at [College 41] in a variety of departments.

This kind of embedded mid-level requirement is an attempt to structure the middle of a writing curriculum. The expectations for the writing instruction these courses provide, however, are unclear. If the institution wishes to assess student writing across the curriculum, this embedded requirement provides a place to begin, but without sufficient faculty development and leadership, the courses will in all likelihood lack a clear focus on writing instruction. This type of requirement, therefore, may be a challenge for a WPA to support, since the first step will be to develop guidelines and common goals for these courses that still do justice to faculty and departmental autonomy. As with so many embedded requirements, however, such a conversation is also an opportunity to increase the visibility of writing and writing instruction on a campus.

CAPSTONE WRITING REQUIREMENTS

The number of schools in the sample with thesis or other capstone requirements is comparable to those with first-year requirements. Ninety-five schools in the sample have some sort of capstone requirement (including theses) at the level of the college, honors program, or department. But these requirements were much more difficult to code than those in the first year, and this category challenged our distinction between embedded and explicit writing requirements. Forty-one respondents identified a senior thesis or other capstone as one piece of their institutions' writing curricula. When we initially examined websites, however, we found that only twenty-nine of these schools have online statements regarding this requirement. On closer inspection, we found that some institutions mandate that all students must complete some sort of capstone exercise in order to graduate. Other institutions specify that such a capstone is required for honors, but not for graduation. Still others leave such culminating exercises to the discretion of individual departments. The explicitness of the writing component of these requirements, and their position in the vertical writing curricula, fall on a continuum from schools that had an explicit "Paper in the Major" for all students, to schools where only a handful of departments require a thesis.

We consider capstone exercises presented as the culmination of a vertical *writing* curriculum and a major or liberal arts education to be *explicit* writing requirements. This is the case with College 6:

> The Paper-in-the-Major is the capstone writing experience in the [College 6] curriculum. Researched and written in the senior year . . . this paper demonstrates students' command of their major's perspectives, methods, and body of knowledge, as well as their ability to communicate these skillfully in writing. . . . Specific topics and formats for the Paper-in-the-Major are determined by the faculty in each department.

We can see how College 6 carefully balances disciplinary variation and college-wide writing goals with this requirement, specifying the paper itself as a college-wide graduation requirement, while allowing each field to define the exercise in a way that reflects its own discursive practices. The writing curriculum at College 6 is consistently explicit and WAC-based. It begins with a first-year writing seminar; students must then take one W course by the end of sophomore year. Then, senior year, students must complete the Paper-in-the-Major requirement, a more WID-focused assignment.

College 7, by contrast, mandates that every major have a culminating capstone experience, but does not specify what form it must take. Instead, each department determines the most useful type of intellectual exercise. Many of the majors at College 7 require a capstone exercise that is writing-focused; some are theses and others are senior-level seminars, as in the case of the English department:

> ENG 400 is a capstone course that assigns the student primary responsibility, through independent reading and research, for promoting the intellectual aims of the seminar. As part of the capstone experience, each student researches, writes, and revises a substantial, sophisticated essay and gives a public presentation based on it. Each English major is required to complete one seminar.

Writing is just one of several goals for the capstone experience at College 7. The capstone courses at College 7 are presented as opportunities for students to engage in disciplinary "reading and research," exploring a particular topic in depth, while also demonstrating their development as writers.

When writing is embedded into capstone exercises, they remain focused on their disciplinary function, allowing students to work intensively as scholars in the field. They can also help departmental faculty understand how and where they need to improve writing instruction within their major curricula in order to better prepare students for that culminating experience. For example, at Diffusion College, a school where every major requires a "senior exercise," the Department of Linguistics recently grew frustrated with the quality of their seniors' thesis work. They felt that seniors were prepared for the kind of linguistic analysis they needed to do, but were decidedly unprepared to write about linguistic data with the sophistication they expected. They therefore revamped the focus of three lower-level courses in the core major curriculum to provide more specific writing instruction. In doing this, the faculty did not consult directly with the WPA. They did, however, draw on his materials, which they had from participating in Diffusion's WAC-based first-year writing seminar program. In this case, then, the embedded writing requirement at the capstone level catalyzed the revision of a department's curriculum in ways that make it more focused on teaching disciplinary written inquiry. The conditions at Diffusion are such that this happened under the influence of the WPA's expertise, even though he had no direct authority over the Linguistics (or any other departmental) curriculum at the college. Writing-focused capstone exercises thus provide writing administrators with opportunities to work collaboratively with departments across campus to revise how writing is taught within major curricula. This can extend writing instruction vertically at the same time that it fosters a more conscious, reflective culture of teaching writing throughout an institution.

TRENDS

Research from longitudinal studies (see, for example, Carroll; Thaiss and Zawacki) demonstrates that the lessons of first-year writing must be reinforced and extended throughout students' college careers. Writing-rich environments at small liberal arts colleges allow some of that reinforcement to happen tacitly. Similarly, the prevalence of writing-focused capstone exercises (heterogeneous and localized as they are) suggests that these are institutions committed to students' development as scholars, and therefore writers, in their chosen fields of study. Many schools have turned to W course requirements at the mid-level in order to help students move from the first year's introduction to written critical inquiry to the more specialized kinds of writing they do in the various discursive communities of the college. Table 6.2 shows the configurations of first-year writing (both explicit and embedded) and W courses in the sample. (We do not provide full configurations, including mid-level courses and capstones, because of the difficulty of analyzing those data.)

The configurations of requirements speak to the writing across the curriculum culture of these schools. Of the forty schools with only one first-year writing requirement, over half (23) take a WAC-based approach, either explicit or embedded. Thirty-nine schools have some sort of first-year writing requirement in conjunction with a W course requirement, building some verticality into their curricula. In addition, respondents reported changes in the last decade which suggest that these schools are committing more fully to this approach. Fourteen schools have moved from first-year composition to first-year writing seminars in that time. This suggests that the faculty of these institutions are taking increasing responsibility for, and ownership of, writing instruction.

Table 6.2 Verticality of Writing Requirements.

Type of requirement	Number of schools (n=100)
FYWS only	18
FYC only	12
FYS only	5
Core only	5
W courses only	5
More than one FYW requirement but no W courses	15
FYWS + W courses (beyond FYW)	20
FYC + W courses	14
FYS + W courses	1
Core + W courses	2
Other FYW + W courses	2
No Writing Requirement	1

In addition, many schools in the sample have moved in the direction of formalizing their writing requirements. Six schools added an entirely new explicit writing requirement in the last ten years. Twenty-eight additional schools expanded their requirement, including schools that have given more weight to the writing component of an existing requirement—for example, by turning a first-year seminar program with an embedded writing requirement into a first-year writing seminar. This is a subtle but significant shift in terms of institutional culture and resources. It also includes schools that have added verticality to their writing curricula, building structures through which students proceed into the discursive communities of their major fields. This increase in verticality has, at some institutions, produced tension between the ambitions for writing across the curriculum and those for writing in the disciplines. Faculty at small colleges typically believe in writing as a tool of learning and communication, so there is little resistance to WAC. However, questions arise for a WPA when writing becomes an embedded departmental requirement. Where this tension has arisen, we have observed anecdotally that there is a lack of formal, ongoing, faculty development and leadership. When writing is embedded in departmental curricula, it does not necessarily fall within the WPA's purview; he or she may then justifiably question how it is assigned, taught, and assessed in mid-level courses and in senior culminating experiences. It may be that such embedded requirements suffer from this lack of professionalized leadership. While we discuss leadership configurations in relation to writing requirements in Chapter 8, it is worth noting here that of the twenty-five schools that have added WPA positions in the last ten years, twelve have expanded their writing requirements. As schools, particularly those with a WAC focus, add formality and explicitness to their structure of writing requirements, they seek out expertise from the field of writing studies by hiring a WPA and/or a WCD.

In understanding institutional cultures and writing curricula, it is important to look for embedded as well as explicit writing requirements. This brings to the surface the verticality of a writing curriculum. It also reveals how the tension between faculty governance and autonomy shapes the delivery of writing instruction at a particular school. Institutions in the sample take very different approaches to balancing these two values; in some cases, the result is a leadership vacuum, in which a requirement is designed without the necessary leadership for its success. The questions of implementation explored in the next two chapters turn on trade-offs. These touch on issues of expertise, which in turn hinge on issues of staffing and leadership.

7 Staffing First-Year Writing

> *[T]wo kinds of work . . . now both go under the rubric
> of "composition": The first is disciplinary in its focus on
> rhetorical theory, on the analysis of cultural discourses, on
> the practices and processes of literacy, and on the history of
> teaching writing. The second is programmatic in its ambi-
> tion to improve the teaching of first-year and basic writing.
> . . . To become a discipline, rhetoric and composition does
> not need to colonize and administer first-year writing; to
> teach writing well, one does not need to be a composition-
> ist. Once we distinguish between these two kinds of com-
> position, between the disciplinary and the programmatic,
> I think we will find that we can support both.*
>
> —Joseph Harris

The question of how to staff first-year writing has been a vexed
one for at least a century. In John Morton Payne's *English in American
Universities*, Fred Newton Scott argues that the time- and contact-in-
tensive nature of teaching composition makes small classes an urgent
necessity (121–23). Marc Bousquet, Tony Scott, and Leo Parascondola's *Tenured Bosses and Disposable Teachers* is perhaps the most recent
indictment of a system that, nationwide, overwhelmingly relies on the
underpaid labor of temporary faculty. Both Scott's and Bousquet's
analyses—indeed, the entire debate itself—hinge on the intersection
of pedagogical value and institutional wealth. Staffing is a key issue
of teaching composition because questions of class size are embedded within it. Although the schools in the sample are not uniformly
wealthy, the data set does include some of the wealthiest institutions
in the country. Perhaps more importantly, the fact that these are private institutions means that they control their own budgets. Small colleges have consistently devoted resources to maintaining the value they

place on small classes taught by permanent faculty. As a result, the philosophical and material questions about staffing writing courses center on issues of intellectual expertise rather than labor conditions.

The writing programs in the sample have benefitted from how these schools understand undergraduate education more broadly. Schools in the sample have been able, by and large, to keep class sizes in writing courses relatively low. They have also been able to maintain a commitment—central to the small college structure of feeling and to their promises to potential students—to staff most writing courses with full-time faculty. In this chapter, we present these data in more detail, first focusing on the material parameters of class size, exemption, and staffing within first-year writing. While analyzing the data, we realized that the question of *who* should teach first-year writing was a central philosophical question for small college writing programs, given the prevalence of WAC-based requirements and the WPA's responsibility for faculty development. We shared this finding with focus group participants in order to hear their take on this issue.

Our analysis here focuses on explicit first-year writing requirements for several reasons. First, these are the most common types of requirements. Second, as we've noted earlier, the field of rhetoric and composition can be said to have emerged out of first-year writing requirements and programs. Nonetheless, the most common first-year requirement in the sample is not the composition course that dominates the national field. Analyzing how first-year composition and first-year writing seminar programs are implemented, then, allows us to extend our comparative analysis of small college writing programs. Throughout the chapter, when we refer to "first-year writing" we are therefore indicating only explicit requirements. Embedded requirements are excluded from this discussion.

Class Size, Exemption, and Staffing

Enrollment caps and exemption policies are fundamental parameters to staffing first-year writing courses, since they determine the number of faculty the program needs on a regular basis. The CCCC *Statement of Principles and Standards for the Postsecondary Teaching of Writing* recommends that "[n]o more than 20 students should be permitted in any writing class. Ideally, classes should be limited to 15." (For research establishing the logic of these standards, see Horning, "Definitive

Article.") Figure 7.1 shows the percentage of schools with specific enrollment caps in the sample; throughout the data set, we found relatively low caps on first-year writing courses.

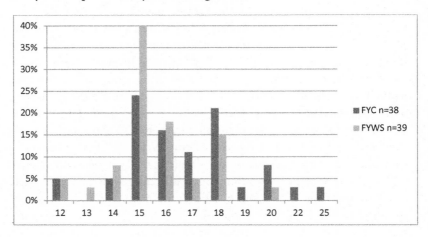

Figure 7.1 Enrollment Caps for FYC and FYWS.

All but two of the seventy-seven schools that provided class size data comply with the CCCC guideline of keeping class sizes below twenty, and 44% meet the ideal of fifteen or smaller. These figures contrast sharply with national norms. Anne Ruggles Gere reports in the "Initial Report" on the 2009 CCCC survey of its membership (which did not account for institutional size) that only 20.2% sections of first-year writing capped enrollment at eighteen or lower; another 47.4% had a range of nineteen to twenty-four students per class. Small colleges' commitment to small classes and low student-to-faculty ratios clearly carries over to this realm.

When we compare the thirty-eight first-year composition to the thirty-nine first-year writing seminar programs within the sample, we find only one school with a FYWS requirement cap enrollment above eighteen, while six of the schools with a FYC requirement do so. This may be because first-year writing seminar programs distribute the burden of staffing the requirement across the entire institution, rather than pulling personnel entirely from a single department. It may also be that the smaller class is important to incentivizing faculty across the college to teach in the program. FYC programs, staffed by a single department, may have the impossible choice between increasing class size in first-year writing, offering fewer courses for the major, or hiring temporary faculty. As we discuss below, the last option is rare. Most small colleges strenuously resist habitually relying on part-time and/or temporary faculty, and very few schools in the sample have graduate programs from which to draw writing instructors.

In some cases, enrollment caps are specified in the language of the requirement itself. This is one way for a school to make a public commitment. In such cases, when college-wide enrollments grow (as we know anecdotally they have done at a number of schools in the sample), the institution may choose to increase staffing resources, or it may choose to create a policy by which students can place out of the requirement. (Such resource-driven concerns are not the only reason for exemption policies, of course.) Roughly one-third of the sample (thirty-two schools) indicated that they had some method (AP, SAT or IB scores, placement exam, portfolio, or a paid test) by which students could be exempted from the first-year writing requirement. Of these schools, twenty-eight have first-year composition as their primary first-year writing requirement, and four have first-year writing seminars. Of those with first-year composition, ten have an additional first-year writing requirement (FYWS, FYS, or core) that students cannot place out of; ten require a W course beyond the first year (seven of which do not have an additional first-year writing requirement); one school has a portfolio requirement. The four schools with a requirement *other* than FYC that allow exemption do not have an additional first-year writing requirement, but all have a W course requirement. This means that only ten schools exempt students entirely from the writing requirement. The average percentage of students who exempt from the twenty-five schools that provided this information is 14%, although that average is raised—somewhat misleadingly—by the nine schools that exempt more than 15%. Those nine schools have additional requirements, so that students who place out of FYC still need to fulfill other first-year and WAC requirements.

These data demonstrate small colleges' historic commitment to writing instruction and, more specifically, to requiring at least one writing course of all students. The writing curricula at these institutions exist to develop all students as writers and critical thinkers, to engage them from the outset in the kind of mental discipline celebrated by the *Yale Report*. Requirements do not seem to be designed to address a deficit in the writing of a sub-set of student writers or to measure for competency. (Only twelve schools list competency as an explicit goal of their writing requirement.)

Nonetheless, material questions of resources and recruitment affect individual schools' abilities to make their first-year writing course the foundation of the liberal arts education they offer. In a focus group discussion, one respondent meditated briefly on the ramifications of having all students take a particular course:

> When we moved from a four-division type of curriculum—this was about four years ago—to this new foundation curriculum where everyone has to take a first-year writing seminar, there was this clause that said in the transitional years we will continue to accept the AP credit, if they get a 4 or 5. That was supposed to expire I think two years ago, and it's still going, and part of the reason is we just don't have the faculty to staff more sections. So—and also it's a recruitment issue because students want to get out of that class, and they want—you know, whatever. So right now we're still accepting the AP, and that is automatic, it's a 4 or 5. A student can say, "I don't care about the credits, I still want to take the class." Some do.

The "first-year writing seminar" discussed by this participant is actually a first-year composition course taught by English department faculty and adjuncts. At this institution (whose enrollment cap on FYC courses is fifteen), one-third of incoming students are exempt from this requirement, but the school also requires students to take two W courses. This participant is a solo WPA/WCD, and may well be stretched thin in her efforts to lead first-year composition, WAC, and the writing center. Such a lean leadership configuration for this curriculum may also indicate that the program is under-resourced.

The concern with recruitment at this institution is not representative of the sample as a whole. More often, the schools in the data set rhetorically and instrumentally align the first-year writing requirements with their values—and sell them to students as a package. In fact, we found that many schools eliminate exemption policies as they move from FYC requirements to FYWS. This may reflect a philosophical discomfort with exemption. Such policies may therefore be resource- rather than pedagogically-driven. Because first-year writing seminar programs distribute the responsibility for staffing a required course more evenly across the institution, they may allow schools to dedicate more faculty hours to that work.

Figure 7.2 shows the trends in staffing first-year writing courses at small colleges. These analyses are drawn from the 68 schools that have either first-year composition or first-year writing seminar requirements, and for which we have staffing data. There is a clear commitment to having tenure-line faculty provide writing instruction at these schools—a commitment that is unsurprising in a set of schools focused specifically on undergraduate education and close colloquy between faculty and students.[1]

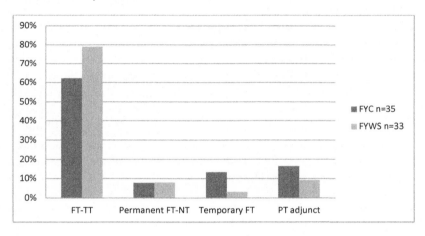

Figure 7.2 Comparison of First-Year Writing Faculty Status (average by percentage of total writing program staff).

Thirty-three FYWS programs reporting staffing data use 79% full-time, tenure-track faculty, and thirty-five of the FYC programs use 62% full-time, tenure track faculty. (This average of 71% compares favorably to the 2009 CCCC survey, which reports 16.9% nationwide.) At thirty out of the sixty-eight schools, ninety to one hundred percent of the people teaching in the writing program are tenure-line faculty. (In some cases, it's possible that the only writing instructor not on a tenure line is the WPA.) One-third of these schools have first-year composition, and two-thirds have first-year writing seminar programs. This may be in part because at many FYWS schools, seminar faculty are also incoming students' advisors. The WPA may then share responsibility for faculty recruitment for these courses with department chairs, the registrar, or a dean of academic or student affairs.

At the other extreme, only nine schools have a first-year writing staff that comprises fifty percent or more of temporary labor, either full- or part-time. (Six schools use fifty percent or more part-time temporary labor, and three schools use fifty percent or more temporary labor, both full- and part-time.) Of these nine schools, seven have a FYC requirement, so the reliance on temporary labor may be due to the limitations of staffing a required course with faculty from one department.

Overall, staffing and exemption issues at the first-year composition programs in the sample are comparable to those of the field as a whole, although the small college commitment to small classes carries over here. First-year writing seminar programs, by contrast, are almost entirely staffed by tenure-line faculty, have fewer large classes, and rarely exempt students from the requirement. The issues for these programs center instead around expertise in writing and faculty development.

This is visible in Figure 7.3, which compares the percentages of first-year writing sections taught by individuals who only teach academic writing courses, those who teach academic writing and English courses, and those who teach academic writing courses and courses across the disciplines. Few small colleges rely completely on specialists in rhetoric and composition to teach writing.

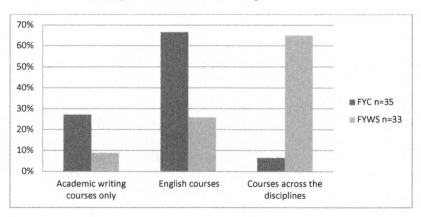

Figure 7.3 Comparison of Types of Courses Taught by FYC and FYWS Faculty (average by percentage of sections taught).

Very few faculty teaching first-year writing at small colleges specialize in the field of rhetoric and composition. Only 27% of the sections of first-year composition and only 9% of the sections of first-year writing seminars are taught by writing specialists. This is even true in the case of the nine institutions with independent writing departments or programs. In fact, seven out of the nine have a FYWS, FYS, or core requirement instead of FYC, sharing responsibility for teaching of writing across the curriculum. It is, in fact, rare across the sample to have *any* general education requirement be the province of a single department; small colleges are more likely to require a course in mathematical reasoning (which can be fulfilled by courses in math, computer science, logic, or statistics) than they are to require that all students take a particular math class. The WAC focus of these schools and the premium they place on shared ownership of the curriculum are additional philosophical differences.

The majority of faculty teaching FYWS (65%) teach courses across the disciplines (91%, if English is included) in addition to teaching first-year writing. We discussed many of the administrative pros and cons of staffing first-year writing with faculty from across the institution in Chapter 6. In brief, FYWS programs are powerful vectors for WAC pedagogy. The main challenges facing FYWS programs in terms of staffing are those of faculty recruitment, faculty development, and programmatic alignment (which we might also think of as consistency). In order to staff such programs and maintain low enrollment caps, faculty must be actively recruited into the programs from across campus. For many small college faculty, teaching a first-year writing seminar is an opportunity to develop a new course or to experiment with a new topic. For others, it is a way to teach a more interdisciplinary course than their usual rotation affords. Institutions ensure an adequate roster each year in a variety of ways. One approach is the connection between first-year advising and teaching the FYWS already noted. Another is to offer course development money for such seminars. Some institutions consider teaching in the FYWS program important service to the college, and reflect that in their review procedures. (See Hanstedt on the importance of service at many small colleges.) Other institutions focus on recruitment at the departmental level, because every course a department gives to the seminar program is one that it cannot offer for its major curriculum. Some institutions develop target contributions for individual departments based on full-time equivalencies and others offer additional resources to departments that commit to regular participation in the program. All of these strategies are ways of ensuring that the institution delivers on its commitment to share writing instruction among the faculty as a whole.

The job of the WPA in a first-year writing seminar program is to work with a diverse group of faculty of all ranks and from across the college, in order to provide expertise and to move them toward delivering at least somewhat consistent writing instruction. Such work poses challenges and significant opportunities for disseminating WAC pedagogy. The strong culture of faculty autonomy at these schools can make it difficult to suggest new pedagogical strategies. In addition, faculty do not typically teach in the program every single year, and so rotate in and out of faculty development conversations. As we identified this staffing model as present at a significant number of the schools in the sample, we decided to ask the focus groups to meditate on its philosophical implications. We therefore asked an open-ended question: "How do you feel about faculty across the college sharing responsibility for teaching writing?" In response, participants in one focus group debated how consistent or well-informed writing instruction could be in such WAC-based programs: How could non-compositionists have the expertise needed to deliver writing instruction?

All four participants in this focus group have some version of writing across the curriculum at their institutions. As they reflected on our question, they began to debate the relative merits of what they ended up calling an "infiltration" model. (Townsend describes this as "the 'infusion' model" of writing across the curriculum ["Writing Intensive" 237].) In this approach, the WPA's expertise influences writing instruction throughout the college via faculty development. This contrasts with what we might call the *expert* model, in which writing is owned by dedicated rhetoric and composition faculty with doctoral training in the field.

Speaker 1, a WPA from a school with first-year writing seminar and W course requirements, was the first to respond:

> Obviously, we wrestle with this a lot. And the way I've sort of made my peace with this in a sense is that I think that, in fact, yes, language and writing practices are universal. We have them, they are not all the same, but to that extent they are—I'm never comfortable saying "skills," but I think there is something that as long as I can help faculty understand better ways of teaching it, they can do what needs to be done. On the other hand, I think that it's possible, not at my college—

this isn't going to happen, and I'm not going to push for it—but that we could have, well we actually have a rhetoric major at our college. But I'm not in that department, I'm in English. But we could have a writing studies major that would require specialization.

Here, she distinguishes between writing as an interdisciplinary field of study and writing as a means of communication to use across the curriculum. As Joseph Harris notes in the passage from "Thinking Like a Program" used as an epigraph to this chapter, there is a tension in the field between the desire for rhetoric and composition to take its place alongside the many other disciplinary and interdisciplinary fields of study that make up the modern university, and the conviction that writing and writing instruction are an invaluable component of all fields. At the small college, the focus has been on the latter. This is not because small colleges routinely devalue writing studies as a field, but because writing instruction is already deeply embedded in their curricula. As small colleges become aware of the emergence of writing studies, they are tapping into this expertise through the WPA as leader of WAC initiatives—rather than unilaterally creating large departments to deliver writing instruction.

We can see this shared interest in teaching writing in part when Speaker 1 mentions in passing the need to "help faculty understand better ways of teaching" those aspects of writing she describes as "universal." She then continues to meditate on this tension by bringing in an example from a different discipline:

> *Speaker 1*: But to the extent that we ask anybody graduating from [College 18] should be able to make some kind of sense of statistical information, for example, and that none of us should let our students use it badly, but I don't need to call in the math department to do that for me every time. . . . I guess I think that I'm happy in my environment with my students that they are learning to write not simply at a minimal level of producing a thin argument—some do, thin argument.

> *Speaker 2*: Some sort of formulaic prose, yeah.

> *Speaker 1*: But that they are becoming to a certain extent rhetorically savvy and that they can use writing to participate in civil discourse and civic life. And that seems to me pretty

good, and that that can be accomplished by faculty shared across the curriculum.

We can see that as the conversation develops, Speaker 1 clarifies what she sees as the goals of writing instruction for faculty across the curriculum. Her focus shifts from directly answering the stated question to how she feels about faculty across the college teaching writing, demonstrating her approval of that approach in all its complexity. The writing goals she evokes are general—students are becoming "rhetorically savvy"—and consonant with the rhetorical and developmental orientation of the small college structure of feeling. These are students who are learning to "*use* writing to participate in civil discourse" (emphasis added).

As the discussion continues, Speaker 3 (who describes her school's writing requirement below) turns the conversation to the dilemma of expertise, raising questions about the qualifications of the English department in comparison to those of faculty from across the college:

> *Speaker 3*: Well, I think at schools like ours, though, we don't really have any other option. When I think about the—at [College 4] the English Department is almost entirely responsible for teaching composition. We have a second first-year class required, but that's across the curriculum, and writing instruction is not necessarily going to happen. But even those people in the English Department are not trained in rhetoric, and so you know, and I don't think [College 4] is so unusual in that respect, as a small liberal arts college.

> *Speaker 4*: Well, that seems a strength of these small liberal arts colleges. It may be a weakness that there's not that kind of depth, but the strength here is that in an R1 university, you can't tell me that physics, science people ever even take one single, you know, rhetoric course, but that you have the opportunity to, in fact, to *infiltrate*, if you will, the departments across—it's a small enough place that you really can have some influence. (emphasis added)

Speaker 4's institution has a first-year writing seminar program. Here, she adds to Speaker 3's argument by explaining how the size of these institutions allows the WPA to "infiltrate" departments across the college in order to "have some influence." She suggests that even though schools such as hers and Speaker 3's do not have a cadre of writing specialists to teach writing, she can use her own expertise to educate her colleagues about best practices for writing instruction. The SLAC WPA may need to think about how to use her expertise within her institution—how to infiltrate teaching practices across the college in order to infuse writing instruction throughout (to use Townsend's term). In the case described by Speaker 4, expertise in this context is best used to train faculty from across the curriculum rather than to teach writing to students directly.

A bit later, Speaker 3 raises another tradeoff in writing instruction at a small college:

> Yeah, so I don't know necessarily that the study of rhetoric [. . .] my concern about limiting it as it is at [College 4] is that when the others don't have that responsibility, they don't share that responsibility for teaching, they see the English Department as responsible for inoculating students, and if they are not properly inoculated for literacy errors, then we become the responsible people. We're supposed to have insured that there are no literacy errors, in addition to you know the transition to college and learning how to cite properly and how to use the library, all of those many things that first-year seminars are supposed to do. There is this misunderstanding, even that they've gone through it themselves, curious, there's this misunderstanding about how long it takes to develop those literacy skills, and there's a kind of token, "Well, yeah, I assign writing in my science class or math class," but that further development of writing abilities and sensibilities and rhetorical skills, we all know needs to continue, but we all know that when it's limited to a certain group, there isn't this shared responsibility, that the liberal arts are supposed to be taking on.[2]

Here we see that Speaker 3 is identifying a perceived limitation of housing writing instruction within one department. Within such a culture of writing, the sense that responsibility for student learning is the collaborative responsibility of the faculty as a whole gets lost, since faculty in other departments assume that the English department "owns" writing instruction. This pinpoints one of the most vexed tradeoffs in WAC: If writing instruction is housed solely in one department, other departments may come to understand it as beyond their scope—and, as a result, fail to reflect on the rhetorical and discursive nature of knowledge construction in their fields. If writing instruction is not under the purview of a single department, on the other hand, it can be difficult to survey courses and expectations enough to insure consistency across the requirement. These two scenarios require WPAs to use their expertise differently. When no single department "owns" writing instruction, WPAs can use their expertise to infiltrate and educate these colleagues on best practices. There may be less resistance because faculty outside of English may value a WPA's expertise and wish to learn from it. However, it may be easier to build a shared vision for writing within a single department—although there is no guarantee, of course.[3]

Up to this point we have looked at decisions based on resources and institutional philosophy, but WPAs do not come to their positions as blank slates. They have their own philosophies of how writing should be taught based on experience teaching and perhaps doctoral training. It is possible that some of these philosophies—cultivated before coming to a small college—are invested in individual power in ways that are subtly at odds with the collaborative nature of the small college structure of feeling. Speaker 2 demonstrates this tension when he raises the question of whether faculty from across the curriculum have the necessary rhetorical knowledge to teach writing at the same level as specialists in rhetoric and composition:

> *Speaker 2*: I don't think that we should expect our disciplinary colleagues to have rhetorical knowledge. I don't know what they would do with it, even. But I do think that as long as we believe that anyone can teach writing—I actually don't agree that that is so. I mean, I don't think that is a fair expectation to democratize this work that widely, just like you know not everybody can repair cars or whatever else in the world.

> *Speaker 4*: So who can teach writing?

> *Speaker 2*: Well, I mean, I don't know how to answer *that*. Lots of people can teach writing as they teach it in different ways. Not everyone can teach the same kind of writing, but I think that one of the problems is that at schools where we have this odd sort of labor arrangement, there's another question is how much can we expect those people to be doing in innovative and strong ways? And I think that it's kind of an irony that

the more we democratize this work, the tougher it becomes to actually kick up the volume in the courses themselves at some times. That's all, right. And it's kind of a dilemma . . .

The conversation has shifted from focusing on practical concerns to exploring the philosophical underpinnings of each speaker's view toward writing instruction. Speaker 2 emphasizes the dangers of a WAC-based approach to delivering writing instruction. If writing instruction is "democratized"—that is, assigned to all faculty at the college, regardless of their fields of specialization—he worries that the courses themselves cannot provide as rigorous and theoretically sophisticated writing instruction as they could if all writing instructors were rhet/comp specialists.

Researcher 1 then pushes Speaker 2 to think more deeply about the implications of his claim. She asks, "So does it make you nervous, this trend that we're noticing, which is sort of SLACs being much more dependent on faculty across the curriculum instead of what it used to be, which was more of an English Department or Rhetoric Department?" Speaker 2 responds:

> *Speaker 2*: Well, I don't think—traditionally English Departments have been trained in teaching literature, they haven't been trained in teaching writing, so that wasn't necessarily a better arrangement. I guess I am, you know, maybe it's just my age and when I came up in the field, but I continue to be struck by our inability to claim an institutional space of our own.
>
> *Researcher 1*: Us being, meaning rhetoric people?
>
> *Speaker 2*: Yes, yeah. In a more regularized way. How is it that that was accomplished by every other discipline except ours. I just find that troubling. I think it delimits our work and makes us become jack-of-all-trades, jill-of-all trades, and make us become sort of ambassadors of social, psychological, professional contingencies. You know, why should we be asking ourselves, how do we get faculty to do this without fear?

Speaker 2's elaboration conflates two issues. At first, he raises the issue that rhetoric is not currently seen as a discipline that is equal to others. He then shifts focus, raising the separate dilemma of non-rhetoric faculty who are afraid to teach writing. In conflating the issues, Speaker

2 may be asking himself and others in the group, "Why should it be the job of the WPA to encourage those who are fearful of teaching writing to do it, when there are specialists out there who would be better qualified and have less fear?" Speakers 4 and 2 then continue the conversation, focusing on the latter point:

> *Speaker 4*: 'Cause that's our context.
> *Speaker 2*: Yeah, but that shouldn't be our job.

Speakers 4 and 2 thus bring up an interesting dilemma between context and responsibility. Speaker 4 draws our attention back to the small college structure of feeling, emphasizing the WAC orientation of these schools: We should be asking ourselves how to help faculty do this, she argues, because at these institutions, teaching writing is part of their job and part of what they value as an element of a liberal education. Speaker 2's quick response suggests a resistance to this aspect of leading a writing program at a small college. In doing so, he shifts the focus of the conversation slightly to questions of status:

> *Speaker 4*: I mean, there are rhetoric programs out there that dedicate themselves to rhetoric.
>
> *Speaker 2*: Yeah, and I think they wouldn't face that same question, right? How do we get people to take this on without fear? You take it on without fear if you've studied it, you take it on without fear if it's part of your professional training and you have a PhD in it, just like the people in biology do, and that's just not—so I don't think that we can have it both ways. I don't think that we can be fully on par, symmetrical in terms of status, and also have lots of other people doing this work.

Speaker 2 hypothesizes that faculty across the curriculum are afraid to teach writing because they have not studied it and cannot call themselves experts. But the question of fear seems to be a red herring; the larger discussion has turned back to the tension Speaker 1 brought up at the outset of the conversation. Speaker 2 is focused on writing as its own discipline at the expense of its pervasive role in all disciplinary education at a small college.

At this point, Researcher 2—operating as a participant observer—questions the paradox that Speaker 2 raises by presenting one of her own:

Researcher 2: Similarly, I'm not sure that we can have rhetoric be a discipline comparable to other disciplines and a program comparable to other programs *and* say that rhetoric and attention to writing infiltrates the entire curriculum. I mean, I think it cuts both ways; I think you're absolutely right there are trade-offs, which is why we termed the question originally in terms of pros and cons, but I think in both directions, it cuts both ways.

Speaker 2: I mean, infiltration is kind of an interesting metaphor for it because that already suggests a sort of, I don't know, not surreptitious, but a kind of sneakiness, a kind of way of getting us in.

Researcher 2: I'm actually ok with that aspect.

Speaker 2: Politically you feel like that's a viable way to think of it? Infiltrating?

Researcher 2: Yes. That's a much longer conversation. . . .

Speaker 2: It's interesting.

Speaker 4: But I would be interested in hearing how you think you can develop a writing-rich curriculum in a small liberal arts college without that sort of infiltration?

The tensions this discussion identifies are simultaneously pragmatic and philosophical. The question of who "owns" writing instruction— or is best positioned to provide it—has implications for how schools staff their writing programs and for how they imagine those programs fitting into the larger educational missions of their various institutions. It is not feasible for small colleges to have a single department largely dedicated to a single requirement, because the staff size would be disproportionate to other departments and programs on campus. This type of department would be different in that it would not grant majors; instead, its main mission would be to implement a requirement that has historically been assumed as part of the collective ownership of an undergraduate education.

At the end of the conversation, Speaker 3 makes a distinction between change and "a return to something" in regards to the delivery of writing instruction:

Speaker 2: This isn't going to happen in my lifetime, I can tell you that. That kind of change is not on the horizon.

Speaker 3: But it's interesting that it would be a return to something as opposed to a change.

Researcher 2: I think in some ways it would and in some ways it wouldn't. In many ways, the place of rhetoric in a classical curriculum is like the place of writing in a writing-rich curriculum today. I think that, I see WAC as a really direct heir to the role of rhetoric in the classical curriculum.

Speaker 3: Except that don't you think that composition is more instrumental than, than—

Researcher 2: Composition is—I guess I'm making a distinction between WAC and composition. From what I've been learning about the classical curriculum and the liberal arts and so on in the nineteenth century, and particularly before 1875 or so, it was a kind of infiltration model. You were paying attention to rhetoric and communication at all points, but I think not sometimes in some of the ways we think of it when we think of classical rhetoric as a kind of stand-alone subject because of the ways it was appearing everywhere all four years and so on. And I think there are ways in which, unless we're going to go back to a four-year entirely prescribed generalist education without majors, I actually think WAC in some ways is a really interesting reinvention of some of that curriculum goals.

Researcher 2 here sums up one of the key claims throughout this book: Writing has been a mainstay of the small college structure of feeling for a very long time. In other words, a WAC-based approach to writing instruction at a small college is less a *change* from practice-as-usual than it is a *recognition* that the values of many such institutions align with the philosophy of the writing across the curriculum movement. This recognition comes as these colleges formalize the place of WAC in their curricula—to varying degrees—by providing opportunities, mandates, and resources for faculty development. Such a focus on faculty development arises from small colleges' focus on faculty as teachers (as well as scholars), and can help to mitigate the lack of consistency and expertise that may exist when writing instruction is a shared responsibility across the curriculum.

Faculty development encompasses a significant space in the small college WPA portfolio: 98% of WPAs in first-year writing seminar programs, and 84% of WPAs in first-year composition programs, listed faculty development as one of their responsibilities. Of the 82 respondents who answered the question of whether faculty development was a shared responsibility, 42 (or 51%) say that this is not a solo responsibility, but one shared with other entities on campus (most commonly a committee or dean). The types of faculty development the respondents offer are listed in table 7.1.

Table 7.1 Faculty Development at Small Colleges.

Type of Faculty Development offered	Number of Schools
Required seminar or workshops	30
Optional semester-long seminar	5
Workshops	79
One-on-one consultations	72
Meeting with Departments	39
Monthly lunches	20
Informal meetings	86

Respondents may use more than one approach. Although—as with the range of writing requirements beyond the first year—the types of faculty development activities are common and in line with national trends, it is striking how many respondents included "informal meetings" and "one-on-one consultations." This reliance on informality and individualized attention is consonant with the SLAC structure of feeling, specifically with the value it places on individual relationships as essential to teaching and learning. It also connects closely with the informality of the WAC movement and the heterogeneity of WAC programs more generally, which Susan H. McLeod discusses in more detail (see "Writing Across the Curriculum: An Introduction"). In advising a new small college WPA in one of our focus group discussions, an experienced WAC director underscored the centrality of this kind of flexible approach: "These places run on relationships," she pointed out, "and you ignore that at your peril. The worst thing you could do is not do the kind of reaching out that you're doing."

For many of our respondents, a primary goal of their faculty development efforts is—in Rutz's formulation—to make "the implicit explicit" (69), or, as one focus group participant suggests, to "infiltrate." In other words, they seek to provide workshops and other opportunities for faculty to have conversations that articulate what they value in student writing and how they teach it. To do this, they are much like the WAC directors McLeod describes, although with other titles: "listeners as well as talkers, learners as well as facilitators of learning" ("An Introduction" 6). Small colleges are fertile ground for such conversations because of the value the faculty and the institutions already place on teaching. Reflecting on the success of the faculty development program at College 19, the writing program administrator observed that after coming to one of the workshops tied to teaching in the first-year seminar program,

> [P]eople would come say, "You know, we go to so many stupid meetings. This is the only thing that I like. This is the only thing that matters. This is so gr—refreshing." So that has been really tremendous. We have over 100 (out of 285) faculty across the curriculum who participate in that, so that has really opened the door to have other conversations about the teaching of writing.

Faculty development at a small college needs to blend the WPA's expertise from the field of writing studies, the faculty's value in teaching, and the small college ethos of shared responsibility for student learning. Small college WPAs will be most effective if they listen to what faculty have to offer before jumping in to profess their own expertise. Just as in the classroom, when we scaffold for our students how to write for different genres and audiences, the WPA at a small college needs to scaffold between what are known to be best practices, and what faculty have been doing for years in their courses. As the comment from College 19's WPA shows, small college faculty are interested in discussions around pedagogy, and with the right finesse, a WPA can *infiltrate* these discussions with knowledge from the field.

8 Redefining Small College Writing Programs: Leadership Configurations and Writing Requirements

Most of the conversation about collaborative administration is contained within the traditional understanding of writing programs as first-year composition programs (either within large universities or small colleges, or within separate writing departments). Increasingly, however, writing programs extend beyond traditional boundaries to include all the units and people across a campus who are involved in the evaluation and instruction of writing.

—Diane Kelly-Riley, Lisa Johnson-Shull,
and William Condon

To date, there has been no comprehensive analysis of how different types of writing requirements (and sets of requirements) are typically led at different institutions. Conversations about such questions tend to be narrower, focusing on whether or not writing across the curriculum should be housed in English, for example (see Blair; Howard, Hess, and Darby; Kirsch, Finkel, and France; Smith, "Responds" and "Why English"). More recently, the debate has turned on whether first-year writing instruction is best served by being separated from English (see, for example, Anson, "Who Wants"; Deis, Lowell, and Weese; J. Harris, "Thinking"; and Spellmeyer). But such narrow discussions about the location of a particular component of a writing program beg the questions we raised in Chapter 4 about program-wide *configurations* of leadership positions. The notion of "program" remains elastic at most SLACs, which makes it more difficult to define the leadership responsibilities, positions, and the institutional home of writing at any one particular institution. The leadership configurations presented in Chapter 4 illustrate what programmatic structures currently exist at small colleges, and what tendencies toward change are inherent in them. The configurations also invite analysis, because the philosophical orientation of a school's approach to writing instruction is embedded within the leadership configuration it has developed. It is important to ask questions about how a school came to its present arrangement. A particular leadership configuration does not automatically indicate a specific orientation. For example, a school with a *WCD Only* configuration may indicate a deficit model of writing instruction, because the school understands writing instruction as something that supports needy students. On the other hand, that same configuration may indicate a developmental model, because the school is focused on supporting all students as writers.

While local, historical analysis helps answer these questions, it is also essential to analyze the writing curriculum of a school in relation to its leadership configuration in order to fully understand the philosophy of the writing program. If a *WCD Only* school has a single writing requirement that most students place out of, and has no professionalized leadership, it becomes clear that the school believes that writing instruction is only for some underprepared students—not all students. Bringing the data from leadership configurations and requirement structures together allows us to analyze what types of requirements are most closely associated with what types of leadership positions—and, just as importantly, what types or sets of requirements are most often governed by which configurations of leadership positions. These two components form the skeleton of any writing program; understanding their interaction is therefore essential to understanding a program's functioning and underlying philosophy. In this chapter, we begin by presenting data that shows the most common requirement structures across the four most common leadership configurations. We then examine first-year writing requirements more closely, analyzing the ways in which first-year composition and first-year writing seminar programs are most often led. These analyses show some of the directions from which change emerges for small college writing programs. We therefore conclude the chapter discussing pressures and considerations for change. (Appendix F presents a set of questions external and in-

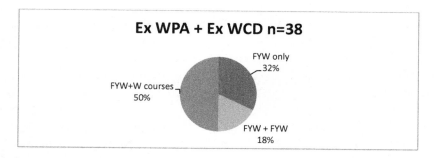

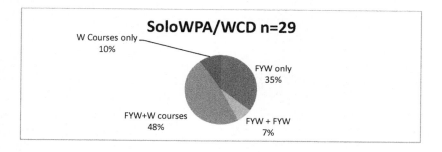

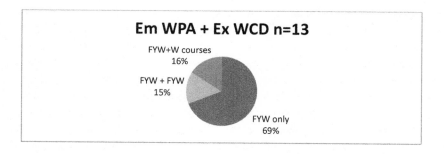

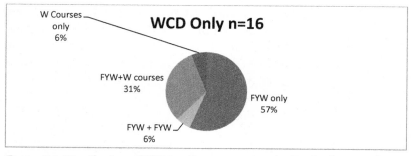

Figure 8.1 Distribution of Writing Requirements over Leadership Configurations.[1]

ternal reviews can use to frame this type of analysis of a small college writing program.)

The requirements data presented in Chapter 6 illustrate the trend that small colleges have begun to add verticality to their writing programs. Figure 8.1 breaks down the first-year writing requirement and W courses across the four most common leadership configurations. The *Explicit WPA + Explicit WCD* (19 out of 38) and *Solo WPA/WCD* (14 out of 29) configurations are most prevalent within a vertical writing curriculum; however, most *Embedded WPAs* (9 out of 13) work within a single, first-year writing requirement. The majority of schools (9 out of 16) that employ a *WCD Only* require only one first-year writing course.

As we noted in Chapters 6 and 7, the writing requirements at small colleges reflect the historic affinity between these schools and writing across the curriculum. In examining their curriculum-centered programs, we find that schools with explicit, vertical writing curricula are most likely to have a leadership configuration that includes an explicit writing program administrator. In other words, the presence of explicit WAC beyond the first-year requirement seems to make institutions more likely to feel the need for professionalized leadership, perhaps because of the importance of faculty development and assessment to successful WAC programs (see Young and Fulwiler). As more courses are added to the writing requirement, the need for more leadership may also become apparent, as the requirement may grow beyond that of a single department or program.

We see further complexities in program structures as we continue the comparison of first-year writing seminar and first-year composition programs that we began in Chapter 7. Figure 8.2 looks at the data from the perspective of the requirement rather than the leadership configuration. Here, the data is broken down as follows: We compare schools that have only one first-year writing requirement (FYC-only and FYWS-only); those that have one first-year writing requirement plus a W course requirement (FYC+W and FYWS+W); and those that have more than one first-year writing requirement, with or without an additional W course requirement (FYC+FYWS and FYC+FYWS+W).

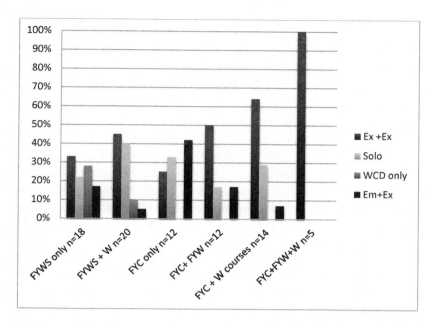

Figure 8.2 Comparison of Leadership Configurations in Relation to FYC and FYWS.

Of the sixteen schools that employ a *WCD Only* configuration, none have a first-year composition requirement. In the total sample, if there is first-year composition, there is also some kind of WPA—a trend unsurprising given the strong association of those two entities, historically. In addition, first-year composition, as we have defined it, is a department-based requirement. It must, then, be managed by someone in that department, whether that individual is the department chair (an embedded WPA) or a compositionist whose title includes recognition of those responsibilities (an explicit WPA). When there is a W course requirement in addition to FYC—that is, when the writing curriculum becomes explicitly vertical—the leadership configuration is typically more explicit. (This could happen either through the revision of the existing position, or through the addition of a new position.) We can see this in that 42% of the programs with only first-year composition requirements are led by embedded WPAs, while only 7% of the programs with FYC + W courses have that particular leadership configuration. Similarly, 25% of the FYC-only schools have explicit WPAs, while 64% of the FYC + W courses schools do. (That same addition of the W course to the FYC requirement shifts *WCD Only* configurations slightly into the middle of the Venn diagram, as *Solo WPA/WCDs*: 29% with FYC-only versus 33% with FYC + W courses.) We speculate that this increase in the explicitness of leadership when verticality is added through a writing across the curriculum requirement occurs because the "program" has started to move beyond the purview of a single department. The requirement structure needs broader faculty support, ownership, and development.

Among the schools in our sample, WPAs charged with the oversight of first-year composition requirements are typically housed in departments of English (36 respondents). Two are housed elsewhere (one in an independent writing program and one in a rhetoric department). In these cases, at least a portion of what we would call the writing program and the WPA are housed in the same department. However, when an institution takes a WAC-based approach to its writing requirement—either through an FYWS or a W requirement—it becomes significantly more difficult to predict the institutional homes of either the WPA or the "writing program" itself. Among the schools in our sample, WPAs charged with the oversight of FYWS have more diverse institutional homes. Eighteen respondents reported an English department as their home, including three of the administrators in a *WCD Only* configuration; four report a writing and rhetoric department; another four report the provost or office of the dean of faculty; and others report interdisciplinary studies (2) or the writing or learning center (4). For five respondents, the position rotates, and institutional home depends on who is currently serving as WPA.

The overwhelming majority of all writing administrators in the sample (55 out of 80, or 69%) identify English as their home department. Some respondents, however, reported that this did not necessarily reflect the full truth of their institutional location. After indicating "English" on the survey, one respondent qualified in her response: "I'm partly in the English Dept, partly an administrator—specifically so I can work across departments. I'm the only person in the university to have such a position. It's designed to let me work freely across the curriculum." For others, the connection to the English department speaks to the catalog designation and disciplinary location of the courses they offer, but not of their administrative work.

The WAC-based first-year writing seminar requirement is less often associated with embedded leadership overall. Only 17% of the

FYWS-only and 5% of the FYWS + W course requirements are led by embedded WPAs. Perhaps because these requirements are already centered outside a single department, the addition of a W course requirement to FYWS does not make as dramatic a change in leadership configuration as it did in the case of first-year composition. But we do see that *WCD Only* schools are unlikely to have both a vertical and WAC-based requirement. Instead, *Solo WPA/WCD* is more common when a WAC-based curriculum goes vertical. This may be due to a shift in responsibilities to include more faculty support and assessment (see discussion in Chapter 5). This verticality may make the need for the writing administrator to support faculty, as well as students, clear and pressing.

One reason for schools to identify embedded sites of writing instruction is because doing so makes it possible to uncover leadership vacuums where they exist. Table 8.1 presents the most common clusters of requirements (presented in Chapter 6) in relation to the four most common leadership configurations (discussed in Chapter 4). It seems that, overall, embedded requirements are associated with more student-centered leadership configurations. For example, for the five institutions whose only writing requirement is the embedded first-year seminar (FYS), we see that 60% (or three schools) utilize *WCD Only*, 20% (or one school) has a *Solo WPA/WCD*, and 20% (again, one school) has an *Explicit WPA + Explicit WCD*. The WPA at this last school is a rotating member of the faculty. Thus, even though this was coded as an explicit WPA position, it still raises the issues we discussed in Chapter 4 in the case of such positions. There is no guarantee of writing expertise, and there is the possibility that some individuals will not fully invest in the program for the long haul.

For the FYS requirement, verticality does not seem to make a significant difference, although with a single school in this category, it is difficult to generalize. (The one school with an FYS + W requirement has neither a WPA nor a WCD.) One danger of an entirely—or almost entirely—embedded writing requirement, then, is that it does not seem to warrant systematic, curriculum-focused, professional leadership. At some of these schools, the writing center director may provide some faculty development and leadership. At other institutions, it seems that there is little to no leadership for writing on campus. The institutions themselves may not recognize these embedded sites of writing as just that.

Table 8.1 Distribution of Leadership Configurations over Writing Requirements.

	Ex +Ex	Solo	WCD only	Em+Ex
FYWS only N=18	33%	22%	28%	17%
FYC only N=12	25%	33%	0%	42%
FYS only N=5	20%	20%	60%	0%
Core only N=5	40%	20%	20%	20%
W courses only N=5	0%	40%	60%	0%
FYW+ FYW N=15	47%	13%	7%	13%
FYWS + W courses (beyond FYW) N=20	45%	40%	10%	5%
FYC + W courses N=14	64%	29%	0%	7%

One striking finding is that the only requirement scenario that never exists in conjunction with an *Explicit WPA + Explicit WCD* leadership configuration is that of W courses only: Sixty percent of the schools (n=3) with this requirement have *Solo WPA/WCD* and 40% (n=2) employ *WCD Only.* It is likely that this reflects a committee-based structure, in which the requirement was initially proposed by a faculty committee, some version of which continues to have oversight over it. Some version of that committee, then, typically approves courses for the W designation. We speculate that moving from no writing curriculum to a W course requirement is the first step for an institution to make its embedded culture of writing explicit. It may therefore be some time before an institution can realize that it needs ongoing, professionalized, explicit leadership for such a requirement. When it does, these schools typically start with a *WCD Only* configuration and organically shift into a *Solo WPA/WCD* position as the writing center director assumes more responsibilities directly related to the W course requirement.

PRESSURES FOR CHANGE

This study offers a snapshot of a set of institutions in the midst of change. This is likely true of any study of a social organization. But in coming to understand the curriculum-centered structures and leadership configurations within the sample, we were struck again and again by the vivid presence of historical origins—what Raymond Williams would call residual structures—and looming changes. Changes in personnel create opportunities for institutions to examine and re-evaluate their curricular structures and their cultures of writing more broadly. (These changes can be catalyzed by retirement or other departures and through new hires.) Just as structures of feeling are in-progress and are comprised of tensions as well as affinities, writing programs only appear static when we remove them from the march of time.

From our observation, the greatest change currently seems to be taking place at institutions with *Solo WPA/WCD* or *Explicit WCD Only* configurations. In the other cases—as far as we have been able to tell—pressures for change are not as dramatic. In particular, when institutions adopt an *Explicit WPA + Explicit WCD* configuration there is little inclination to change this configuration. When they revise their writing requirements (shifting from FYC to FYWS or adding verticality), they maintain their commitment to this configuration of leadership, although the new requirements may catalyze different kinds of (or more) collaboration between the two administrators.

During the period of our research, several participating institutions arrived at significant crossroads for their delivery of writing instruction and several others reported seeing such moments of re-evaluation and decision coming soon. We have observed two basic approaches, two main roads that fork at these moments. In such a moment, institutions re-commit to their established writing program structures, continuing to tweak or refine them with available resources. On the other hand, they can determine that something fundamental in the culture of writing needs to change, and set out to shape a writing program in line with the new, ideal culture of writing to which they aspire. In addition, we have found that changes to a small college writing program most often grow out of changes in personnel (retirements and other departures) or dissatisfactions with the curriculum. As David Russell notes, such curricular initiatives often emerge from changes in the student population (*Writing* 271). Neither of these catalysts predicts which fork an institution will take. In the remainder of this chapter, we consider these different approaches in more detail, drawing on our respondents' narrative comments on the survey and the stories they told in follow-up correspondence, interviews, and focus group conversations.

Personnel-Driven Change

It may be that the *Solo WPA/WCD* leadership configuration is the site of the most flux and change at the present time because such positions have moved into the overlapping space between curriculum- and student-centered spheres as their current incumbents acquired additional responsibilities over the course of long careers. This may have been in response to changes to the curriculum. Nine of the twenty-nine solo WPA/WCDs have been in their positions longer than fifteen years, and nearly all of them spoke of their plans for their positions when they left. In describing her dizzying array of responsibilities at College 25, for example, one solo WPA/WCD underscored the fact of her own initiative while also acknowledging the need for change upon her retirement:

> Well, like most people who run programs, I have several full-time jobs, *by my own choice*. The teaching load per semester for conventional faculty is two courses, for a total of 4 per year. I am supposed to teach one per semester, so in theory I get about half-time off to direct writing programs. I actually teach a great deal more than that, and run many programs, but that's fine: *I choose to do this.* There are huge advantages to functioning this way. Were I to design a position for a successor, though, I'd have to change things. (emphasis added)

Over the course of a thirty-year career, an individual may agree to, or create, a set of responsibilities that are not sustainable beyond that individual. There is no magic formula for any WPA position, and certainly not for any solo WPA/WCD position. But we believe that it is likely that the SLAC structure of feeling itself has shifted in the last thirty years. Changing demographics (of students, faculty, and disciplinary and interdisciplinary fields), as well as shifts in the culture of assessment, have created new responsibilities for writing program administrators nationwide. As long-time writing program administrators retire, whether explicit or embedded, many of these institutions will need to undergo extensive self-examinations in order to redesign their leadership configurations.

What such self-examination leads to will necessarily vary by institution, as the respondents in our sample attest. While in some cases the retirement of a program administrator led an institution to create new position(s), as we discuss below, in other cases it re-committed to its existing program structure. College 26, for example, maintained its status quo by hiring someone from within its writing program upon the retirement of its WPA. That (new) solo WPA/WCD explained:

> I was hired to direct the WP AND to teach 2 sections per semester. Usually College Comp in the fall (around 24 students) and Intro Creative or a Lit class in the spring. My experience comes from two areas: project manager/tech author for 15 years, and a year's adjunct teaching in the English Department. Apparently they loved the depth of my "comments" on students' College Comp papers. The woman who was running the Writing Program took early retirement and put my name on the table as a replacement.

In this case, the WPA's retirement could have launched the institution into a wholesale examination of its writing program. Instead, it decided to promote one of its adjunct instructors into the position. It may be that the college did not have the resources to launch a national search, and this decision may also reveal that the culture of writing at that institution does not understand or value professional WPA expertise. They focused on institutional knowledge and continuity instead. They may have been looking for a manager rather than a leader, someone who would maintain the existing program without significant change.

In the case of College 27, the initial decision was similar—to hire an interim replacement for a departing solo WPA/WCD:

> My full-time position as WC and WAC director was created one year before I was hired. It was a tenure track position, and the first person hired into it left after one year. I was an adjunct at the time and was hired as an emergency replacement with the understanding that it would be for two years. However, I'm now in my fourth year, will be here next year, and the position may be changed to accommodate my credentials; that hasn't yet been resolved.

But at College 27—unlike at College 26—the abrupt departure of the tenure-track, solo WPA/WCD catalyzed a wide-reaching examination of the writing program. While the writing center director position has been reclassified so that our respondent (who does not have a PhD) can remain in it, the position of WAC director has been converted to a rotating position, to be a held by a member of the tenured faculty. It is unclear whether this new structure better supports the goals of the writing program, or if it helps the institution keep someone in the position of WCD at the expense of the WPA position.

Curriculum-Driven Change

Retirements and other departures create one kind of opportunity for an institution to re-examine its leadership configurations. In other cases, however, the drive comes from a sense that the writing requirements—or general education requirements as a whole—need to be examined, expanded, or otherwise changed. Rather than changes in personnel catalyzing such structural realignments or reorganizations, then, curricular revisions can create a need for a new or revised configuration. At College 28, for example, the institution first simply decided that it needed to examine its culture of writing. Speaking of himself and his colleague, our respondent recalls,

> Neither of us was hired to work with the writing program. My second year here, the Dean, who knew that I had directed the writing program at [another institution], where I had a 3-year contract while ABD, asked me to chair an ad hoc committee to investigate writing practices at the college. This was about 1990. We polled the faculty, discovered a lot of consternation about writing, and then over the next few years launched the WAC program.

In this case, College 28 called upon a standing member of its faculty because of his previous WPA experience. His participation in that review ultimately led to the creation of a WAC program and his own location within it. Although this individual was not specifically hired into a WPA position, his expertise in the field allowed him to help the institution review and refine its structure of administration. In essence, he grew into his current WPA role slowly.

Blended/Double Catalysts

Institutions overhauling their writing curricula do not always have the benefit of standing faculty with the expertise they need to foster a vibrant culture of writing. In any case, change can begin on one front, but move into another, which is why institutions need to look at both whenever suggesting changes to a writing program. The case of College 3 illustrates this. Ten years ago, College 3 developed a new writing requirement consisting of two writing-intensive (W) courses. Quoting an internal study that reported dissatisfaction with the quality of writing instruction at the institution, the College 3 committee on educational policy proposed a flexible, slightly vertical requirement structure:

> Students graduating from [College 3] should receive instruction in effectively formulating and supporting an argument in writing. Many of the proposals submitted to the [committee on educational policy] reflect the concern that some of our students lack instruction in this critical intellectual skill. According to recent senior surveys, almost 50% of students feel that their undergraduate experiences did not greatly enhance their ability to write effectively. In alumni surveys, [College 3] rates slightly lower than its peer colleges in making a very important contribution to our students' ability to write. (*Summary of Data Presented at Board Retreat, January 2001,* 11, 16).

> The [committee on educational policy] proposes requiring that all students take two writing-intensive courses: one by the end of the sophomore year and one by the end of the junior year. The committee strongly believes that instruction in writing should take place across the curriculum. We also believe that students will benefit most from writing-intensive courses by taking them early in their college careers and that therefore students should be strongly encouraged to complete the requirement by the end of the sophomore year.

We can see here that, as a result of feedback from faculty, students, and alumni, College 3 identified writing as an area in which it was not satisfied with the education it was providing students. They therefore created and rationalized a new requirement that took a WAC-based approach to writing instruction and focused on the first two years of students' educations.

College 3 also built into the legislation a request to expand the resources that were then supporting the writing center. While we do not have information about whether and how that request was met, we do know that for some time pre-dating this change, responsibilities supporting the writing center tutors had been embedded into the responsibilities of a dean of students. Upon that dean's retirement, the responsibilities shifted to the portfolio of the director of another administrative unit on an interim basis. During that time, the institution designed an entirely new position for a director of writing—what we would call an explicit writing center director on the basis of the job description.

That interim director—our respondent—explained that the new writing center director would not have direct oversight over the W requirement itself. She wrote:

> The Writing Requirement at [College 3] is a curricular requirement and all curricular requirements as I understand it are governed under faculty rules by the [committee for educational policy] . . . The Director of Writing will not have any direct responsibilities for the writing requirement but as is listed in the position description that I've attached will be available to consult with faculty around various writing issues upon request.

At first it seems that College 3 has moved—slowly—to an *Explicit WCD Only* configuration. However, they have also recently instituted a writing fellows program to better support the W course requirement. If that program continues, our respondent explained, since "the courses that are supported are all Writing Intensive courses . . . [t]he director will have administrative responsibilities for the drop-in center and the [writing fellows program]." The trajectory of this institution, then, is from an *Embedded WCD Only* configuration (a structure of administration we have not otherwise seen) through curricular change to an *Explicit WCD Only* configuration. This may well further evolve into a *Solo WPA/WCD* configuration, depending on the new writing director's interests and the evolving needs of the institution. College 3 represents the potential shift in a college's leadership configuration that can occur from the addition or expansion of a writing requirement.

Without understanding the recent trajectory of curricular change, it would be difficult to fully understand the possibilities in College 3's current program.

Writing programs are complex entities. Even at small and bureaucratically streamlined schools, we can see that there are many different approaches to leading writing requirements. It is clear that decisions made on individual campuses reflect particular needs and values that a national study cannot. But mapping the institution and the program—and embracing the messiness of that process and the resultant picture—is necessary to understanding and therefore fostering an institution's culture of writing. Curricular structures and leadership configurations do not exist in isolation; they are bound together, and are further inflected by how the institution positions student-centered writing support.

III

Student-Centered Writing Instruction

9 Writing Centers

It seems to me, then, that in order to conceptualize the writing center in a small college, we require a new paradigm. . . . [A]n ecological paradigm, a model relying on interconnectedness rather than outsiderness, on the whole rather than the parts. Tension doesn't vanish in this model—not at all. What changes, though, is the dualistic relationship between writing center and institution; dualistic, two-way linearity—us and them—is replaced by a network. The writing center is embedded in an institutional network, a web seen as a whole.

—Erika Spohrer

To do their work well, both doctors and WAs [Writing Associates, or peer writing tutors] are constantly making ethical choices. They are involved in balancing good things that are in conflict. They are figuring out how to act rightly in complex, ambiguous situations that often unfold quite quickly. A good WA, like a good doctor, needs to learn how to be a good counselor. A good WA needs practical wisdom.

—Kenneth Sharpe

One of the central metaphors of writing center scholarship is that of margin and center (see, for example, Muriel Harris, "Writing Center Administration" 75–76; Macauley and Mauriello). The writing center's position on the "margin"—of campus, of students' educations— can be variously interpreted as a problem or an advantage (Spohrer 6–7). This metaphor is less useful in the small college context, for both material and philosophical reasons. At a small institution, margins and center simply cannot be terribly far apart. As Julie Neff points out when discussing the University of Puget Sound Writing Center, "A small liberal arts college is in many ways an ideal place for a writing center. Writing center values—writing as process and product, active learning, the worth of the individual—are also the values of the institution" (127).

We argued in Chapter 1 that writing centers are, at least in part, descended from the rhetoricals (co-curricular oratorical performances) practiced at nineteenth-century colleges. Rhetoricals brought curricular and extracurricular writing together within the frame of "laboratory" work on writing. Although small college writing centers in the twenty-first century are typically situated in the realm of student support, they nonetheless retain a closely networked relationship to the curriculum. This derives from the scale of these institutions and from their strong commitment to writing throughout the curriculum. In addition—and perhaps most importantly—it emerges from their strong commitment to students as intellectuals, apprentice scholars, and future leaders.

All of the schools in the study have writing centers in some form; sixteen of those have been established in the last decade. This count includes both explicit writing centers and what we would describe as embedded writing centers—that is, learning or academic resource centers that also provide writing tutoring. We identified *explicit* writing centers as those for which there was an independent identity (such as a website) even if the writing center is embedded in a learning center in terms of physical location or reporting lines. In their survey-based studies, Valerie Balester and James C. McDonald, as well as Dave Healy, count the directors of learning centers that provide writing tutoring as writing center directors (see "Writing Center Directors"). We largely followed this practice; we also relied heavily on self-identification by survey participants. In presenting trends in the data, we focus first on locations on campus and within institutional organizational systems. Small college writing centers, overall, are positioned in ways that identify them as educational entities for both student writers and student tutors. We then discuss the staffing and training of writing center tutors, because the education writing centers provide is both for student writers and for peer tutors.

Although many scholars emphasize the importance of local conditions in writing center design (see M. Harris, "Writing Center Administration"; Mullin et al.), we found striking similarities across the schools in the sample as well as between those small colleges and the writing centers of all sizes described in the literature. Writing centers at small colleges—like writing centers everywhere—work with student writers to help them improve their writing, and learn to navigate the varied discursive communities of the university in the twenty-first century. Many of the writing and learning centers at the schools in the sample provide additional services. These include support for: oral presentations, technological and/or new media composing, PowerPoint, study skills, and subject tutoring. Five of the schools in the sample have speaking as well as writing centers.

Bound up in the fabric of their institutions, small college writing centers seem little worried about being branded places of writing remediation. Both our respondents and scholars contrast large and small schools in this regard. Erika Spohrer recounts her surprise when she came to Eckerd College from a large university to find it a teaching and learning environment already saturated with WAC and active learning pedagogy—and, as a result, with a writing center bound up in the ecology of the school rather than on its margins (8). One respondent offered one more concrete way to think about the comparative centrality of writing centers to small colleges. In this comment shared during a focus group, he speculates that SLAC writing centers may not be seen as remedial at least in part because of the value faculty place on students' learning processes:

> In the larger places where I've worked, writing centers really carried that remedial—that remedial label, stigma, you know whatever you want to call it. And at the smaller schools where I've worked, they haven't carried that as much, and I think it's because the faculty know the students, they can see that students develop as writers over the time that they're there, and so the Writing Center becomes part of that developmental process over the four years that they're with us, whereas at the larger places where I've worked, the Writing Center is "This student can't write. Fix it."

Another participant in this focus group, the writing center director from College 20, agreed, describing how he "hand-deliver[s]" notes and reports to "all faculty members when their students come." Once again, this indicates a connection between institutional size and culture. Not only are the faculty at College 20 interested in the learning their students do at the writing center, but the school is small enough that the writing center director can deliver reports about each consultation personally.

Our respondents argued that this leads students to feel differently about the writing center. The College 20 WCD meditates that "the difference in writing centers for me is that students come back—All the time. They develop relationships with tutors that they don't get at the larger—at the larger school I worked in the writing center." This anecdotal sense is supported by quantitative research. In their recent cross-institutional study of exit survey data from a large public university, a medium-sized private university, and a small liberal arts college, Pam Bromley, Kara Northway, and Eliana Schonberg found that students most frequently came to the writing centers at those institutions for the same five reasons: "an instructor's recommendation, a challenging assignment, the improvement of grades, bettering writing in general, and making sure they are on the right track" (13). They also found statistically significant differences in the extent to which students felt connected to the writing center and their experiences there. Students at the study's small liberal arts college were significantly more likely to report feeling welcome than those at either of the other institutions, and students at the medium-sized private university and the small college were more likely to feel that consultations were productive and collaborative than did students at the large public university (17–18). It would seem, then, that while small college writing centers are structurally similar to those at large universities, institutional size results in a less marginalized place in the educational culture of the school.

Writing Center Locations

Small colleges locate their writing centers in ways that reflect the centrality of writing across the curriculum as well as active, individualized learning to their cultures. As Carol Peterson Haviland and Edward M. White have noted, writing center locations are at once "physical, economic, political, and pedagogical" (212). The fact that the vast majority of schools in the study—82 out of 100—situate their writing centers in academic buildings or libraries signals their pedagogical and political centrality. Table 9.1 presents trends for writing center locations in the sample. The predominance of academic locations for writing centers reflects the close relationship between curricular- and student-centered realms characteristic of the small college structure of feeling.

Table 9.1 Location of the Writing Center on Campus.

Location	Number of schools
Academic Building	47
Library	35
Own Building	7
Dorm	6
Administrative Building	3
Other	1
Multiple locations	1

Six schools, by contrast, emphasize the student-centered mission of their writing centers by placing them in residence halls. We cannot comment on more precise locations; we did not examine where each building was located on each campus, for example, and did not inquire whether writing centers were located in basements or on main floors. Seven institutions give the writing center its own building, but it's hard to know what that indicates without information about where on those campuses those buildings are located.

Political location overlaps with geographic location, but also raises additional issues. Considering questions of writing centers' administrative situations, Haviland, Carmen M. Fye, and Richard Colby emphasize that "[l]ocation is political because it is an organizational choice that creates visibility or invisibility, access to resources, and associations that define the meanings, uses, and users of designated spaces" (85). In their analysis, a free-standing writing center whose director has a short reporting line to the academic dean or provost may have the "greatest autonomy and access to resources" (87), but such a position can also compromise the center's sense of connection to the discipline that grounds it intellectually. For them, a departmental location provides such an intellectual home but, at the same time, may keep a writing center in a "stepsister" or "handmaiden" position (88). They see, furthermore, that a strong connection to a WAC program can help a writing center to resist associations with remediation, but can also further decentralize the center's mission (90). While being embedded within a student services center of some kind allows for synergies between different kinds of tutoring and tutoring philosophies, as well as the opportunity to think about the whole student, it can also bring attention to writing under the rubric of remediation (Haviland, Fye, and Colby 90–91).

The majority (59) of the schools in our data set fall into Haviland, Fye, and Colby's first category, with free-standing or independent writing centers. These writing centers have explicit, dedicated directorial positions to lead them, and those leaders typically have short reporting lines to the provost or academic dean. (See Chapter 5 for a fuller discussion of writing administrator positions.) This configuration can give the writing center a clear, individualized, and professionalized presence on campus, and can make it an excellent home for writing across the curriculum (as Muriel Harris discusses; see "A Writing Center without a WAC Program"). Indeed, the WAC culture of small colleges means that a free-standing writing center is perhaps less likely to suffer intellectual confusion in this location than Haviland, Fye, and Colby imagine—and that culture may also explain why departmental homes are relatively rare in our sample (seven schools).

Thirty-one schools embed the writing center within an academic or student support center, with a variety of names, including: Academic Skills Center; Learning Commons; Center for Teaching and Learning; Center for Academic Excellence; and Academic Resource Center. As Haviland, Fye, and Colby suggest, the inclusion of writing tutoring in a larger center provides increased access to resources. (For fuller discussions of the search for resources to support writing center work, see Faigley; Kail.) But those resources are not then explicitly focused on writing, which may marginalize the role of writing in student learning and faculty development. While the administrative consolidation represented by this approach may reduce costs—and therefore make more student services available—the director may be less likely to have expertise in writing center pedagogy than in the field of teaching and learning. This structure can provide more opportunities for cross-curricular exchange between tutors, but as Haviland, Fye, and Colby point out, can also bring writing (and all other) tutoring under the rubric of remediation.

WRITING CENTER STAFFS

If these administrative and geographic locations demonstrate the academic centrality of writing centers at small colleges, their overwhelming reliance on peer tutors reveals the dual nature of their educational mission. As Table 9.2 shows, 67 schools use only undergraduate or peer tutors, versus five schools, which do not use any undergraduate tutors. Two additional schools were in the process of phasing out their peer tutors during the time of this study. Ninety schools use 80% or more undergraduate tutors, and 92 use at least 60%. It is unclear in our data, however, exactly how the writing administrator's tutoring of students factors into writing center staffing figures. Tutoring students is a job responsibility listed by 13 (19%) of the WPAs and 31 (48%) of the WCDs in the sample. Some but not all of these may have included themselves as professional tutors.

Table 9.2 Staffing of the Writing Center.

Type of staffing	Number of schools
Undergraduate peer tutors only	67
Graduate student tutors only	2
Professional tutors only	3
Combination of peer and professional tutors	26
Data Unavailable	2

In his 2006 essay, "Staffing a Writing Center with Professional Tutors," Steven Strang makes a strong case for using "at least some professional tutors" in any writing center (291). His list of the advantages professional tutors bring emphasizes the kinds of specialized knowledge and expertise they can provide, not just for particular rhetorical tasks, but also for specific types of learners (293–94). Strang ties his argument in part to his institutional context at the Massachusetts Institute of Technology: a large university focused on the sciences and engineering, located in a city with many other large universities from which to draw professional tutors.

Small schools, by contrast, do not typically have local graduate programs or graduate students on whom to draw. While some of these schools are located in places where they could draw on graduate students (or other possible pools of professional tutors) to work in their writing centers, most do not. In addition, their focus on undergraduate education makes faculty at small colleges unlikely to believe that undergraduates are incapable of teaching one another, as Strang notes is the case at MIT (Strang 293; see also Trimbur, "Peer Tutoring" 22). There is, therefore, a less urgent need to turn to professionals in order to "giv[e] an institution's instructors confidence that sending students to the center will result in their receiving good feedback" (Strang 293). In fact, in a small community, the very names of the writing center tutors—often among the strongest students from a variety of disciplines and majors—can lend the writing center greater cachet and status among faculty. Those students, even at schools that do not have writing fellows (course-based peer tutoring) programs, can act as ambassadors of writing center pedagogy.[1]

Peer tutoring at small colleges was, in fact, an important and influential model for early WAC pedagogy, with the example of the writing fellows program Harriet Sheridan established in the 1970s at Carleton College (see Hughes and Hall; Severino and Knight, "Exploring"; Soven, "WAC" and "Survey"). Such programs attach peer writing tutors to courses across the disciplines, often as part of supporting faculty efforts to teach writing-intensive classes. Thirty-one of the schools in our study have such programs; fourteen of those were added in the last ten years, confirming Margot Soven's argument in 2001 that "peer tutoring" was becoming "the new mainstay of many WAC programs" ("WAC" 200; see also Spigelman and Grobman 5). The influence of writing fellows programs on how we think about peer tutoring is allowing us to rethink the presumption that undergraduate peer tutors can provide only generalist support. In fact, recent work takes undergraduate peer tutors seriously as experts in their major fields. While Jill Gladstein's work with tutors negotiating the "gray space" between WAC and WID in working with introductory biology classes shows how they rely on that disciplinary expertise, Carol Severino and Mary Trachsel's study found that their tutors still preferred to work in a generalist mode.

The most recent data published from the Writing Centers Research Project in 2003 provides data on staff size, broken down by institutional enrollments. WCRP reports that writing centers at schools with enrollments under 1,500 employ from 0 to 72 tutors. As tables 9.3 and

9.4 show, our data corroborate those findings. (The enrollment at the schools in our sample is 1,883, on average.) The schools with the largest tutoring staffs in our sample typically have strong writing fellows programs as part of their WAC curricula. As a result, in any semester, many of the writing tutors on staff will not be working *in* the writing center, but will instead be supporting student writers in the context of courses across the college.

Table 9.3 Writing Center Staff Size (Schools with a 100% Undergraduate Staff).

Undergraduate peer tutors only n=67 (range 4–120 tutors)	
4–10 tutors	16 schools
11–20 tutors	31 schools
21–30 tutors	10 schools
31–40 tutors	5 schools
41+ tutors	5 schools

Table 9.4 Writing Center Staff Size (Schools with a Mixed Staffing Model).

Combination of tutors n=26 (range 6–60)	
6–10 tutors	8 schools
11–20 tutors	9 schools
21–30 tutors	5 schools
31–40 tutors	3 schools
41+ tutors	1 school

It seems likely that institutions with larger staffs have each tutor working a smaller number of hours. This is the suggestion of the WCRP data, which included size of tutoring staff and number of consultations held. That study found that schools with 0–1,500 students had a high of 72 tutors and 1,480 consultations (20.5 consultations per tutor). At schools with 1,501–3,500 students, however, they found highs of 50 tutors and 2,405 consultations (48 consultations per tutor). The remaining three categories of schools (with enrollment ranges of 3,501–10,000,

10,001–25,000, and 25,001+) had consultation-per-tutor figures of 50 or higher. The larger institutions presumably had graduate students as well as undergraduates on whom to draw, which corresponds with our finding that schools employing professional tutors typically have smaller staffs than those employing entirely undergraduates.

The preference for peer tutoring among these schools, and for having many students work a few hours per week, may arise from the small college structure of feeling, as well. These institutions may want to make the opportunity to tutor in the writing center available to as many students as possible because they regard it as an extracurricular education itself. (Writing center tutoring is a paid position at all of the participating schools.) These are institutions deeply invested in the learning of undergraduates and in developing undergraduates as intellectuals, apprentice scholars, and future leaders. In her discussion of the writing center at Colorado College, Molly Wingate underscores the ways in which it provides a "locus where tutors learn about and practice teaching" (10). Paula Gillespie and Harvey Kail make this argument about peer tutoring writing centers more generally. They contend that "peer tutoring engages *both* the tutor *and* the writer in active, institutionally supported learning, suggesting that students as well as faculty take writing and reading seriously" (322, emphasis added).

Gillespie, Kail, and Bradley Hughes extend these claims in their work with the Peer Writing Tutor Alumni Project, which examines the written reflections of former peer writing tutors from Marquette University, the University of Maine, and the University of Wisconsin-Madison (see Gillespie, Hughes, and Kail; Hughes, Gillespie, and Kail; and Kail, Gillespie, and Hughes). According to Hughes, Gillespie, and Kail, the participating alumni "assert that they developed" the following through their experiences as writing tutors:

- a new relationship with writing,
- analytical power,
- a listening presence,
- skills, values, and abilities vital to their professions,
- skills, values, and abilities vital in families and in relationships,
- earned confidence in themselves,
- and a deeper understanding of and commitment to collaborative learning. (14)

These lessons from peer tutoring are strikingly similar to the values we have identified as part of the small college structure of feeling, recalling Julie Neff's claim that writing centers and small colleges are a perfect philosophical match. The central terms of small college mission statements echo the categories Hughes, Gillespie, and Kail have uncovered. The mission statement of College 30 promises that education there will enhance students' analytical power by "inspir[ing]" them "to engage in probing inquiry," while that of College 9 promises to prepare students for lives of "ethical leadership." College 14 brings together many of the values listed above in defining itself as a community dedicated to "learning, teaching, scholarship, discovery, creativity and creative thought." Writing centers and small colleges thus share a commitment to the kind of extra-curricular education that not only supports student writers, but also causes the tutors themselves to develop transportable ways of thinking about texts, learning, their peers, and themselves.

Peer tutoring as extracurricular education begins with how peer tutors are trained, although "training" may be a misnomer as it implies that this is the only site for learning within the structure of the peer tutor position. Table 9.5 depicts the kinds of structures the different schools employ. We can see that the most common models are either a course or weekly meetings. Some schools use more than one method, requiring, for example, a course for new tutors and regular meetings of the full staff.

Table 9.5 Training Offered to Writing Center Tutors.

Type of training	Number of schools
Course (half or full credit)	47
Weekly meetings	46
Monthly meetings	7
Workshops before the semester	58
One-on-one consultations with director	5
No training	2*
Other methods	11**

* One school has had the same professional tutors for a long period of time.

** Some respondents listed some form of meetings, but with less regular timing. Other methods include conference attendance, reading of articles, and workshops.

Hughes, Gillespie, and Kail emphasize the collaborative nature of writing center work in producing these qualities. We would extend this, arguing that the writing centers in the sample are grounded philosophically not only in a Vygotskian understanding of learning as social and fundamental (see Bruffee; Vygotsky), but also in David Schön's notion of reflective practice. We know anecdotally that a significant component of many of these courses—at small colleges and nationwide—is writing center research. Peer tutors at many schools in the sample routinely develop research projects as part of a training course or as a separate project in the writing center. Students may pick a topic that relates to their work as peer tutors, read the literature on it, gather original data from their experiences (from their own tutoring, from interviews with faculty members, etc.) and from other published data, and write a paper or create a poster. Such teacher-based research immerses student tutors in writing center scholarship, giving them the opportunity to develop as apprentice scholars in the field of writing studies. In some cases, they may be asked to share their results with the other peer tutors in the program, or as part of on-campus presentations of student research. These kinds of projects thus bring together the reflective and collaborative nature of these courses. At the same time, they develop the profile of the writing center, which becomes further visible on campus as a student-centered research site. These projects have sometimes become the basis for formal presentations at regional or national conferences or been published as papers in such journals as *Young Scholars in Writing*. (See also Podis and Podis, *Working with Student Writers*, which includes essays written by peer tutors about writing center tutoring.)

In many of the writing centers in the sample, tutors are asked to reflect in writing after individual consultations and at key points during their tutoring careers. This kind of reflection on practice is essential to the learning Hughes, Gillespie, and Kail report (26–27; see also Schön). Reflecting on her work as a tutor, a graduating senior at College 53 focuses in particular on how she has transferred the lessons in reflective practice from the writing center context to other areas:

> I have already seen the impact of the Writing Program's reflective practice upon other parts of my life. As someone who was always told she was a good writer, I had often taken my own writing process for granted before I began the [training] class. . . . However, the frequent attention that we paid to re-

visiting and reevaluating the writing process in [the training class] demonstrated to me that 1) there is literally always room for improvement, be it in the writing itself or in the writing process, and 2) taking out the time to honestly reflect on writing was a way of paying respect to a practice that is deeply important to me. From its influence on my writing process, the Writing Program's reflective practice has also spilled into other roles and processes I engage in, such as my leadership of [an advocacy project] (where I began instituting individual and shared reflective practices, such as regular one-on-one meetings with newcomers to discuss their feelings about their progress in the group).

We see in this small college writing tutor the kinds of learning Hughes, Gillespie, and Kail identify as typical of peer tutoring alumni at their institutions. She has developed confidence through peer tutor work, confidence that has shaped the way she leads the advocacy project. She has transferred the individualized and reflective learning practices from her writing center training to that project. Her reflection thus testifies to the centrality of writing centers to "the education of undergraduate students as writers, readers, listeners, creative problem-solvers, and liberally educated human beings" (Hughes, Gillespie, and Kail 39).

Speaking at the twenty-fifth anniversary of the Swarthmore College Writing Associates Program, political scientist Kenneth Sharpe argues that a well-designed, peer-tutoring writing center causes the tutors themselves to learn "practical wisdom." Drawing an analogy to medical students learning to become doctors, he explains that this education combines practice, reflection, and formal training: "You can't learn through trial and error unless you learn to recognize your errors as they happen; to figure out what went wrong in this particular case. You need to learn the courage to admit mistakes and to pick yourself up to try it again" (14–15). Writing tutor training, he continues, "is structured to 'cause reflection to be learned'" (15). In catalyzing such learning in student tutors—in helping them develop practical wisdom—writing centers are doubly bound up in the ecology of small colleges. What the individualized learning tutors do is caused by, and catalyzes, similar kinds of learning in the students they tutor, providing a one-on-one education in writing that blurs the line between curricular- and student-centered domains.

10 Supporting Diversely Prepared Writers

*I do not argue that we should sidestep or stand in igno-
rance of writers whose needs are greater than others in
our college communities; rather, I argue that calling these
writers something "special"—even if that label is accommodating, welcoming, or generous in spirit—connotes a
historical baggage that Mina Shaughnessy attempted to
diminish but instead reified as a label available to some
and not others within first-year writing programs.*

—Kelly Ritter

The small college structure of feeling, as we've noted, typically pro-
duces a highly individualized and non-bureaucratized approach to education. This may be particularly true in the case of the writers "whose
needs are greater than others" in their local communities. We have
found that small colleges resist systematically identifying or labeling
those students. At the schools in the sample, writing centers are often
the site of support for the students who find themselves struggling with
the school's expectations for student writing. As Ritter argues, *all* institutions have student writers who struggle more than others and who
need more support. The resistance of small colleges to naming those
students may have roots not just in their focus on individual students,
but also in the fact that most of these institutions understand themselves as selective: They are for the most part premised on the notion
that they have chosen the students who come, which can make them
resistant to the notion that some of those students might be "underprepared" or somehow not quite "ready." At the same time, and in recent
decades, many small colleges have made conscious efforts to diversify
their student bodies, focusing on initiatives that target international
students and, within the US, groups that have been historically un-

derrepresented in higher education (especially at private institutions). The latter efforts include developing partnerships with organizations that focus on supporting those students' efforts to attend college (for example, the TRIO program; the Posse Foundation; Questbridge; and the Jack Kent Cooke Foundation's Community Transfer Initiative).

Institutions can deny a systemic issue when they focus support for these students in the student-centered rather than the curricular realm. But these shifts in population are forcing schools to pay more systematic attention to how they provide writing support. This brings up not just questions of support, but also of identification: How do you systematically and yet with individual attention support *diversely* prepared writers? In this chapter, trends in the sample allow us to explore the complexities of this question in the small college context, presenting how the difficulty of identification complicates these institutions' desire to support all student writers. We then argue that systematic directed self-placement provides the necessary balance between bureaucratic formality and pedagogically-oriented flexibility.

Needs Greater Than Others

Questions of identification and support are closely intertwined in the basic writing literature. In order to design appropriate systems for supporting those writers who need it most, we also have to design processes by which we can identify them from year to year. Andrea A. Lunsford and Patricia A. Sullivan note that the definition of a "basic writer" varies "from college to college" and also "from year to year within a single academic setting" (19). Building on this, Kelly Ritter calls for "a re-definition of *basic* in composition studies using local, institutional values rather than generic standards of correctness" ("Before" 12). Their orientation toward students as intellectuals and apprentice scholars means that one key goal of the schools in our sample is that students emerge at the end of four years as sophisticated critical thinkers, readers, and writers. (We see this clearly in the prevalence of "critical thinking" or "critical writing" in the goals of first-year writing courses of all types.) Elite institutions, as Neal Lerner argues, have an incentive to overlook the presence of struggling or underprepared writers on their campuses in order to maintain or emphasize their elite "brand" (Lerner, "Rejecting" 14).

The survey included five closed questions about how underprepared students were identified and supported; we therefore limited what participants could tell us about these students and the culture of writing support on their campuses. This was due to the length of the survey; we imagined that at this point survey fatigue might set in. Additional data collection led us to realize that these closed questions did not capture the complexity of these discussions. They did not, for example, permit respondents to address the fundamental question of whether or not their schools *had* underprepared students—or even how their institutions defined that term.

The term we now use for this chapter—"diversely prepared writers"—reflects the rich ambiguity of this type of designation. (This is perhaps true at any institution, but it's clearly the case at small colleges.) In focus group interviews, we posed these kinds of general questions. Specifically, we asked how prepared WPAs found students for the expectations of their institutions, and whether they thought that faculty at their institutions would agree with this assessment. In the first focus group, one participant (from College 19, with an acceptance rate of 33%) re-framed the issue more broadly:

> *Speaker 1*: I feel there's a really big leap that happens between high school and college writing—cognitively, intellectually— and that's why I think AP 5 doesn't do it or almost anything that you can do in high school is not like college writing, so they're prepared to sort of begin, but they're not—they don't write college-type papers. It's maybe more a genre aspect. They just don't—the level of complexity that's asked for in most college papers I don't see most high school students being able to do that off the bat.

Speaker 1's focus is developmental. She does not isolate a particular group of students as being under- or differently prepared; rather, she argues that almost all students need to make a "big leap between high school and college writing," and explains that for this reason, she sees all students as unprepared for the expectations of her institution. Students may not be prepared "cognitively, intellectually" or for "the level of complexity that's asked for in most college papers." Her focus seems to be on what students need to be prepared to *learn* rather than on what they should already *know*.

This sense that undergraduate education will be a transformative discipline—which we saw in the *Yale Report*, and remains a value of the small college structure of feeling—is picked up by the next speaker. Speaker 2 (from College 21, with an acceptance rate of 68%) continues the conversation by agreeing with Speaker 1 that most students are not prepared for the expectations of her institution:

> *Speaker 2*: I agree completely, and [to] the students who come in who say, "But I made A's on all my high school papers," I say, "But you're not writing high school papers anymore, and you have to learn to move the quality of your analytical thinking and the level of your style." You know, no one comes in there—well, I take that back. There probably are students, maybe one or two students in every class who are far beyond the other students, but most of them it varies wildly. I mean, some of them have no skills at all, and some of them are functional but they don't write college-level papers.

There is wide consensus in the field that "college-level papers" are different from "high-school level" papers (see, for example, the essays collected in Sullivan and Tinberg). The goals for first-year writing at small colleges emphasize detailed argumentation, sophisticated analysis, and critical thinking; this suggests that the expectations for these students are high. (Such expectations are of course not limited to small colleges; see Bartholomae). While Speaker 2, unlike Speaker 1, makes distinctions between the preparedness of different groups of students, she still emphasizes the question of preparation as an issue for nearly all entering first-year students. She implies that all students, except "maybe one or two students in every class," are not ready for what faculty expect of them, but points out that the remaining students have a variety of needs. The consensus between these speakers is thus that faculty at their institutions have high expectations for students as intellectuals, and that the purpose of their schools is to transform *all* of those students. The scale of these institutions makes individualized identification and support mechanisms possible, if it is only one or two students per year. On the other hand, we see here a characteristically small college desire to focus on what *all* students will learn from the institution, to see *all* students as individual learners.

In the second focus group, a dialogue amongst the four participants took place around the question of "How well prepared for the expectations of college writing do you feel first-year students are at your institution?" The group began their conversation similarly to the first focus group, meditating on the ways that "very few of [the] students can write in the way I expect them to be able to adjust to writing for college" (Speaker 1). She continues, "[t]hey come fairly well prepared, but they don't come prepared to *think* in the way, and that I think is the real shock for many of them" (emphasis added). Speaker 1 (from College 4, with a 50% acceptance rate) suggests that while high school has prepared most of the students she sees to *begin* to write in college, it has not prepared them to think in the more nuanced and critical ways they will need to. Speaker 2 (from College 5, 34% acceptance rate) picks up on this point:

> *Speaker 2*: I agree. And I take the developmental view on that, actually, I mean I really believe that—you know, I don't blame the high schools at all, although there is some pretty bad high school teaching out there, and there's some very good high school teaching out there. But even the really best students, and I would say that probably we all get the very best students from their high schools, right? And they come and they're so confident and they're so polished and they're so really wonderful, and even the ones who aren't confident and polished and wonderful have something going on. But you know I fail a third, fully a third, of my first semester writing—
>
> *Speaker 3*: Really?
>
> *Speaker 1*: Wow, that's impressive.
>
> *Speaker 2*: I do.
>
> *Speaker 3*: That is impressive.
>
> *Speaker 1*: Good for you!

Speaker 1 and Speaker 3 (from College 22, with an acceptance rate of 26%) both question Speaker 2's claim that she fails a third of her first semester writing class. We cannot tell from the transcript whether their surprise at, and respect for, Speaker 2's practice comes from the fact that one-third of the students fail or from her willingness to stand by a tough grading standard. (Speaker 1's final "Good for you!" suggests the latter, at least in part.) Speaker 2 then further explains her "developmental view" of students:

> *Speaker 2*: Well, it's painful, and then I have to teach them
> in my spring course where everybody . . .but I do, I really do
> take the developmental view that they really weren't, regard-
> less of how well taught and trained they were in high school,
> they were simply not ready to make the intellectual leap that
> we're asking them to make—that they can sort of pose as ex-
> perts, even if they're not, where they can actually formulate
> important and interesting ideas and arguments, either in op-
> position or on the back of some real expert, right, and then
> run with it, you know, and then use that evidence usefully
> and carefully, you know, and do it temperately. You know,
> almost no 18-year-old can do that, but I don't think it's a fail-
> ure of high school, I don't think it's a failure in preparation,
> and I always just assume that what we get are the really, really
> good ones. And that our job—that's why they call it school,
> right? They're not supposed to come already knowing how to
> do this!

Speaker 2's expectations for students echo those of David Bartholomae
in "Inventing the University": the students must "pose as experts,"
demonstrating discursive understanding and disciplinary knowledge
before they have actually mastered it. She also clearly believes that
eighteen-year-olds are, for the most part, not developmentally ready
for that task. The consensus between the two focus groups is thus that
students cannot be prepared for college-level work when they arrive on
campus; the focus of first-year writing therefore needs to be on helping *all* students make the transition from high school- to college-level
thinking and writing.

In this context, making distinctions between students can feel complicated, despite the earlier Speaker 2's awareness that most students'
skills "var[y] widely." Nonetheless, the second focus group began to do
just that, echoing the progression of the earlier conversation:

> *Speaker 1*: But you know what's really curious is that I want
> often to talk about this kind of thing [as] a lack of intellectual
> curiosity, but as I hear you talking I think that's not right
> because we have students, for instance, who come through
> the Posse program, and if you're not familiar—Posse. It's a
> national service to recruit students from under-represented
> groups. And these students have ideas like mad, right, but

they don't have a way to express them, whereas our students who come from very privileged backgrounds, they know their P's and Q's, but they dare not.

Speaker 4: They have beautiful records.

Speaker 2: They're so risk-averse. They're so risk-averse.

Speaker 1: Right, right, and so there's a carefulness and a re-servedness that they're not even conscious about. And I think most of my colleagues would agree—colleagues on my cam-pus—would agree about that, and [College 4] has had that reputation. And we're more and more beginning to get stu-dents who want to take those intellectual risks, and are will-ing and able to.

Here, Speakers 1, 2, and 4 distinguish between those students "who come from privileged backgrounds" but are "risk-averse" to use the skills they have acquired in high school, and those students who come from "underrepresented groups" who "have ideas like mad, right, but they don't have a way to express them." The speakers seem to be iden-tifying two distinct groups of students who are unprepared for the intellectual work of college in different ways. In comparing these dif-ferent ways of being prepared for college-level work, the participants are mapping different skills sets onto different groups of students. This is clearly a generalization, but the WPAs are here trying to do justice to the diversity of the students they see. In addition, this distinction recalls the emphasis on sophisticated and nuanced critical writing and thinking as learning goals, because neither group of students meets that standard.

Speaker 4 (from a school with a 60% acceptance rate) ends by ex-panding the discussion to meditate on how her colleagues see students' level of preparedness:

Speaker 4: I, I, I actually think most of our students are [. . .] they're quite well prepared, they have not been, they haven't thought about writing as a way of solving problems. They've thought about it as a way of performing, but they've got a cer-tain skill set that they're very shocked to learn isn't all about spitting back, and I think that's very exciting. And the longer we are in the college colloquium business, which is our fresh-man seminar, the more my across the curriculum colleagues are beginning to go, "Oh, I see." They actually have a fair amount of skill set, they're shocked about, they didn't realize this wasn't another application of crescent wrench, so they have to learn again, and I have fewer and fewer colleagues every year who go, "My students can't write" just because they have comma splices. So I think that the process of, yeah, I think you're right, I think that's exactly it. They're pretty well prepared in ways that we can work with, but they go, "Oh, but my AP teacher told me . . ." And I go, "Yes, exactly right. Did you think that you were coming here to show me what you already knew? We expect to teach you here."

Throughout both focus groups, the participants share their assumption that students come to their institutions needing to learn how to write for a new set of intellectual expectations. Students must "pose as experts," learning to "take intellectual risks" and to think about "writing as a way of solving problems." These WPAs clearly believe that the institutions' cultures of writing should focus on helping students to make that transition. There is little mention of students who have "needs greater than others" overall and therefore struggle. Instead, there is a shared assumption that writing instruction is tied to developing all students as intellectuals—the wider goal of the institution. As a result, these participants agree that the students who come to small liberal arts colleges want to learn—and can.

But these focus group discussions also reveal awareness that students need different types of support, and that the institution needs to support all learners. What we don't see here are the mechanisms by which the schools in the sample identify and support diversely prepared students, and so we present the trends in the two sections below.

IDENTIFYING DIVERSELY-PREPARED WRITERS

In order to identify the students who might most benefit from these supports, small liberal arts colleges do, in fact, employ a variety of mechanisms in order to identify which students might benefit from additional writing support. Table 10.1 shows the responses to our question, "How do you identify underprepared writers?" Twenty schools reported that no identification occurs at their institution. This is a surprising response, given that "self-identify" and "faculty identification" were both choices. In addition, eighteen of these schools have an explicit first-year writing requirement (10=FYC, 8=FYWS), where we would imagine faculty are paying attention to whether or not students need additional writing support.

Table 10.1 Methods of Identification of Underprepared Students.

Method of identification	Number of schools
Self	51
Faculty	46
SAT scores	43
Advisor	23
Placement exam	21
No identification	20
Other methods*	13

* "Other" may be GPA, admissions office or materials, a first year dean, or the academic resource center. Portfolios and tutor identification are other possibilities.

Several of these schools did respond affirmatively to our questions about how the institution supports marginalized writers, including that students could self-select into a particular writing course; work with a writing center tutor (either peer or professional); or work directly with the WPA or WCD. It may be that these participants were responding to connotations of the term "underprepared," and that they were making a silent distinction between identifying those writers and identifying all writers who need additional support. Nonetheless, how such writers come to be aware of resources at the twenty "no identification" schools remains something of a mystery.

Many schools use more than one method of identification, triangulating data from (for example) SAT scores and a writing placement exam. The most common system was one that allowed for multiple avenues of referral: students can self-identify, but they can also be identified by faculty who advise them or teach them in class. A comparatively large number (43) of schools utilize SAT scores in some way to identify students who may need additional writing support. There is, however, widespread consensus that such standardized test scores have little predictive value (see, for example, Hamp-Lyons; Norris et al.), and so make inefficient and even dangerous placement mechanisms. Using such a crude mechanism is particularly surprising in a set of schools that pride themselves on valuing the whole student. It may well be that schools are using SAT scores (as well as other data) to identify students who, for a variety of reasons, might be good candidates for summer bridge programs; it is also likely that SAT and other standardized test scores are primarily a starting point for more qualitative methods more in line with the SLAC structure of feeling.

Twenty-one schools identify marginal writers at least in part through a placement exam. This is a long-standing component of many writing programs nationally. Indeed, the field of rhetoric and composition has been said to have been inaugurated with the infamous entrance exam instituted at Harvard in 1869. The best of these provide students with a rhetorical introduction to college writing. Drew University, using a form of directed self-placement via iMoat, has students take a "'Placement Confirmation Test' . . . which includes 1) an essay synthesizing three articles; 2) checklists for each level of the class; 3) an essay in which students use the checklist and their reading and writing experience to argue that we should accept their self-placement decision" (Jamieson; see also MIT/Microsoft). Sandra Jamieson points out that "[t]he difficulty of the synthesis essay gives [students] a sense of what we expect—quite a few who have already registered change their registration (wisely) after taking the test, so it does function to guide them." (On the advantages and dangers of placement tests, see CCCC, *Writing Assessment*.)

The two most common approaches to identifying writers in need of supplemental support are more holistic: by having faculty identify students who struggle in their classes (46 schools), and by having students identify themselves (51 schools). The former resonates with the method of identification used in the studio approach to basic writing, described at length by Rhonda Grego and Nancy Thompson (see "Repositioning Remediation" and "The Writing Studio"; also Lalicker), although it is much less formalized than in their description. This method ties identifying marginal writers directly to the writing tasks expected of them at the institution. At schools that take a WAC-based approach to first-year writing, this potentially involves all the faculty of the college in thinking about the challenges students face in making the transition from high school. Nonetheless, the informality of the process at many institutions can make it challenging to feel confident that students are getting support as early and consistently as they need it. We don't have data on how these mechanisms function at each institution—for example, to whom students are identified.

The fifty-one schools in our study that offer students the opportunity to self-identify a need for writing support may appear to be offering a kind of directed self-placement. The diffuse and unsystematic nature of the support available, however, makes it difficult to make that claim. The respondent at College 3 offered the following, not atypical, gloss: "There is no systematic way that underprepared writers are identified currently." She then described a loose and determinedly non-stigmatizing approach to outreach in concert with tutorial-based support:

> I give an address to each incoming class during the Welcome to Academic Life section of Orientation where I amongst other things talk about the resources that "smart" [College 3] students avail themselves to [sic] early and often. Those services include the range of peer to peer supports as well as me. Over the last two years there has been a pre-orientation for First Generation and International Students. I address each of these groups and emphasize amongst other things the availability of my office as a supplemental advising/mentoring resource and the availability of one-on-one writing tutors throughout the semester or year upon request. A number of these students have seemed to hear these directed messages so that I have been one of the folks who has strongly encouraged the continuation of these pre-orientation assemblies. I've intentionally tried to focus on "inclusive academic excellence" or "enhancement" for all students as opposed to the stigma that the label "underprepared" can have with the result that those students who need the interventions the most will avail themselves the least in a "selective" environment if services seemed based on a "deficient model."

This institution—one of the most selective in our sample—offers students a buffet of individualized support options from which they can choose: "a range of peer to peer supports as well as" working directly with this Director. The Director seeks to present that buffet as available to and benefitting *all* students—"the resources that 'smart' [College 3] students" use; at the same time, she advertises it directly to

the populations she thinks may be most in need of writing support—
first-generation college students and international students. If students
associate these services with remediation, the Director worries, "those
. . . who need the interventions the most will avail themselves the
least."

The ease with which writing center-based support for struggling
writers blends in with opportunities and services writing centers provide to the entire college community is one of the strengths to this
approach. For international students, the relative informality of the
writing center also helps to acculturate students in a safe, low-stakes
environment. On the other hand, this approach may make it more difficult for some of the neediest students to seek out available support.
This may be because some students are reluctant to self-identify as
needing support, while other students may not be savvy navigators of
even the relatively simple bureaucracy of a small college. But peer tutoring—like any form of support—cannot reach everyone. Some students may fear revealing their struggles (or disabilities) to peers, and so
may be reluctant to seek assistance from them. As Pamela Bedore and
Deborah F. Rossen-Knill point out, there may also be some learning
issues—deep-seated anxieties related to writing or learning differences
that require work with someone who has more expertise and experience than an undergraduate tutor can provide (56–57).

College 3's approach is representative of that of many schools in the
sample. Students are informed of the tutoring resources and of supplemental writing classes, but there is little guidance offered to help them
figure out whether or not they might need such resources. Directed
self-placement (DSP) addresses the gaps in this informal approach to
identification and support. In essence, it formalizes a process already
in place at many of the schools in the sample—self-identification—by
providing designated moments and guiding questions.

DIRECTED SELF-PLACEMENT

Daniel J. Royer and Roger Gilles describe directed self-placement as
"any placement method that both offers students information and advice about their placement options (that is the 'directed' part) and places the ultimate placement decision in the students' hands (that is the
'self-placement' part)" (*Directed Self-Placement* 2). The specific nature
of the direction varies from institution to institution, as do the place-

ment options facing the student. At Grand Valley State University, where Royer and Gilles developed the approach, students must choose between English 98, which is a basic writing course that does not count toward students' required credits for graduation, and English 150 (standard first-year composition) ("Directed Self-Placement" 55). To help them with their decision, students are asked whether or not a series of statements about literacy practices describe them:

- I read newspapers and magazines regularly.
- In the past year, I have read books for my own enjoyment.
- In high school, I wrote several essays per year.
- My high school GPA placed me in the top third of my class.
- I have used computers for drafting and revising essays.
- My ACT-English score was above 20.
- I consider myself a good reader and writer. ("Directed Self-Placement" 56)

These statements are not simply about current practices; they touch upon confidence levels, high school training, and academic success. Students are advised that if many of the statements do *not* describe them, they should consider taking English 98 ("Directed Self-Placement" 57). Royer and Gilles argue that traditional placement mechanisms, such as placement exams or scores on standardized tests, "send . . . a message oddly discordant with the basic educational values of agency, choice, and self-determination" ("Basic Writing"). Directed self-placement, by contrast, fosters the students' agency and replaces a technocratic focus on the validity or reliability of the measures "with something akin to rightness" ("Directed Self-Placement" 61-62). As David Blakesley notes, this "simple act of providing students some stake in exercising personal agency in such an explicit way can begin the process of achieving the more noble goal of higher education: to prepare a citizenry to write its own future by deliberating on its past" (29). This vision resonates with the small college structure of feeling.

A number of scholars have emphasized the importance of this reflective component of directed self-placement, arguing in some cases that students need more "contextually rich and relevant information" about the institution's curriculum before they can make appropriate decisions (Bedore and Rossen-Knill 58; see also Nicolay). Some of these critiques focus on the cultural background of particular student populations; for example, Lewiecki-Wilson, Sommers, and Tassoni argue that at their university, many students "have a history of damaged self-image" that might lead them to "misplace themselves out of reticence, fear, or anxiety" (168-69).

Despite the close synergy between the philosophical underpinnings of directed self-placement and the SLAC structure of feeling, however, CompFAQ lists only three of the schools invited to participate in our study as using this. (The only published account of directed self-placement at a small college is Cornell and Newton's essay on DePauw University, in Royer and Gilles' *Directed Self-Placement*.) While we recognize the above cautions and limitations, we argue that this model offers an opportunity to SLACs because of its potential to be adapted to "local, institutional values" (Ritter, "Before" 12). While directed self-placement was developed and has, thus far, been implemented in conjunction with course-based support structures, one could devise a series of questions and imagine a rhetorical situation in which to prompt students to engage in a more reflective process of identifying whether or not they want to seek out a peer writing mentor. While such tutorial support is different than the course-based support Royer and Gilles describe, we can imagine adapting their questions to the context of specific student populations and programs.

In "Responding to Directed Self-Placement," Michael Neal and Brian Huot caution that this approach to writing assessment and placement is still new and relatively untested by validity studies (253). It is likely that small college WPAs moving towards such a system will, of necessity, have to anticipate several years of trial. But as we have noted throughout, small colleges can provide environments supportive of innovation and experimentation. Directed self-placement would build on the strengths of small college writing centers while also creating a more systematic and comprehensive structure around the students whose "needs are greater than others" (Ritter, *Before* 130).

SUPPORTING DIVERSELY PREPARED WRITERS

In "A Basic Introduction to Basic Writing Program Structures," William B. Lalicker identifies a "baseline and . . . alternatives" for the delivery of basic writing instruction. Although his schematic is useful, we have found more heterogeneous groupings in our data set. Lalicker's baseline is what he calls the "prerequisite model," in which students are required to take a non-credit-bearing class before they are eligible to take the standard first-year composition course. Additional models include the stretch model, which "stretches" the work of the standard course over two semesters; the "studio" model, which clusters students from a number of different sections to work together in small tutorial groups; the "intensive" model, in which the basic writing sections garner more credit hours and include supplemental meetings with the instructor; and the "mainstreaming" model, in which "students address deficiencies in their writing through their own initiative."[1] Our data suggest that some institutions mainstream while others retain a prerequisite model; others still have gone on record as having a stretch course in place (see Jamieson).

Table 10.2 presents the types of support available. The focus here is not on what students are required to do (after being somehow identified as needing additional writing support) but what the institution recommends for them. Although thirty-one institutions had indicated that they had "additional writing requirements" for students identified as underprepared, further analysis indicates that sixteen of those schools required courses, while the other fifteen made a variety of other recommendations. These data are drawn from the following question: "How does your program support underprepared writers? (check all that apply)." This question provided respondents a chance to indicate what kinds of support are embedded in other structures on campus, including the writing center or the WPA/WCD's portfolio of responsibilities.

Table 10.2 Support Provided to Underprepared Students.

Type of Support	Number of Schools
College offers summer bridge program	18
Student self selects into a writing course	46
Peer tutor works with student	84
Professional tutor works with student	30[2]
WPA/WCD works with student	19
WC offers workshops	20
Other opportunities for support**	22

* Respondents could indicate multiple opportunities.

**Students may be required or recommended to take a course; they may get assistance from their professors, or they may participate in mentoring programs and other support programs.

Six schools indicated that they provide "no support," although interestingly all but one of those schools have strong peer-tutoring writing centers. The most common support structures at small colleges are tutoring-based (eighty-four schools use peer tutors and twenty-three use professional tutors). This is consonant with the SLAC structure of feeling, which prizes one-on-one interactions between students and between students and faculty. Twenty-two schools indicate they only offer one type of support for struggling writers; of those, sixteen (73%) rely on peer tutors. This heavy reliance on peer tutors to provide writing support is one of the ways writing centers are woven into the fabric of students' educations at small colleges. As Donna Nelson points out,

> The one-on-one approach used by writing labs has proved successful not only for basic writers, but for average and even gifted writers as well. . . . When a writing lab is conceived as a place where all students can be helped in this manner . . . all students will benefit—and basic writers won't be as likely to slink through the writing lab doorway, feeling embarrassed or as though they are being punished for some misdeed. (192; see also Cobb and Elledge)

On the other hand, this reliance can also mean that faculty—and the institution as a whole—has delegated a significant portion of writing instruction to students.

Sixty-five schools in our sample report that the writing program or writing center provide support that specifically targets the needs of English Language Learners (ELL). Most of those schools provide this support through individualized tutoring; only eighteen schools offer a course for these students. (That may be the course identified earlier for all struggling writers, rather than a course specifically focused on teaching writing for ELL students.) Thirty schools support ELL students through the usual work of the writing center and nineteen schools offer tutoring with some sort of ELL professional. Among the thirty schools that provide tutoring through the writing center, some offer a peer mentor program where an ELL student can meet regularly with the same peer tutor. These mentor programs are often wide-ranging in mission. College 10, for example, describes their "Writing Partnerships" as "semester-long tutorial[s] that focus . . . on the individual needs of a writer," and so hides from view the fact that many or most of the writers seeking such mentoring may well be struggling with the expectations of college-level writing at the institution. Some scholars have observed that such one-on-one approaches can prevent ELL students from building constructive alliances with one another to learn collaboratively (see Braine; Elbow; Matsuda and Silva; Silva; and Smoke; see also the CCCC *Statement on Second Language Writing and Writers*).

Given the responsibility small college writing centers take for this area, it is unsurprising that many schools report providing additional training for tutors who will be working with ELL students.[3] In addition, one trend we've observed anecdotally is toward hiring a member of the professional staff with specific ELL expertise. Many of the schools in the sample have been consciously and deliberately diversifying their student bodies in the last decade. This has meant a greater focus on the recruitment of international students. In some cases, this has also resulted in outreach to historically underrepresented minorities (which may include resident ELL students). While the populations brought to these schools through these endeavors are different in many ways, these combined efforts have placed new pressures on the writing support provided for ELL students (both resident and international) and, in some cases, have resulted in the creation of new positions in the writing center or writing program.

Our analyses thus show that there is a wide range of support structures available at small liberal arts colleges for the diverse students who attend them—an unsurprising finding about a set of schools that pride themselves on how much they value students as individual learners. But these schools' reliance on individualized relationships and diffuse discussion of support may make it harder than it needs to be for the students who would most benefit from these courses and tutorials. The reliance on peer tutors to provide writing instruction to the neediest students may indicate that the institution has abdicated a key responsibility. Small colleges may be reluctant to systematically identify their needier students through an unconscious resistance at the institutional or individual level to commit to any official labeling of students. These schools may fear that any formalized identification might name (and thus create) a community through intellectual marginalization. A well-designed program of directed self-placement, by contrast, inaugurates students' educations by asking them to reflect on and understand their rhetorical knowledge and literacy practices. Coupled with an appropriate and flexible set of support offerings, such a program can scaffold the learning of a diverse set of students by honoring them all as individual learners.

IV

Small College Writing Programs

11 Assessment

[T]ruth means doing our epistemological best. Before we make a knowledge claim (for example, Here is how writing is valued in our writing program) that carries with it serious consequences for students, faculty, and society, we need to conduct the best inquiry we can.

—Bob Broad

A longitudinal study is currently underway to examine the totality of students' academic experience at [College 29], including the nature of their writing in relation to other factors. We are also beginning studies, in collaboration with other institutions, of students' thesis-writing, and students' quantitative writing. We prefer studies that are more research-oriented than assessment-oriented.

—Survey respondent

In the introduction to *What We Really Value: Beyond Rubrics in Teaching and Assessing Writing*, Bob Broad extends Brian Huot's 2002 call for a theory and practice of writing assessment that is site-based, locally-controlled, context-sensitive, rhetorically-based, and accessible (Huot, *[Re]Articulating* 105; see also Broad 13–14). In this chapter, we present the current state of writing assessment at small liberal arts colleges. Most of these practices are deeply embedded in the local cultures and programs of these schools; we therefore analyze the practices of three schools in detail after describing the overarching trends across the sample. Assessment at its best can bring together curriculum- and student-centered writing instruction, catalyzing data-driven conversations about all the sites of writing instruction at a school. It can also be a way for a WPA (and an institution) to own embedded sites of writing. Although embedded sites can be more difficult to assess than explicit ones, undertaking an assessment inquiry can be a way to better understand the goals and functioning of those sites. As Broad and our respondent point out differently in the epigraphs to this chapter, the first step is research.

At large public institutions, assessment is often driven by government mandates and bolstered by hierarchical structures such as offices of assessment The program narratives of the University of Kentucky and George Mason University, both highlighted by CWPA as models of localized assessment, are good examples. This can lead to pressure to adopt standardized measures, what Edward M. White has called the "truck scale measurement model," instead of the more localized, rhetorical, and contextualized approaches advocated by scholars in the field (*Teaching and Assessing Writing* 248). Assessment at private liberal arts colleges is more often driven by re-accreditation. Seventy-two of our respondents listed accreditation as one of the factors motivating writing assessment. The scale of these institutions, however, makes it easier for them to implement assessments that would result in overwhelming amounts of data at larger schools. In 2001, for example, William Condon pointed out that some small liberal arts colleges were already collecting and evaluating student papers as part of their assessment of writing across the curriculum (43). It may be that small colleges came early to such an approach to writing assessment not just because their size makes such approaches feasible, but also because their relative autonomy as private institutions gives them more leeway to design their own measures. Direct assessment of students' performances is clearly tied to teaching and learning, and therefore speaks to the small college structure of feeling.

Condon highlights the "developmental portfolio" assessment at Alverno College, but the portfolio assessment at Carleton College is currently the most widely known, as a result of Carol Rutz's research. As Rutz and Jacqulyn Lauer-Glebov describe, prior to the implementation of a sophomore-level portfolio requirement in 1998, students were required to take a "writing-rich" seminar in their first year. In addition to assigning final grades for all the students who took the course, faculty would indicate that some students had "*earned* WR" credit for writing proficiency (82). "However," they report, "no specific guidelines existed to help faculty measure proficiency, nor was there an effort to coordinate pedagogy in WR courses" (82). By instituting a sophomore-level portfolio requirement (a process described in

Rutz and Lauer-Glebov 83–84 and Rutz, Hardy, and Condon 9–13), Carleton developed an ongoing approach to assessment that combines the direct assessment of student writing with faculty development both through faculty development workshops every December, and through the conversations over student portfolios during the portfolio reading session each June. As Rutz details in "Delivering Composition at a Liberal Arts College," the portfolios provide faculty direct evidence of students' experience as writers at Carleton, and therefore let faculty see the variety of writing students do across the curriculum (Rutz 64–65, 67–68). Portfolios also inculcate reflection on writing and learning at a key point in a Carleton education and allow for a more systematic evaluation of student writing with immediate feedback to students (65–66, 68–69). Finally, this approach "affirms the effectiveness of delivering writing instruction through a WAC model" (68); writing assessment at Carleton, Rutz writes, "has evolved from chronic complaints about a steady decline in student performance to active, creative change in teaching to foster learning" (69).

Some small liberal arts colleges resemble Carleton prior to the implementation of the portfolio assessment. In such cases, "[g]ood writing [is] preached—and taught—in many ways" (Rutz and Lauer-Glebov 83), but without systematic data-based discussion. Rutz argues that "writing assessment [can be] a means to uncover and improve writing instruction—to make the implicit explicit" and encourages liberal arts colleges to undertake "a close examination of their writing cultures" (69). The programs we highlight below have undertaken such close examinations, and have had experiences similar to that of Carleton. The institution of assessment and/as regular faculty development has allowed all three of these schools to articulate and evaluate what they mean by "good writing." They have all undertaken the inquiry Broad calls for to uncover what they really value and, as a result, have flexible, sustainable, and robust assessment processes in place. We situate these models in the context of the trends across the sample. We can't do justice to the variety of writing assessments in place at small colleges because they are too localized to aggregate. But the assessments in place at Spelman College, Illinois Wesleyan University, and Occidental College provide a representative sampling of the ways in which small colleges are using assessment to better understand their cultures of writing—including the embedded components of those cultures—and to further their historic commitment to student writing.

Trends in Writing Assessment

In 2006, Carol Rutz observed that "many liberal arts colleges do not attempt to assess student writing, whether at the individual, course, or program level" (61). Three years later, nearly half (49) of the institutions in our data sample reported assessing random samples of student writing; twenty-nine schools do some type of portfolio assessment. (Some of those institutions may do both.) In addition, thirty-three institutions survey faculty about student writing, and fifty-one schools survey students about writing.[1] The comparatively high rate of student surveys may be a result of schools' participation in national surveys, such as NSSE (the National Survey of Student Engagement). A small set of the invited schools do not use NSSE, but do use the COFHE (Consortium on Financing Higher Education) survey, which is also a survey of student engagement and progress. Fifteen of the schools have joined the Consortium for the Study of Writing in College (see CWPA-NSSE). It isn't clear how the NSSE or COFHE data are used on these campuses; WPAs at some institutions that administer NSSE were unaware of the fact. (NSSE has experienced a similar disjunction nationwide; see Jaschik, "Turning Surveys.")

Most of the writing administrators in the sample reported being responsible for assessment. This is, unsurprisingly, more true of those with curricular responsibilities: 84% of the WPAs (including solo WPA/WCDs) reported being responsible for writing assessment, compared to 47% of writing center directors. The number of writing center directors responsible for assessment increases to 62% when no WPA is present in the leadership configuration. In trying to learn more about what kinds of direct assessment of student writing these schools undertook, we asked: "What kinds of writing assessment does your institution do regularly?" Table 11.1 presents the types of assessment institutions reported.

The distinction between "writing courses" and "other courses" in this question is one that respondents made in a variety of ways. The category of "writing courses" at some institutions may include departmental courses that fulfill the W requirement while at others it may include only courses taught under the purview of the composition program. The major trends, however, are for: assessment in the context of "writing" courses (as they are locally and variously defined) as well as some other courses; assessment in light of college-wide goals or criteria; the impact of peer tutors on student writing; and longitudinal studies that track student writing over the course of four years. Strikingly, assessment is only tied to passing a requirement at ten schools and to proficiency at twenty.

Table 11.1 Types of Writing Assessment at Small Colleges.

Type of Assessment	Number of Schools
Student writing in writing courses	63
Student writing in other courses	28
Student writing over four years	25
Student writing in connection with college writing goals	40
Faculty development program	12
Impact of peer tutors on student writing	25
Students passing a writing requirement	10
Students' writing proficiency	20
No assessment	17

Since there are no national studies to which we can compare these data, we can simply speculate that small colleges are unlikely to take these approaches because, in the former case, most requirements are defined in terms of courses (rather than other tests or assessments) and, in the latter, because of the relatively low incidence of proficiency requirements. The most common assessment practices in the sample—of student writing in writing courses and in connection with the college's writing goals—are clearly driven by the schools' emphasis on student learning.

Seventeen schools—roughly one-sixth of the sample—reported doing no institutional assessment. However, more than half of those respondents reported that they are responsible for writing assessment on their campuses (those included explicit WPAs, solo WPA/WCDs, and WCDs). This discrepancy may arise from the lack of an institutional mandate, with writing assessment serving a programmatic purpose or occurring solely within the context of program review. It may also be that those institutions are in the planning stages, meaning that the institution is not regularly assessing student writing right now, but that the WPA or WCD has been charged with developing a plan.

One WPA in this situation ruefully reported that assessment was solely her domain: "Rubrics, alignment, training. It's all me." In other cases, the collective governance characteristic of these schools may make it difficult to initiate assessments. One respondent noted, for example, "Assessment of writing is on the [horizon]. Because no one owns writing instruction at [this particular college], it is difficult to assess and make recommendations for change." Our respondents expressed the perception that their institutions were behind the curve with writing assessment, reporting that "there has been no regular assessment until very recently," and that "the assessment landscape at the institution is changing currently, but that's a slow process of change." At many of these institutions, the problem seems to be the fact that the rhetoric of assessment arrives on campus through accrediting agencies; as a result, "assessment" is associated with accountability—and not with teaching and learning. One respondent puts this cogently:

> The word "assessment" is used exclusively with respect to Middle States Assn and administration initiatives. The rest of us wish we had never heard of it. The work I do to make sure the courses and the curriculum is working properly for students and faculty is "assessment," but it was not considered such by the "assessment" machinery required by Middle States.

What we see in the models below—as in the case of Carleton College, described above—is that small colleges are unlikely to undertake writing assessment until they see how it will enhance the learning of their students. While these institutions may be late to the assessment party, they are able to learn from the best practices developed by the field. Within the context of their particular structure of feeling, they can then adapt those practices to the institution's goals. Over the course of this research, we've heard anecdotally about moments when writing assessments catalyzed change. In some cases (including Illinois Wesleyan), this took the form of a new commitment to the existing requirement; in other cases, it has produced new requirements and even new positions to lead them. We would speculate that these changes arise when a writing assessment helps an institution see the embedded components of its writing program more clearly, leading it to capitalize on the opportunities such sites of writing represent.

SMALL COLLEGE MODELS OF WRITING ASSESSMENT

Spelman and Occidental Colleges and Illinois Wesleyan University are geographically far-flung, serve different populations of students, and have different historic missions. With Carleton, however, they represent thoughtful, well-designed approaches to writing assessment that carefully balance the mandates of accrediting agencies with the local structure of feeling. In addition, all of these writing assessments take the form of feedback loops, with each iteration leading to new insights about student writing, writing pedagogy, and the school's writing curriculum. Furthermore, each of these initiatives is broad-based. While our respondents are leaders on their campuses, they articulated a strong sense of the range of stakeholders and partners that make these ongoing efforts successful.

Illinois Wesleyan University in Bloomington, Illinois is unusual in our sample in that it offers nursing and eight pre-professional programs as well as a traditional liberal arts curriculum. It was founded by a group of "lawyers, doctors, teachers, tradesmen, mechanics, farmers, and ministers" in 1850 as an all-male institution affiliated with the United Methodist Church (Illinois Wesleyan). IWU admitted its first African-American students in 1867 and its first female students in 1870; its first international students were admitted in 1889 (Illinois Wesleyan). It retains the affiliation with the Methodist Church today. The current study body is 2,100, with an average class size of seventeen and a student-to-faculty ratio of 11 to 1.

Our informant for this study was Dr. Joel Haefner, Writing Coordinator and Lecturer in Computer Science, with whom we corresponded over email and interviewed over the phone. Haefner directs the writing center and partners with Mary Ann Bushman, the WPA, on program assessment; both report to the Associate Dean of Curriculum. Illinois Wesleyan's writing program consists of an explicit WPA and WCD; it has an entirely explicit writing requirement, which consists of a first-year writing seminar, called the "Gateway Colloquium," and two W courses.

Assessment at IWU has focused on explicit requirements with implicit expectations. The findings of Teagle-funded assessment research across six Midwestern small colleges revealed in 2007 that, while the IWU first-year writing seminar was helping students improve, there was little writing development occurring beyond the first year. (Students were, in fact, postponing the fulfillment of their writing-intensive course requirement until their senior year.) In an email, Haefner explained that these results were a "big wake-up call" to the IWU faculty, and led to a desire to "reviv[e] and restructur[e]" the writing program through assessment and faculty development. This led to a three-year project funded by the Mellon Foundation. The funding allowed IWU to bring in a number of outside speakers in the planning stages, and then to hire Bob Broad and William Condon as consultants. Haefner had earlier traveled to Carleton College to observe their faculty portfolio reading sessions. Haefner explains in his email that

> As we thought about assessment in our campus culture, we realized that we wanted assessment that was meaningful but not intimidating, assessment which engaged faculty from as many disciplines as possible but which might also speak to students and families, assessment which tied directly into the teaching of writing and which was still cost-effective.

The first goal has been to bring to the surface the embedded values of the institution by generating an IWU writing learning outcomes statement using dynamic criteria mapping (see Broad; Broad et al.). Haefner explained in the phone interview that the IWU outcomes statement works in conjunction with paper scoring rubrics, which are—to use his term—"living documents" that will be revisited with new faculty, if the university is able to sustain the initiative beyond the grant funding.

Condon helped IWU develop a three-year plan for scoring and assessing student writing according to these rubrics. They now assess the writing of first-year, senior, and mid-career students. In his email, Haefner describes the assessment event:

> [E]ight faculty members scor[e] around sixty papers, based on an eleven-dimension rubric we developed earlier and which we revisit each year. Besides establishing data which we can compare for a campus-wide, longitudinal analysis of student writing, this quantitative assessment catalyzes excellent faculty discussion. We always conclude our quantitative assessment with a discussion of faculty development foci and specific development events which the data and our assessment experience suggest.

Haefner describes here how IWU established a feedback loop between assessment and faculty development. The assessment meetings "always conclude" with a discussion of what pedagogical concerns have emerged from the evaluation of student writing. In addition, the process is largely faculty-driven. The drive to assess student writing arose from the faculty's dismay at the Teagle study's results, and has been attentive throughout to what faculty across the university value in student writing. It has thus turned tacit norms into explicit standards by developing rubrics through dynamic criteria mapping.

Haefner and Bushman partnered on these efforts, which is a clear collaboration between the writing center director and writing program administrator, and hence between the curricular- and student-centered realms. In addition to making the implicit explicit, then, IWU's assessment brings a desire to support students as writers into direct conversation with how the writing requirement is administered, structured, and taught.

Occidental College is located in Los Angeles, California. Founded in 1887 by a group of Presbyterian clergy and laymen, the school has always been co-educational. (Occidental became nonsectarian in 1910.) Occidental has been designated as a community engagement institution by the Carnegie Foundation because of its commitment to collaboration with its surrounding communities, and has a longstanding commitment to "equity and excellence" (Occidental College). It is consistently named one of the most diverse liberal arts colleges by *U.S. News & World Report* (see also Dreier and Gottlieb). Occidental is one of the most-filmed campuses in the sample, appearing in films as early as 1920. The student body is currently 1,863, with a student-faculty ratio of 10 to 1.

Our informant was Dr. Deborah Martinson, a tenured associate professor of English Writing and also the writing program director. We interviewed Martinson over the phone and also in person during the 2011 CCCC conference in Atlanta. Occidental's leadership configuration is *Solo WPA/WCD*; the three members of the English Writing department share and rotate responsibilities for administering all aspects of the writing program, including its writing center. It has an explicit writing requirement comprised of a two-semester first-year writing seminar requirement followed by a junior-level WID requirement. Both have a proficiency component. In the first year, students submit a portfolio including one paper from each semester of the FYWS, as well as a timed writing. Students who do not have two out of three passing scores must take a sophomore-level writing course. (Roughly 20% of the first-year class is required to take the course; many other students take it of their own accord, so there is no stigma attached.) The second stage of the proficiency requirement varies as to discipline and disciplinary methods of assessment. Many departments require students to produce a paper that achieves a grade of B- or higher in a course within their major during the junior year. These papers are read by more than one professor, although the specific criteria are embedded within the departments. In an email, Martinson contended that the Occidental faculty's "very real commitment to . . . diversity" makes them attentive to student writing and to student learning outcomes.

The first stage of the Occidental writing assessment lies in the evaluation of students' papers from each of the first-year writing seminars according to a what Martinson calls a "features rubric" (Appendix E) that she and a faculty committee developed in 2004, drawing on the CWPA "Outcomes Statement" and other publications. These papers are from early in the fall semester and late in the spring semester, providing data of students' trajectories over the course of their first year. On the phone, Martinson explained that the features rubric used for the first-year writing also forms the basis of "research rubrics" (Appendix E) used to evaluate the junior-level writing. The requirement structure thus provides Occidental with two significant moments to reflect collectively on students' progress as writers, and to adjust pedagogy and curriculum in light of those findings.

In 2004, Martinson, with help from an associate dean at Occidental, developed a longitudinal study of fifty random students who were members of the class of 2009. For this longitudinal study, Occidental used the rubrics already mentioned and developed an additional qualitative rubric that provided space to indicate students' development over the course of their four years. (A full description of the plan for the longitudinal study is available in Appendix E.) Martinson described in her email that she triangulated the faculty evaluation of student writing by conducting interviews and/or email reflections with the study participants. This has led to a rich data set of students' writing lives at Occidental.

This approach to assessment arose out of the evaluation of student writing for the purpose of determining whether or not students had passed a requirement. But with the longitudinal study, the approach has come to meld student assessment with program assessment, by creating a feedback loop between student writing performances and writing instruction. At each stage of the writing assessment (first-year, junior year, senior comprehensive), Martinson reported the results and implications of the assessment to the entire faculty and posted the report on an internal website. In a follow-up email in June, 2011, Martinson told us that more departments have worked with the writing program to develop their pedagogies, curricula, and assessments as a result of this internal publicity. The Occidental assessment thus catalyzes more focused faculty development and the general growth of the school's culture of writing. The English Writing department is a curricular entity charged with supporting student writers; its faculty spend part of their teaching time meeting with students individually in the writing center. This approach to assessment thus blurs the lines between curricular- and student-centered realms.

Spelman College is a historically black college (HBC) for women founded in 1881 in Atlanta, Georgia. The college's mission emphasizes community engagement both locally and internationally: "[O]ur goals include integrating and globalizing learning, teaching creatively and rigorously, leading from our authentic core, living sustainably, improving ourselves continuously, and collaborating to better our city's quality of life" (Spelman College). The college has approximately 2,343 students and a student-faculty ratio of 12 to 1.

We interviewed Dr. Anne Warner, our Spelman informant, over the phone and also in person during the 2011 CCCC conference in Atlanta. Warner's official title is "Director of the Comprehensive Writing Program" (CWP), which she classifies as a writing center director position. Spelman has an *Embedded WPA + Explicit WCD* leadership configuration. The writing curriculum at Spelman is comprised of both explicit and embedded elements. The explicit requirement consists of first-year composition (English 103, administered by the English department) and a writing portfolio (administered by CWP), which is due at the end of the first year. The embedded requirement is the core curriculum, "The African Diaspora and the World." Students also take a year-long first-year seminar that does not require writing. In that seminar, however, they do produce writing that is included in the writing portfolio, which Warner described in her email as "part of a broader, developing institutional project." The Comprehensive

Writing Program is a freestanding academic unit consisting of three computer labs with multimedia assistants and a space staffed by peer tutors. The program reports to the academic dean within the office of undergraduate studies, though Warner herself is a tenured member of the English department and has chaired it for seven years. Now, she noted over the telephone, her "energy and attention are totally focused on the CWP."

The Spelman College Electronic Portfolio Project (SpEl.Folio) "develops students' ability to think critically about the connections among their intellectual, professional, and personal lives. . . . SpEl.Folios enable assessment on multiple levels: self-assessment by students, course and major-based assessment, and institutional assessment of designated learning objectives" (SpEl.Folio, "Mission Statement"). This college-wide project was initiated in 2007; the First-Year Writing Portfolio has been folded into it although, in an evolving form, the portfolio has been in place since 1993. Warner dates its development to Jacqueline Jones Royster's advocacy of that approach when she directed CWP in the 1980s. (For Royster's reflection on a decade of WAC at Spelman, see "From Practice to Theory.") Two grants were also key to the project's development. Warner explained in the phone interview that they were able to use the "tail end" of a Bush-Hewlett grant for faculty development and student learning. In a follow-up email, she mentioned that Bill Condon "served as consultant for assessment of multimedia materials." A Mellon grant funded the overall SpEl.Folio project. In addition, CWP has faculty development support from Title III.

The writing portfolio includes a reflective cover letter and three academic argument essays, two of which students may have submitted to any course. The third essay, an "independent argument," is written solely for the portfolio. The first-year seminar includes two sessions on selecting and preparing particular elements of the portfolio. The portfolio requirement is thus supported in both the curricular- and the student-centered realms. In the phone interview, Warner argued that the portfolio process is ideally suited to Spelman's student population, some of whom feel that they do not "test well"; by contrast, Warner offers, "no one ever says, 'I don't portfolio well.'"

In her email, Warner identified 2004 as a watershed moment in the portfolio's evolution. The combination of new faculty (including Margaret Price, an English department colleague who Warner describes as her "assessment mentor") and consultant Michael Neal helped the college to move from "a very basic set of standards to a more comprehensive and descriptive scoring guide created with full input from the jury readers." Now, Warner assembles a "jury" of faculty reviewers each year; this group represents disciplines across the campus and includes some external participants. With Neal as facilitator, they evaluate the portfolios during the course of a week using a holistic approach to scoring. The first session is a calibration of faculty scoring, during which the group reads, evaluates, and discusses their evaluations of three sample essays. Warner noted in the phone interview that, as a facilitator Neal has been able to provide an "expert balance between creativity and possibility" (for more on Neal's approach to assessment, see Huot and Neal; Neal).

"While no formal program evaluation is done in this context," Warner wrote us, "every year we exchange information and perspectives, working especially with how peer tutors may support core course assignments." Through the efforts of the CWP, the portfolio composition and submission process yields a cross-curricular writing experience, with CWP providing writing resources to the courses that comprise Spelman's core curriculum (which do not consistently include writing instruction as a goal), as well as workshops and peer tutorials to students in English 103 and the core courses. The assessment project, then, becomes a writing process that engages not only the individual student whose writing is being assessed, but also the peer tutors who collaborate in the process.

IMPLICATIONS

We have highlighted these three programs because we believe that they provide models for writing assessment in the small college context that are worth further consideration. Illinois Wesleyan's experience with dynamic criteria mapping offers a strategy for revitalizing an existing WAC-based requirement. Through that process, faculty at IWU have re-committed to their approach to writing instruction and are working to improve the specificity and transparency with which they communicate their writing values to students. At Occidental, a multi-stage proficiency requirement has inspired a longitudinal study that provides detailed data about students' writing lives, in turn providing concrete data to departmental and FYWS faculty as well as to the writing center. Finally, Spelman's writing center-administered electronic portfolio bridges the gap between curriculum and student support by providing both explicit course-based instruction and tutorial help in "how to portfolio." At all three institutions, writing assessment adheres to the "Principles of Effective Writing Assessment" outlined in the NCTE-WPA White Paper. These practices are, for example, derived from current research; they employ multiple measures and provide a "foundation for data-driven, or evidence-based decision-making" (NCTE-WPA). Their focus in all three cases is on how to improve teaching and learning at those institutions, and in all cases is based on "continuous conversations" (NCTE-WPA). With teaching (and hence teachers) at the center of their assessment practices, these three programs both solicit and foster faculty and student discussion about writing. Through their participation in developing rubrics, evaluating portfolios, and discussing student papers, faculty cultivate a reciprocal relationship to the assessment process, shaping it as well as being informed by it.

As Condon observes, the best assessment practices are complex, doing justice to the rich messiness of learning and teaching writing. The structure of feeling of small colleges—their size, the immediacy and pervasiveness of faculty governance, not to mention a penchant for individual experimentation—make these institutions potentially rich sites of assessment innovation. Rutz and Lauer-Glebov evocatively conjure "a campus where accountability takes a back seat to curiosity, where faculty ask themselves how to help students become better writers without worrying about accreditors' views about the matter" (81). Freed from many of the mandates and external pressures facing state institutions, small colleges have at their disposal the means to design meaningful, context-driven assessments that inform their local contexts and the field as a whole.

12 Conclusion

> *In these terms, the role of the WPA may be thought of as a relatively stable ensemble of activity footings whereby the WPA continually reworks his or her relations to the complexly layered systems of professionalism, coordinating and integrating them with one another and with other spheres and histories of personal experience and culture. That identity formation, already problematic for any professional in composition/rhetoric, is further complicated for WPAs by the ways they shiftingly align and attune themselves and their offices to disciplinary, collegial, and/or workplace frames, each shift highlighting certain streams of activities and contested interpretations within them.*

—Louise Wetherbee Phelps.

This project began with a deceptively simple question about what writing programs and writing program administration at small liberal arts colleges look like in the early twenty-first century. As the writing program administrators at two small liberal arts colleges, we wanted to know how our institutions compared to their peers. The complexity of this initial question became apparent as we understood the two questions that underwrite it. One is methodological: "How do you find out what writing programs look like?" The other is contextual: "Are small liberal arts college writing programs somehow distinctive? If so, in what ways?" *Writing Program Administration at Small Liberal Arts Colleges* answers these questions.

Understanding writing programs requires more than just survey data. Using a mixed methods approach has deepened our analysis in ways that we both could and could not anticipate. Analysis of site documents at once clarified and complicated our interpretations of survey responses. Follow-up correspondence allowed us to be true to both our respondents and our interpretations. Conversations in focus groups and one-on-one interviews helped us understand the philosophical orientations and personal stories hiding inside the aggregate information. Historical research helped us see how the current moment is inflected by particular institutional histories. Finally, grounded theory required a constant dialogue between data and concepts, each reframing the other as we sought to understand this similar and yet heterogeneous set of schools.

In *Writing Program Administration at Small Liberal Arts Colleges*, we have therefore developed a grounded theory of writing program administration at small liberal arts colleges by analyzing data from a set of one hundred such institutions. We have drawn on existing scholarship about small colleges, site documents, quantitative survey data, and qualitative data from individual and focus group interviews to generate this multi-layered analysis. Working with a defined set of schools has allowed us to articulate the complexity of these writing programs and administrative positions. It has also allowed us to identify some of the ways in which the delivery of writing instruction at small colleges differs from the norms assumed in the field of rhetoric and composition. We have identified possible (if partial) explanations for these differences in the history and material conditions of the schools in the sample.

Size, it seems, does indeed matter. The culture of all institutions is materially grounded and determined by their individual histories. Private small liberal arts colleges today share with one another some of those conditions and parts of that history. As a result, they exist within a common structure of feeling that emphasizes developmental, non-vocational learning through individual interactions in a face-to-face community. Change is not over-burdened with bureaucratic hurdles or compulsory standardization. Due to a deep respect both for tradition and for faculty autonomy, institutional change typically evolves, and often results from, carefully built consensus. While no two small colleges will emphasize precisely the same aspects of this structure of feeling, the ways in which any of these institutions delivers writing instruction is conditioned by this set of values, history, and material conditions.

As we discuss in Chapter 2, we sought to understand small college writing programs in terms of

- Where writing instruction is situated and delivered;
- How leadership for writing instruction is defined and located; and
- How the sites of writing instruction and those positions charged with leading it are put in relation to one another.

Our most significant findings cut across all three of these categories of analysis. They demonstrate that identifying the embedded and explicit aspects of a writing program can help an institution or WPA both to better understand that program's local conditions and to professionalize the program's leadership positions. Writing instruction at small colleges is significantly more rooted in writing across the curriculum approaches than seems to be the case at large universities. Out of the one hundred schools in the sample, ninety-two have some form of writing across the curriculum. The most common single requirements in the data set are first-year writing seminars (44 schools) and W courses (45 schools). Schools are re-evaluating their approach to first-year writing and in some cases are shifting from a first-year composition requirement based in a single department to a first-year writing seminar requirement where the teaching of writing is shared by faculty across the college.

We have found that writing instruction operates at a number of different levels at small colleges. Writing may be highly visible, in the form of explicit requirements, established committees, and other formal structures. It may be visible but embedded in other entities, as we have noted throughout. Most challenging of all, it may be diffused throughout the institution and in the pedagogical practices of the faculty. Most small college faculty believe in the importance of writing and, at the very least, assign it regularly. The challenge for small college WPAs, then, is not just to identify their institutions' sites of writing and writing instruction, but to also uncover the practices informing them. To what extent is writing *taught* rather than simply *assigned*? What kinds of support are available for teaching writing?

Many colleges in the sample are moving toward more explicit leadership configurations. This seems to derive from new information about students' learning. Many institutions in the sample are in the process of developing assessment tools and other mechanisms that allow them to build greater verticality into their writing curricula. They are identifying ways to make the writing instruction they already provide more explicit and intentional. As a result, many schools are recognizing their need for positions charged with leading both curricular- and student-centered writing instruction.

The trend toward a writing requirement that consists of both first-year writing seminars and W courses is one indication of this shift. As schools move from first-year composition to first-year writing seminars or add verticality to the writing curriculum, they are in many cases moving from embedded to explicit WPA positions. This shift may also be occurring as embedded WPAs retire and institutions discuss alternative approaches to administering and leading the writing program. In addition, as colleges add new explicit writing requirements, they appear to be creating positions that are in some ways responsible for overseeing their delivery. This shift bodes well for the cultures of writing at these schools. The creation of such positions and opportunities creates more local excitement for faculty development centered on the teaching of writing and for assessment projects that allow a community to identify best practices.

The prevalence of writing centers in the sample (all participating institutions have one, in some form) supports this WAC orientation of these schools. Writing centers foster a process-oriented culture of writing that cuts across the boundaries of particular departments or requirements because they are located on the student-centered side. The predominant reliance on peer tutoring means that these institutions rely on students as well as faculty to deliver writing instruction. While that can be a way for the faculty of the institution to abdicate from one pedagogical responsibility, it also creates significant learning and leadership opportunities for the peer tutors themselves. In addition, by relying on comparatively large numbers of peer tutors, the writing centers in the sample infuse writing pedagogy into the cultures of these schools from the ground up. Students as well as writing instructors are disseminating the idea of writing as both a rhetorical act and recursive process.

Six position-based leadership configurations emerged from our data—rich, detailed descriptions of how deeply complex administration and staffing can be, particularly as they are defined and distributed in multiple configurations that do not necessarily confine themselves to traditional "WPA" and "WCD" designations. Explicit positions are those that line up most easily with the scholarly literature. We found, however, that understanding the full configuration of leadership at a school was essential to understanding the possibilities and limitations of any individual position. A writing center director position, for example, has different responsibilities and opportunities depending on whether it is paired with an explicit, embedded, or no WPA. (Indeed, in the last case, what may at first look like a *WCD Only* configuration may turn out to be a *Solo WPA/WCD*—one of the most exciting, if perhaps also the most exhausting, configurations we identified.) Some embedded WPA positions seem first and foremost about supporting what is in place, managing and maintaining the existing requirement(s). But it was far more likely the case that the WPA has hidden agency (or perhaps individual and/or institutional motivation) to consider moving the school in new directions, directions that include redefining the position itself.

One challenge both for the WPA and the small college is to determine, as one of our respondents asked, "How to conceive of jobs on the borders of departmental designations? How to imagine (and, pragmatically, fund) lines of work that are malleable and hybrid?" Small colleges complicate the notion of "program" as these institutions maintain their commitment to diffused leadership structures and general resistance to formal structures, while at the same time maintaining shared ownership for the development of all students as writers. The configurations of leadership help to define the contours of a writing program and give us insight into the history and values that have shaped any given program. Analyzing the leadership configuration of a school in light of its particular requirement and student support structures will help the institution and the writing administrator understand the program's historic mission and philosophical underpinnings—and, as a result, if and how it needs to change.

FUTURE RESEARCH

While *Writing Program Administration at Small Liberal Arts Colleges* answers the general questions with which we start, it has also generated specific questions that invite further investigation. These questions emerge from a number of different points. Some emerge from features distinctive to small colleges, such as the first-year writing seminar approach to first-year writing instruction. Some arise from our preliminary analysis, such as investigating the responsibilities of the various administrative positions at these schools. Some, finally, develop from the larger heuristic we provide, such as what leadership configurations are typical of large universities. Here we meditate on some directions for future research on writing programs at small colleges.

The parameters of this study did not allow for a detailed comparison of first-year composition and first-year writing seminar programs. While we have outlined the programmatic differences between these two approaches to first-year writing instruction, more research needs to be done to more fully understand the effectiveness of both approaches. In addition to more textual analysis of goals statements, then, comparative analysis of syllabi, assignments, and even student writing will further illuminate these types of requirements. As a field, we haven't systematically examined the impact of having faculty across the institution take responsibility for first-year writing instruction—on institutional culture, WAC, or student learning. A related question is whether student writing from the two different types of programs differs: "How does writing from the different requirements compare with the WPA outcomes statement?"

Further investigation is also needed to understand the writing curricula of these schools beyond the first year. While it may be that our difficulties in coding the data reflect the deep heterogeneity of these requirements, it may also be that a more focused study of capstone requirements (for example) would provide us with a number of specific models currently in operation. Given that many schools are struggling to define the "murky middle" for themselves and their students, this is also an area ripe for further research. It may be that a set of case studies would help both individual schools and the field as a whole see that necessarily messy moment in the curriculum more clearly.

All schools in the sample have a writing center in some form, but we know little about the daily operations of these centers. Who uses the center? How often? How is it viewed by students and faculty? What is the relationship between the writing center and other campus entities? Our analysis of the writing centers in the sample identified the fact that some of these writing centers are embedded in other campus entities, but we need not have the space or the data to explore the impact of that position. This is an important question for writing center scholarship, as well as for the strategic benefit of writing center directors. What does it mean to be part of a learning commons? Similarly, there is little empirical research to date on the impact on student learning of peer versus professional tutors. More research needs to be done in order to better understand the differences between these ways of delivering writing instruction. Research has shown the positive value of peer tutoring for the tutors, but what does it mean for institutions to completely rely on this type of support? Are small colleges relying too much on undergraduates to deliver writing instruction?

Our exploration of how the schools in the sample account for the diversity of students' degrees of preparedness ran into what are perhaps characteristically SLAC difficulties. If the purpose of an institution is to focus on and promote individual development, how does it develop procedures or structures to support those students who may experience the most difficulty transitioning to college? One fundamental question is to learn more about whether or not these schools think that they have diversely-prepared students, and (if so) how they are identifying the challenges for all their students. We identified directed self-placement as one possible approach for small colleges, since it provides both structure and flexibility. More research is needed, however, to better understand the approaches currently in place at these schools and to measure their effectiveness.

Finally—but also most importantly—we have consistently resisted any evaluative claims about different leadership configurations. We offer them as a heuristic for understanding how a particular writing program (or set of programs) works and how to unearth the embedded history and values with any given configuration. It may be that some leadership configurations can be shown to be empirically more likely to foster a vibrant culture of writing than others. Similarly, it may be that some configurations are less stable and more likely to catalyze either positive or negative change. Further research could begin to understand the role a leadership configuration plays in the longevity of a program.

A related question moves from leadership configurations as a whole to particular positions. Our analysis shows the ways in which the responsibilities and status of different administrative positions tend to vary by configuration. We also argued that no one factor (status, responsibilities, or configuration) alone can determine the truth of a particular position. A staff position may have less authority than a tenured position at a small college, but it may not have less influence over the culture of writing—depending on its responsibilities and place in the leadership configuration. We were not able to go into full detail in this analysis. Given the importance of tenured WPA positions to the field as a whole, it is important to understand in more detail what impact all these factors have on WPA work. The focus on status may mean that we do not yet fully understand the complexity of WPA authority.

We developed the leadership configurations as a heuristic for understanding data from small college writing programs. (In true grounded theory fashion, they emerged from the data and then helped us interpret them.) We do not yet know how transferrable they are to large institutions. Can they help university WPAs understand their local contexts in relation to the full field of writing program administration? Our sense is that larger programs will, at the very least, have more positions that define their leadership configurations. As has been the case in our research, however, the most insight may be gained by comparing programs with similar configurations to one another—or by identifying how and why one institution's configuration is different from another's with a similar set of requirements.

The nineteenth-century college casts a long shadow and size, it seems, really does matter. The goal of this research has been to describe and analyze writing program administration at small colleges in order to help the field—and our fellow small college WPAs—better understand the types of writing programs currently at place at this type of institution. Writing programs at small colleges are typically more flexible and elastic than the norm in WPA literature. As a result, they have a greater variety of leadership structures and sites of writing instruction than the literature routinely describes. This variety may come from these programs' strong philosophical and administrative affinities with writing across the curriculum. They are, in fact, most likely to move toward professionalized leadership positions when they recognize and support that WAC orientation. Small colleges typically draw on faculty from across the institution rather than a single department to deliver writing instruction. They draw on undergraduate writing tutors to teach writing to their peers and to disseminate writing pedagogy across the college. Leadership positions at small colleges are comparable to those nationwide in terms of status and responsibilities, but small college WPAs operate in less hierarchical and power-driven contexts. Some small college WPAs are isolated and over-burdened; more have a field-specific colleague (or two) and—just as importantly—regard faculty across the institution as their colleagues and peers, sharing the work of teaching students to write for the university and the world.

At its core, this has been an action research project. It would not have existed without our fellow small college WPAs—our fellow SLAC-ers. The initial impetus for this consortium-based research was not only our curiosity about writing programs at other small liberal arts colleges, but also our desire for a community of writing administrators who face similar dilemmas, challenges, and opportunities on a day-to-day basis. The SLAC-WPA Consortium emerged from the same impetus as this research process, and the two have continued to sustain one another. It is our hope that *Writing Program Administration at Small Liberal Arts Colleges* helps that community of SLAC-WPAs continue their work for local change, just as the knowledge of SLAC-ers has galvanized this research.

Appendix A: List of Schools Invited to Complete the Survey

Agnes Scott College
Albion College
Albright College
Allegheny College
Alma College
Amherst College
Augustana College
Austin College
Bard College
Barnard College
Bates College
Beloit College
Bennington College
Berea College
Berry College
Birmingham-Southern College
Bowdoin College
Bryn Mawr College
Bucknell University
Carleton College
Centre College
Chatham University
Claremont McKenna College
Coe College
Colby College
Colgate University
College of St. Benedict
College of the Holy Cross
College of Wooster
Colorado College
Connecticut College
Cornell College

Davidson College
Denison University
DePauw University
Dickinson College
Earlham College
Eckerd College
Franklin & Marshall College
Furman University
Gettysburg College
Gordon College
Goucher College
Grinnell College
Guilford College
Gustavus Adolphus College
Hamilton College
Hampden-Sydney College
Hampshire College
Hartwick College
Harvey Mudd College
Haverford College
Hendrix College
Hiram College
Hobart and William Smith Colleges
Hollins University
Hope College
Houghton College
Illinois Wesleyan University
Juniata College
Kalamazoo College
Kenyon College
Knox College

Lafayette College
Lake Forest College
Lawrence University
Lewis and Clark College
Luther College
Macalester College
Manhattan College
McDaniel College
Middlebury College
Mills College
Millsaps College
Monmouth College
Moravian College
Morehouse College
Mount Holyoke College
Muhlenberg College
Nebraska Wesleyan University
Oberlin College
Occidental College
Oglethorpe University
Ohio Wesleyan University
Pitzer College
Pomona College
Presbyterian College
Randolph College
Randolph-Macon College
Reed College
Rhodes College
Ripon College
Roanoake College
Rollins College
Saint Anselm College
Saint Mary's College
Salem College
Sarah Lawrence College
Scripps College
Skidmore College
Smith College
Southwestern University
Spelman College
St. John's College
St. John's College, Santa Fe
St. John's University

St. Lawrence University
St. Olaf College
Susquehanna University
Swarthmore College
Sweet Briar College
Transylvania University
Trinity College
Trinity University
Union College
University of Dallas
University of Puget Sound
University of Richmond
University of the South
Ursinus College
Vassar College
Wabash College
Washington and Jefferson College
Washington and Lee University
Washington College
Wellesley College
Wesleyan College
Wesleyan University
Westmont College
Wheaton College
Whitman College
Whittier College
Willamette University
William Jewell College
Williams College
Wittenberg University
Wofford College

Appendix B: Writing at SLACs Survey

Identifying Information

1. Please tell us the name of your home institution:
    _____

2. Please tell us:
    Your name: _____
    Your position title(s): _____

3. How long have you been at the College?
    _____

4. Are you the writing program administrator or writing center director? Do you direct an aspect of the writing program?
    _____

5. If no, does your school have a person with the responsibility of directing any aspect of a writing program?
    _____

6. If you answered yes to question #4, how long have you been in your current position as Writing Program Administrator (WPA) or/and Writing Center Director (WCD)? _____

7. Your preferred email address: _____

8. Your program's website: _____

Your position

9. To whom is your Writing Program accountable? Under what department(s)/which individual's purview(s)?
    _____

10. How would you classify your position?
    o WPA/WCD position is classified as tenure-line faculty
    o WPA/WCD position is classified as non-tenure line faculty (full-time)
    o WPA/WCD position is classified as non-tenure line faculty (part-time)
    o WPA/WCD position is classified as both faculty and staff (full-time)

o   WPA/WCD position is classified as both faculty and staff (part-time)
o   WPA/WCD position is classified as staff only (full-time)
o   WPA/WCD position is classified as staff only (part-time)
o   Other (please specify): _____

11. If your position is on a tenure line, where does the tenure reside?
o   English
o   Rhet/Comp or Writing
o   It isn't on a tenure line
o   Other (please specify): _____

12. What percentage of your time is spent:
o   Teaching academic writing courses:_____
o   Teaching non academic writing courses:_____
o   Administering the writing program and/or writing center:____

13. As WPA/WCD which of the following are your job responsibilities? (check all that apply.)
o   Teach academic writing courses
o   Assess all or aspects of writing program
o   Assess the development of student writing on campus
o   Conduct faculty development
o   Supervise professional staff (asst. director, admin asst.)
o   Supervise tutors (professional and/or peer)
o   Hire professional staff
o   Hire tutors
o   Schedule writing courses
o   Schedule writing center
o   Place students into writing courses
o   Oversee curriculum development
o   Train professional staff
o   Train peer tutors
o   Advertise program
o   Oversee program budget
o   Tutor students
o   Plan events
o   Serve as an academic advisor
o   Offer student workshops
o   Other (please specify): _____

14. Of all of your job responsibilities, which three do you find take the most time? _____

15. Of all of your job responsibilities, which three do you find most useful or rewarding? Why? _____

Program Staffing

16. Are there any staff or faculty members in addition to you who administer a portion of the writing program?

    _____

17. How many? _____
18. What is the position title for the first position?

    _____

19. How would you classify this position?
    o   tenure-line faculty
    o   non-tenure line faculty (full-time)
    o   non-tenure line faculty (part-time)
    o   both faculty and staff (full-time)
    o   both faculty and staff (part-time)
    o   staff only (full-time)
    o   staff only (part-time)
20. If the position is on a tenure line, where does the tenure reside?
    o   English
    o   Rhet/Comp or Writing
    o   Other (please specify): _____
21. What percentage of this person's time is spent:
    o   Teaching academic writing courses
    o   Teaching non-academic courses
    o   Administering the writing program/writing center
22. What are the job responsibilities of this person's position?

    _____

(Questions 23–32 ask the same questions for a second and third position.)

Administrative support

33. Does your program have any administrative support?
    o   Full-time administrative assistant
    o   Part-time administrative assistant
    o   Intern
    o   Student workers
    o   No administrative support

Faculty support

34. Does your writing program have a faculty advisory committee?
    o   Yes
    o   No
    Please explain: _____

Composition of your writing program

35. Does your school have: (Please check all that apply.)
    o WAC
    o First-year writing
    o Writing Center
    o Writing Fellows
    o No writing program (skip to #37)
    o Other (Please specify): _____
36. Are these different pieces part of a formal writing program? If you answered no, please explain.
    o Yes
    o No
    Please explain: _____
37. Does your institution have a writing requirement?
    o Yes
    o No
38. What does the requirement consist of? (check all that apply)
    o First-year writing seminars taught by faculty across the curriculum
    o First-year composition predominately taught by English and/or Writing faculty
    o Writing intensive courses that are located throughout the curriculum
    o Writing in the major
    o Portfolio
    o Senior thesis or capstone experience
    o Other (Please specify): _____
39. Does your program have a description of the writing requirement online?
    o Yes
    o No
    If yes, please post link: _____
40. Are there explicit goals for your writing requirement?
    o Yes
    o No
    o Sort of
    Please explain: _____
41. Is writing proficiency one of the stated goals?
    o Yes
    o No
42. Do you accept transfer credit for the writing requirement?
    o Yes
    o No

o Sometimes

Please explain if you answered sometimes:

_____

43. Is there a way to place out of the writing requirement either through placement or exemption?

o Yes

o No

Please explain: _____

44. Are there other curricular requirements that do not require writing but encourage it?

o Yes

o No

Please explain: _____

45. Have there been changes to your writing program in the past 10 years?

o Yes

o No

46. If yes, please check which changes have taken place. (check all that apply)

o First-year composition was converted to a first-year writing seminar.

o W courses were added to the first-year requirement.

o The writing requirement was dropped.

o A full-time WPA/WCD was hired.

o The WPA/WCD position was converted to a tenure line.

o The WPA/WCD position was converted to a non-tenure line.

o The WPA/WCD position was converted to a faculty position.

o The WPA/WCD position was converted to a staff position.

o The WPA/WCD position was converted to full-time.

o The WPA/WCD position was converted to part-time.

o A writing major or minor was added. (Not creative writing)

o A Writing Center was added.

o A Writing Fellows program was added.

o The Writing Center expanded its services to include more than writing.

o Additional full-time positions were created. (Please explain below if multiple positions added.)

o Peer tutors were replaced with professional tutors.

o Professional tutors were replaced with peer tutors.

o Other (please specify): _____

47. If you're willing, please explain the process or rationale behind any of these changes: _____

First-year writing

48. How many semesters of first-year writing are required?
    o   0
    o   1
    o   2
49. If you have a required first-year writing course(s), is it (check all that apply.)
    o   English literature-based
    o   genre-based
    o   cross-disciplinary
    o   interdisciplinary
    o   topic-based
    o   connected with first-year experience courses
    o   Other (please specify): _____
50. Are there explicit goals for first-year writing?
    o   Yes
    o   No
    If yes, what are they? _____
51. Approximately how many sections of first-year writing are offered during each semester?
    o   Fall semester: _____
    o   Spring semester: _____
52. What is the enrollment cap for sections?
    o   12
    o   15
    o   18
    o   Other (please specify): _____
53. What percentage of sections is taught by:
    o   individuals teaching only academic writing courses including the first-year writing courses:_____
    o   individuals teaching academic writing courses (including FYW courses) and English courses:_____
    o   individuals teaching academic writing courses (including FYW courses) and courses in other disciplines:_____
54. Of the people teaching in your first-year program, what % are:
    o   Full-time tenured or tenure track faculty:_____
    o   Permanent full-time non-tenured faculty:_____
    o   Temporary full-time faculty (may be instructor or lecturer):__
    o   Part-time adjunct:_____
    o   Other: _____
55. Is there a common syllabus for the first-year writing course?
    o   Yes
    o   No
    Please explain: _____

Writing Intensive Courses

56. How many writing intensive courses are required beyond the first-year requirement?
    o   0
    o   1
    o   2
    o   3
    o   4
    o   5
    o   6
    o   Other (please specify): _____

57. How long has the current W course requirement been in existence?
    _____

58. Are there explicit writing goals for these courses?
    o   Yes
    o   No
    If yes, what are they? _____

59. What are the criteria for a writing intensive course? Feel free to provide a link to online information about the courses.
    _____

60. Do some courses taught in a foreign language qualify as W courses?
    o   Yes
    o   No
    If no, please explain: _____

61. Do some courses in creative writing qualify as W courses?
    o   Yes
    o   No
    If no, please explain: _____

62. Who certifies that a course meets the criteria? (department, curriculum committee, etc.) _____

63. Does the designation stay with the course and/or the professor?
    o   Yes
    o   No
    o   Maybe
    Please explain: _____

64. When are writing-intensive courses typically offered? (please check all that apply)
    o   first-year seminar
    o   across the curriculum at the introductory level
    o   across the curriculum at the mid-level
    o   across the curriculum at the upper level (predominately for majors)
    o   as part of a senior capstone exercise (for example, senior thesis)
    o   other (please specify): _____

65. Of the choices selected in question # 64, approximately what percentage of each are taught in relation to the total number of W courses offered? For example: 50% first seminar, 40% at the upper level, and 10% in senior capstones.
   o first-year seminar: _____
   o across the curriculum at the introductory level: _____
   o across the curriculum at the mid-level: _____
   o across the curriculum at the upper level (predominantly for majors): _____
   o as part of a senior capstone exercise (for example, senior thesis): _____
   o other: _____
66. Where are W courses distributed across the curriculum? (Ex: 40% humanities, 20% social sciences, 20% natural sciences, 20% interdisciplinary. Estimates are fine.) _____
67. Do W courses need to be completed by a certain time?
   o Yes
   o No
   Please explain: _____
68. Does your program or institution provide an incentive for faculty to teach W courses?
   o Yes
   o No
   Please explain: _____

Writing Center

69. Does your institution have a writing center or a learning center with writing tutors?
   o Yes
   o No
70. Is the writing center free-standing or part of a larger institutional unit?
   o Free-standing
   o Part of a larger institutional unit
   Name of larger unit: _____
71. Where is the writing or learning center located?
   o Academic building
   o Library
   o Own building
   o Dorm
   o Other (Please specify): _____

72. How large is your staff of WC tutors? _____

73. What percentage of your tutors are:
    o Undergraduates
    o Graduate students
    o Professionals who also teach in the writing program
    o Professionals who tutor only

74. How are they initially trained? (check all that apply)
    o full credit course
    o weekly meetings
    o workshops before a semester
    o they do not receive training
    o other (please specify): _____

75. Does your WC provide online tutoring?
    o Yes
    o No

76. Besides the standard services that a writing center offers, does your center offer additional services? (ex: help with oral communication, PowerPoint, new media, etc.) _____

Writing Fellows (course-based writing tutors)

77. Does your program have a writing fellows program? (Course-based writing tutors)
    o Yes
    o No
    o Other (please specify): _____

78. Do your writing fellows work both as fellows and in the writing center or are fellows and writing center employees two separate groups?
    o WFs do both jobs
    o Two separate jobs
    o Other (please specify): _____

79. What percentage of your tutors are placed in the following courses?
    o First-year composition: _____
    o First-year seminars: _____
    o Introductory courses throughout the curriculum:
      _____
    o Upper level courses throughout the curriculum:
      _____

80. How are your writing fellows trained?
    o In the same course as described for writing center tutors
    o Through additional training
    o They do not receive training
    Feel free to explain your answer: _____

Faculty Development

81. Are you responsible for faculty development?
    o Yes
    o No
82. If yes, is this responsibility shared with another unit on campus?
    o Yes
    o No
    If you answered yes, please explain.
83. What do you do for faculty development?
    o Facilitate a required workshop or seminar
    o Conduct an optional semester-long seminar
    o Conduct optional workshops
    o Conduct one-on-one consultations
    o Meet with departments
    o Host monthly lunches on a given topic
    o Meet informally with faculty
    o Other (please specify): _____

Assessment

84. What kinds of writing assessment does your institution do regularly? (Check all that apply.)
    o Assessment of student writing in writing courses.
    o Assessment of student writing in other courses.
    o Assessment of student writing over their four years.
    o Assessment of student writing in connection with College writing goals.
    o Assessment of the faculty development program.
    o Assessment of the impact of peer tutors on student writing.
    o Assessment for the purposes of passing a writing requirement.
    o Assessment to demonstrate students' writing proficiency
    o No assessment
    o Other (please explain): _____
85. Are you primarily responsible for any of these assessment projects?
    o Yes
    o No
    Please explain: _____
86. What kinds of data/assessment mechanisms do you use for these projects? (Check all that apply)
    o student surveys
    o faculty surveys
    o essay exam
    o random sample of student writing

o student portfolios

o other (please explain): _____

87. What is motivating assessment initiatives on your campus? (check all that apply)

o Accreditation

o College Mission

o Faculty interest

o Your own goals

o Other (please specify): _____

88. Does your school administer the NSSE?

o Yes

o No

89. If yes, how do you use these data within your writing program?

_____

Writing support

90. How do you identify underprepared writers? (Check all that apply)

o SAT scores

o Placement exam

o Faculty recommendation

o Student advisor

o Student self-identifies

o No identification takes place

o Other (please specify): _____

91. Are there additional writing requirements for these students?

o Yes

o No

If yes, please explain: _____

92. How does your program support underprepared students? (check all that apply)

o summer bridge program

o self-selection into a writing course

o writing center peer tutor

o writing center professional tutor

o WPA/WCD works with student

o workshops

o no resources available

o other (please specify): _____

93. Does your program/center offer additional support for students whose primary language is not English?

o Yes

o No

Please explain: _____

94. Does your program/center offer additional support for students with disabilities? Please explain.
    o Yes
    o No
    Please explain: _____

Overall role of writing

95. What initiatives do you wish to put into place in your program over the next 5–10 years? _____
96. Is there anything else you would like us to know about the culture of writing at your institution? _____
97. Our next step is to interview a subset of SLAC-ers about their writing program. Are you interested in being interviewed?
    o Yes
    o No
    o If yes, let us know if you are interested in a phone and/or in-person interview.

Appendix C: Initial E-mail
Invitation to Complete the Survey

Dear X,

I am writing to tell you about an exciting project and to request your help. Dara Rossman Regaignon, Lisa Lebduska, and I are conducting research on the role of writing and writing program administration at small liberal arts colleges (SLACs). This interest began when we created the SLAC consortium and through our analysis of the first SLAC survey. Now we want to expand the survey in order to flesh out a richer picture. The information gathered through this expanded survey will be used to write a book on small college writing program administration. We already have a book contract with Parlor Press.

Below is a link to our survey. We'd appreciate if you'd take some time to complete it. You'll notice that some of the questions are similar to the first survey. During the first round we discovered that people interpreted some questions differently than we intended or that we need more detailed responses in order to properly assess patterns. We also realize that even though our schools are similar, a simple survey may not capture the complexities of our local contexts. Throughout the survey you'll see many opportunities to "please explain" your response. Feel free to go into as much detail as you wish. We also realize that some programs may focus on more than writing and there are places in the survey that speak to this diversity.

The survey can be completed in multiple sittings as long as you use the same link that is in this message. We have set up the survey so you can go back and forth between questions and edit your responses as you go or up to two weeks from the time you begin the survey. If multiple people wish to work on the survey, you will need to access it through the same link in this message. We need only one survey from each school.

By completing the survey you are giving us permission to use the data. The data will be presented as a collective whole unless we seek additional permission from you to include you or your institution's name. Once we analyze the survey, we will be interviewing a sub-set of SLACers in order to create case studies. Unless we gain this additional permission the only place where the institution's name will appear is in a list of schools in the Annapolis Group, the data set for our project.

Besides our gratitude we can offer those who complete the survey an advanced copy of an article we have written using data from the first survey. In this piece we share data on writing requirements at SLACs and an initial portrait of the SLAC-WPA position. A few SLACers have already used these data to make cases on their own campuses.

The survey will remain open until June 15, 2009. If there are any problems while completing the survey or if you have any questions, please let me know.

Thank you in advance for your time and cooperation.

Appendix D: Supplemental Tables

Table D.1 Age of W Course Requirement.

Number of years of W course requirement	Number of schools
1–5 years	7
6–10 years	14
11–15 years	6
15–20 years	3
20+ years	13
Data UA	1

Table D.2 Length of Time as the WPA.

Number of years	Number of schools
0–3 years	33% (n=27)
4–5 years	7% (n=6)
6–10 years	17% (n=14)
11–15 years	10% (n=8)
16–20 years	12% (n=10)
21–30 years	5% (n=4)
31+ years	2% (n=2)
Unknown	13% (n=11)
Total:	N=82

Table D.3 Number of People Involved in Administering Writing "Program."

Number of people	Number of schools
0	2
1	35
2	47
3	12
4	4
Total	100

Table D.4 Number of Course Releases Assigned to WPA.

Regular course load	# of course releases	# of schools
2–2	1	1
	2	3
2–2–2	4	1
2–3	0	3
	1	8
	2	9
	3	2
	Varies	1
	Data unavailable	1
3–1–2	3	1
3–1–3	1	1
	2	2
3–3	0	3
	.5	1
	1	8
	2	11
	3	2
	4	1
	Data unavailable	1
3–4	0	2
	2	3
4–4	0	1
	4	1
6–6	2	1
6 blocks	0	1
4.5	0	1
5.5	1	1
Data Unavailable	—	11

Appendix E: Assessment Materials from Occidental College

Writing Assessment for First-Year Students

To be conducted in 2005–2006, 2006–2007, 2007–2008, 2008–2009. The Director of Core and Director of the Writing Programs have decided to continue this writing assessment for first-year students as it alternates in some meaningful way with third- and fourth-year student assessments.

- Fall CSP Seminar faculty will collect an early fall semester writing sample from each student. If the first assignment is not academic in nature (e.g., personal narrative), then they should collect the second sample. All papers, along with the writing prompt, will be forwarded to the Core Program Office.
- Spring CSP Seminar/Colloquia faculty will collect the final researched paper from each student. All papers, along with the writing prompt, will be forwarded to the Core Program Office.
- The Associate Dean for Curriculum will ask the Registrar to generate a list of 75 randomly selected freshman students who completed their first full year at Occidental. This list will be generated in order (i.e., not alphabetized).
- The Core Program Office will begin at the top of the list above and select the first 50 students for whom we have all three writing samples:
    o A sample of writing from early in the fall semester CSP course
    o The timed writing exercise essay (retained by the CAE after the February timed-writing exercise)
    o The final researched essay from the spring semester CSP course
- In addition to the 50 students above, all students participating in the CSP 89 1-unit credit experience "Information Literacy/Library Research," who are not already part of the sample of 50, will be added to the sample. [This was added in 2006–2007 as a way to examine the impact of CSP 89 on students' researched papers.]
- This selected group of students will be compared with the general frosh class on the basis of demographic and incoming academic ratings by the Director of Institutional Research, and any significant differences will be noted in the final report.
- The Core Program Office will blind all these writing samples, and will be the only place information will be kept on who the samples were from.
- The Associate Dean for Curriculum and the Director of the Writing Program will work together to engage 8–10 faculty members, includ-

ing some who will teach in the CSP program in the subsequent year, to participate in the assessment of student writing. These faculty, along with writing program specialists, will participate in a day of training and evaluation during the summer.

- Each writing sample will be scored using the 6-point rubric from the Writing Program Essay Scoring Guide.
- An additional qualitative rubric by which strengths and problems of each students' writing over time can be noted. Examples may include Critical Analysis, Thesis and Topic Sentences, Evidence, Structure, Power & Authority, etc.
- At the end of the day of evaluation, the group will take approximately one hour to debrief together, with the Associate Dean for Curriculum keeping notes, problems that were seen consistently throughout the writing, strengths that were heartening, themes that may help us as future CSP and writing instructors.
- Quantitative data from these assessments will be compared with the existing assessments for these students:
  - o Fall CSP writing evaluation done by each individual CSP faculty
  - o Timed writing exercise evaluation from spring
  - o Spring CSP writing evaluation done by each individual CSP faculty
  - o If possible, we can also compare this information with external measures for these students (e.g., SAT, writing scores prior to Oxy)
  - o Quantitative data and measurement of change may also be examined correcting for certain measures (e.g., SAT, writing scores prior to Oxy)
- Qualitative data will be assessed by the writing program specialists and documented in terms of:
  - o Common writing problems
  - o Problems that are improved over time
  - o Problems that are not improved over time
  - o And others as identified
- A final summary report of quantitative/qualitative findings and the debrief, along with specific recommendations, will be prepared jointly by the Associate Dean for Curriculum and the Director of the Writing Program. This document will be shared with the faculty generally and the CSP faculty in particular, and be used to modify the existing workshops for CSP on writing instruction and guidelines for the CSP courses.

Writing Assessment for Third-Year Students

Conducted Summer, 2009.

- Early in the spring semester, the Associate Dean for Curriculum will notify students who were chosen in the first-year assessment cohort two years previously (who still remain at the College), that they are part of a randomly selected group who have been chosen to participate in our college-wide writing assessment.
- Students will be asked to submit one thesis-driven argument or analysis paper that they have written or will write in their third year, along with the faculty prompt for this paper. It should be noted that papers will come from students writing across the curriculum, although the papers must be written for a course, and must be for the academic discourse community. Preferably, this paper will be drawn from a course consistent with the junior writing requirement process within her or his major. Often, in 2009 however, students turned in papers for other upper level courses.
- An incentive scheme should be developed to encourage wide participation. It wasn't in the 2009 iteration.
- These papers will be reviewed in the same summer meeting as the writing assessment for first-year students. They will be rated with the same 6-point rubric from the Writing Program Essay Scoring Guide. The qualitative rubric used in the assessment of first-year writing will also be used, with the focus was on the complexity of the assignments and writing tasks and the maturity and the sophistication of the writing. Additionally, an academic research rubric will be included, permitting reviewers to assess students' use of appropriate research in the context of the text (assignment, class, discipline,).
- The quantitative rubric rating will be compared against those given these students in the first year. This, however, is secondary to the attention given to the features rubric and the research rubric.
- If necessary, in certain instances, the Director of Core and Director of the Writing Programs, and the writing specialists will review both first-year papers and this third-year paper from this sample, looking in greater detail at whether assignments and student writing has matured and become more sophisticated and complex. This review is dependent on the conduct and discussion of the reviewers in the assessment session.
- A report on third-year writing will be included in the final summary report noted above under first-year writing.
- A writing evaluation in NISSE was done for the first time in Spring 2009. Data garnered from this instrument will be included in the final report—once it is made available.

Future Possibilities in Writing Assessment
for Third- and Fourth-Year Students

- Interview members of the cohorts—talk with a selected focus group of students from the cohorts near the end of their junior year or in their senior year about the writing instruction they have or have not received, whether they feel they have improved or not in their writing, and student feedback and suggestions on writing instruction and development at the College.
- In students' fourth year, collect the final written work associated with the comprehensive projects for all students in each cohort and review these, again in relation to their previously collected work.

Initially drafted: June 8, 2006

Revised to reflect current practice in first-year writing assessment: September 12, 2007

Revised to include third-year writing assessment process: July 12, 2009

Table E.1 Occidental College's Features Rubric.

	Exxcellent	Good	Adequate	Thin	Problematic
Evidence which:					
supports thesis					
offers relevant background					
explains methodology					
provides examples or exhibits					
General Source Use (kind, context, relevance)					
Appropriate number of sources					
Connection to broader academic conversation					
	Yes	No			
Citation Method Consistently Used					

Table E.2 Occidental College's Research Rubric.

COLLEGE WIDE WRITING ASSESSMENT FORM

Early Fall Sample
Timed Writing Sample
Spring Research Essay

Individual Papers

Writer Number: _____

Reader Name: _____

Use the grid rubric below to assess the student's writing overall - all three papers. Circle one choice in each column, and underline specifics in each category that were especially strong or especially problematic. Note explicit themes of interest or areas of improvement/concern in box below.

	Critical Analysis	Thesis/Topic Sentences	Evidence	Structure	Power & Authority
High Proficiency	Clear, specific, compelling argument; good claims backed by evidence, sophisticated insights tying together several concepts learned in college. Anticipates reader's needs.	Fresh, challenging idea. Precise. Adds "so what?" to thesis to push it to greater complexities; clear relationship b/w thesis & TSs; arguments have substance; not obvious.	Claims supported well with reliable, high quality sources cited well; evidence analyzed thoroughly, quotes not too long, no descriptions; sufficient quantity and quality. Excellent citation style.	Sequence of ideas is effective. Clearly makes sense and engages reader while supporting analysis. Sentences cogent and effective, as are transitions. Nice relationship b/w intro & concl. Clear TS & "so what?".	Confident, mature syntax & diction precise, appropriate, advanced. Tone is mature, not banal or grandiose; dynamic; good vocab; edits effectively.
Proficiency	Good understanding of texts; fully explores prompt, still not addressing why reader should care about this topic &/or interpretation. Good style may be masking slightly shallow analysis.	Contains a clear argument central to essay, but could deepen it by adding "so what", all TSs tie into thesis, supporting it, although TSs could have a bit more variety & depth.	Pursues thesis; clear major points are clearly linked to cited sources, either relies too much on citations (rather than analysis) or needs more evidence or better evidence. Cited well.	Well-constructed paragraphs & sentences. Good use of opening & closing. May have some confusion of topics or sequence within paragraphs. Occasional sentence infelicity.	Employs a variety of sentence structures, though perhaps uneven control. Mostly avoids clichés, diction accurate, generally appropriate for content though less advanced. A few errors.
Some Proficiency	More a report or an account than an analysis, needs to discuss consequences of thesis. Analysis may contain contradictions, tends to be superficial.	Thesis is too general - needs to answer "so what" or discuss importance or consequences of argument; may need to define central terms. TSs not clearly related to thesis.	Limited consideration or use of evidence, excessive quotes or not nearly enough; needs to tie evidence better to claim; Needs to learn and use a citation style.	Distinct units of thought in each para, but sequence of ideas may be off. May not yet use TS effectively. May need to tie TS to thesis and improve transitions. Sentences too often flawed. Intro & concl may not be working together.	Sentences show little variety, simplistic. Diction somewhat immature. Problems with grammar or spelling; analysis impaired by style. May have good ideas which writer cannot articulate well. Pattern of flaws.
Limited Proficiency	Inadequate command of material; perhaps not arguing or discussing thesis throughout, reporting, not analyzing; little dialogue with college community; just states opinions.	Thesis is descriptive, factual, or not central to argument. Needs to interpret, rather than restate the obvious, no clarifying TSs.	Narrates rather than analyzes; insufficient use of textual evidence or relies too much on superficial sources; OPINIONS rather than dialogue/analysis supported by specific & cited evidence. Citation system off.	Wanders, illogical argument; not yet using/understanding an organizational method. Sentences garbled or incomplete. Expository essay components missing	Superficial and stereotypical language. Oral rather than written language pattern. Serious problems in writing, editing, proofreading, or grammar.

General Notes

Appendix F: List of Questions for Schools to Consider when Investigating Writing Program Structures

- What are the sites of writing? More specifically, what are the explicit and embedded writing requirements (if both exist)? How are those sites delivered, supported, and otherwise sustained?
- What are the positions charged with the administration of writing? More specifically, where are explicit and/or embedded writing program administrators and writing center directors located?
- What is the relationship of both of those WPAs to the explicit and/or embedded requirements? What kinds of power, authority, and influence do they have over them?
- Which sites of writing are not administered by either WPA? How are they administered?
- What are the strengths and drawbacks of a chosen leadership configuration? When is it time to change a configuration?
- Are there systems in place to identify students likely to struggle—for a variety of reasons—and to prevent those students from falling through the cracks? Do those systems provide students with opportunities for agency and the information necessary to make good choices?
- Are the support systems for those students consonant with the institution's culture of writing and structure of feeling? Are they adequately resourced?
- What is the relationship between the curricular side, support side and other institutional structures in regards to diversely prepared students? Do they work collaboratively to identify and support all student writers?

Notes

Introduction: Studying Writing Programs at Small Liberal Arts Colleges

1. Small liberal arts colleges are becoming particularly visible in the historical record. In addition to the chapters by Donahue and Falbo, Garbus, Weidner, and Welsch, all in Donahue and Moon's *Local Histories*, see the excellent archival work of Bordelon, Campbell, Conway, D'Ann George, L'Eplattenier, Lawrence, Mastrangelo, McDonald, Spring, and Varnum. Brereton's invaluable *The Origins of Composition Studies* includes documents from faculty and administrators affiliated with Amherst, Carleton, Centre, Davidson, Hamilton, Swarthmore, Union, Vassar, Wabash, Wellesley, and Williams Colleges and Wesleyan University. Throughout the book, we draw on the work of small college compositionists and writing program administrators, and have placed an asterisk on works in the Works Cited that highlight small colleges in general or specific small college writing programs.

2. Our analysis often teases out differences between the writing *program* administrator positions and writing *center* administrator positions. When not explicitly making the distinction between WPA (writing program administrator) and WCD (writing center director), however, we follow the custom of using the term WPA to encompass all the work of leading, facilitating, supporting, assessing, and developing a culture of writing. (For a pertinent discussion, see Ianetta et al.)

Chapter 1: The Small Liberal Arts College Structure of Feeling

1. The distinction between public and private institutions began to be operative only after the 1819 Supreme Court case, *Dartmouth v. Woodward*. This case was catalyzed by the New Hampshire legislature's attempt to seize administrative and governance control of Dartmouth, including changing the composition of the board of trustees, granting the governor the power to appoint members of the board, and creating a board of visitors with the power to veto trustees' decisions (see Rudolph 207–210 and Tewksbury 64–66):

"Although serving a public purpose, Dartmouth, said the Court, was essentially an expression of private philanthropy" and was therefore subject to the control of its board of trustees, not the state (Rudolph 210). Daniel Webster argued on behalf of Dartmouth College.

2. Page numbers refer to the original 1828 *Report*. For discussions of the *Yale Report*, its contemporary context, and larger implications for histories of U.S. liberal arts education, see Pak; Urofsky.

3. Whether we identify modern WAC with Barbara Walvoord's faculty development workshops at Central College, Harriet Sheridan's writing fellows program at Carleton, or Elaine Maimon's NEH-funded initiative at Beaver—or, more strikingly, with all three—we see that something about the conditions of small colleges makes fertile ground for writing. See Russell (*Writing* 282–86 and "Historical Perspective" 62). On Central College, see Walvoord ("Gender and Discipline"); on Carleton College, see Maimon ("It Takes a Campus" 20–22; Rutz, Hardy, and Condon); on Beaver College, see Maimon ("Beaver College" and "It Takes a Campus").

4. Here and elsewhere, we are drawing on Williams' notion of residual, dominant, and emergent as well as that of structures of feeling (see *Marxism and Literature*). For an in-depth analysis of emergent and counter-hegemonic practices at a small college, see Bruce Horner's discussion of Amherst College's English 1-2.

5. For a general overview of the early curricula and goals of the northeastern women's colleges, see Rudolph (317–19). For more specific discussions of the early curricula of Morehouse, Vassar, Mount Holyoke, Wellesley, and Spelman in particular, see Jones, L'Eplattenier, Mastrangelo, and Read, respectively. Interestingly, Spelman moved away from the classical curriculum and toward a vocational course of study focused on the preparation of its students for careers in nursing and teaching in the 1890s; it shifted again later in the twentieth century.

6. For a fuller discussion of the philosophy and context of the *Yale Report*, see Pak; Urofsky.

7. Many of the moments when these conversations erupt are moments when the college-going population is expanding. This was true in the 1820s and 1830s (see Potts) and between 1850 and 1920 (see Brereton, *Origins* 7). It was true again in the 1950s and the 1970s. These waves of increased diversity and consequent curricular reform are dialectical. The 1820s expansion led to experiments with curricular choice, experiments effectively quashed by the *Yale Report*'s influence. Similarly, the expansion of the college population in the last quarter of the nineteenth century led permanently to greater curricular choice, while that in the middle of the twentieth century led institutions to back away from such choice ever so slightly. Finally, the surge in the 1970s—including at small liberal arts colleges like Carleton—led to a new focus on writing and launched the modern WAC movement. In every case,

the influx of more—and more diversely prepared—students leads to a productive re-examination of some of the fundamental precepts of college-level education. Small liberal arts colleges are at another such moment today, re-examining and re-committing to the liberal arts for the twenty-first century.

8. To protect the identity of the schools in our sample, we treat mission statements, websites, and college catalogs as site documents, which do not require citation. Throughout, when directly discussing a school, we use pseudonyms except in instances (such as in Chapter 11) where the schools have given us permission to name them. Despite our best efforts to protect the confidentiality of our respondents and the participating schools, however, it is always possible that their identities could be uncovered, particularly given that many of the site documents we reference are publicly available. When sharing descriptions of schools from published literature, we left names as presented in those articles.

9. While all institutions expect service of faculty, small schools place a greater emphasis on college-wide service than do larger institutions. At many small schools, faculty are expected to serve on at least one college-wide committee starting in their second year, in addition to departmental service. Hanstedt argues from the context of Roanoke College that "the ways in which [faculty members] have added to the day-to-day life of the college" weigh most heavily on tenure and promotion committees' minds (81). The most elite SLACs, which typically have a 2/2 teaching load and pre-tenure leave, have research expectations closer to those of research universities. Faculty are still expected to have a college-wide presence at tenure time, however, and to have made visible contributions to the institution as a whole. In an essay in *Profession*, Ed Folsom argues that graduate students are best suited for small college jobs when they are "developed as well-rounded departmental citizens" in graduate school, rather than "as emerging scholarly stars" (128).

CHAPTER 2: MIXED METHODS AND GROUNDED THEORY RESEARCH

1. The present moment for this discussion is the 2009–2010 academic year. As we discuss below, the survey was administered in the summer of 2009, with subsequent data collection and analysis occurring through March, 2010.

2. We excluded one school from the HEDS data set because it is a two-year college within a larger university. Because our focus is on four-year institutions, we decided that it was too different from the rest of the set. Our sample includes schools that were listed as members of these two consortia in May, 2009. It is possible that other schools have joined either consortium since then.

3. The latter school's enrollment is actually comprised of the joint figure for two affiliated institutions.

4. As we have pointed out, we each completed the survey as participant researchers and so account for two of the 109 schools.

Chapter 4: Configurations of Writing Program Leadership

1. On the importance of collaboration between writing programs and writing centers, see Carino, "Writing Centers and Writing Programs"; Ianetta, McCamley, and Quick; and Waldo.

2. See McClure. For a series of narratives doing justice to this metaphor, see George's *Kitchen Cooks, Plate Twirlers, and Troubadours*.

Chapter 5: Positioning of Writing Program Administrators

1. For discussion of similar issues, see Thaiss and Porter (538–39) and Enos and Borrowman (14–15).

2. As noted in Chapter 4, for the schools that have both a WPA and a WCD (that is, with either *Explicit WPA + Explicit WCD* or *Embedded WPA + Explicit WCD* configuration), we contacted both individuals so that we could have a full picture of the responsibilities included in those configurations. In Table 5.1, we did not include embedded WPAs because we lack most of those data. There are also no data available for three WCDs and one explicit WPA.

3. For further discussion of the relationships between writing centers and WAC programs, see the essays collected in "Writing Centers and Writing Across the Curriculum: A Symbiotic Relationship?" (Barnett and Blumner, *The Longman Guide to Writing Center Theory and Practice* [410–473]).

4. For more advice, both for candidates and for reviewing committees, see Boyer, *Scholarship Assessed* and *Scholarship Reconsidered*; Roen et al., "Reconsidering."

Chapter 6: Writing Requirements

1. Question number 50 asked: "Are there explicit goals for first year writing?" Approximately 85% of respondents answered affirmatively. (Of the fifteen respondents who reported their first year-writing programs did *not* have goals, seven were first-year writing seminar programs, and four were first-year composition.) Respondents who indicated that their programs *did* have goals were asked on the survey to provide either the text of the goals or a link to where they could be found online. Once we had categorized the first-year writing requirements of the different schools, we sorted the schools

by category (FYC or FYWS) and selected every fourth school within each group, irrespective of their survey response to question 50. For those selected schools (9 FYC, 10 FYWS), we first looked at the response to question 50 and then visited each program's website to see if a goals statement was posted. We felt that this gave us an adequate random sample, comprising 24% percent of FYC schools and 22% percent of FYWS schools, and so did not follow-up further with respondents.

Our textual analysis examined each program's goals statement or program description in comparison to the CWPA "Outcomes Statement" in order to see its concerns and values reflected there. Since none of the goals statements from participating schools provided the detail of the "Outcomes Statement," we looked for language that echoed its categories.

2. The recent "Writing Infusion vs. FYC" thread on WPA-L also addresses this issue, and the difference institutional size makes in this context; see Schwartz et al., "Writing Infusion vs. FYC."

3. Anson and Dannels discuss this type of approach at North Carolina State University; see also the NCTE-WPA White Paper on the importance of such transparency.

CHAPTER 7: STAFFING FIRST-YEAR WRITING

1. We utilized two different measures when asking respondents about who teaches first-year writing. When asking about the status of who teaches first-year writing, we asked in terms of the percentage of staff that holds each level of status. It is possible that ten percent of a teaching staff can be teaching more or less than ten percent of the sections of FYW. However, we also asked what percentage of sections of first-year writing are taught by individuals only teaching academic writing courses, teaching academic courses and English courses, and those teaching academic writing courses and courses across the disciplines.

2. Bracketed ellipses in transcripts indicate an unclear word or phrase that the transcriber was unable to decode.

3. The exchange catalyzed by Catherine Pastore Blair's "Only One of the Voices" addresses these issues in the context of where to house leadership for writing across the curriculum. See Blair, "Only One," and both "Response" pieces; Howard, Hess, and Darby; Kirsch, Finkel, and France; and Smith, "Why" and "Responds."

CHAPTER 8: SMALL COLLEGE WRITING PROGRAMS: LEADERSHIP CONFIGURATIONS AND REQUIREMENTS

1. We did not include categories for either leadership configurations or writing requirements that contained fewer than two schools. Mid-level and thesis requirements were too difficult to factor into this analysis.

CHAPTER 9: WRITING CENTERS

1. On writing fellows as ambassadors, see Severino and Knight, "Exploring." For a discussion of how direct contact with writing center peer tutors can foster faculty respect for the writing center, see Carino, Floyd, and Lightle.

CHAPTER 10: SUPPORTING DIVERSELY PREPARED WRITERS

1. For fuller discussions of the stretch model, see Blakesley; Glau ("The 'Stretch Program'" and "Stretch at 10"). Grego and Thompson ("Repositioning Remediation" and "The Writing Studio") elaborate the studio model, and Segall advocates the intensive model. Soliday (see also Soliday and Gleason) describes mainstreaming; see also the essays collected in McNenny's *Mainstreaming Basic Writers*.

2. The number for professional tutors differs from the data presented in Chapter 9. For some reason, seven respondents who listed a percentage of their staff as professional tutors did not present these same staff as a resource for underprepared students. Perhaps the professional tutors at these schools work with *all* students, so the respondents did not list them as resources exclusively designated for underprepared students.

3. There is a wealth of tutor training literature on this. See, in particular, Blau and Hall; Gillespie and Lerner; Muriel Harris, "Cultural Conflicts"; Muriel Harris and Silva; Myers; and the essays collected in Bruce and Rafoth's *ESL Writers: A Guide for Writing Center Tutors*.

CHAPTER 11: ASSESSMENT

1. The assessment questions appeared near the end of the survey. We therefore worried that respondents would be suffering from survey fatigue and only asked six questions on this topic, all closed. As with any survey, it's possible that respondents interpreted the questions in different ways, responding to the use of the words "regularly" or "institutional" assessment rather than the assessment they may do on their own. These data alone do not allow us to make broad claims about assessment at small colleges. We therefore decided to explore in more depth three schools from the sample with interesting approaches to writing assessment. Our initial knowledge of these programs came from the survey, website analysis, and personal conversations. All three informants reviewed this chapter before publication in order to make sure that their programs and assessment practices were represented accurately.

Works Cited

* Asterisked sources focus on small colleges.

Adler-Kassner, Linda. *Activist WPA: Changing Stories about Writing and Writers.* Logan: Utah State UP, 2008. Print.

*Amorose, Thomas. "WPA Work at the Small College or University: Re-Imagining Power and Making the Small School Visible." *WPA: Writing Program Administration* 23 (2000): 85–103. Print.

Annapolis Group. "About the Annapolis Group." *Collegenews.org.* The Annapolis Group, 2009. Web. 26 Mar. 2010.

Anson, Chris M. "The Intelligent Design of Writing Programs: Reliance on Belief or a Future of Evidence." *WPA: Writing Program Administration* 32.1/2 (2008): 11–36. Print.

—. "Who Wants Composition? Reflections on the Rise and Fall of an Independent Program." *A Field of Dreams: Independent Writing Programs and the Future of Composition Studies.* Ed. Peggy O'Neill, Angela Crow, and Larry Burton. Logan: Utah State UP, 2002. 153–69. Print.

—, and Deanna Dannels. "Profiling Programs: Formative Uses of Departmental Consultations in the Assessment of Communication Across the Curriculum." *Across the Disciplines* 6 (2009): n. pag. Web. 30 June 2011.

Arum, Richard, and Josipa Joksa. *Academically Adrift: Limited Learning on College Campuses.* Chicago: U of Chicago P, 2011. Print.

Balester, Valerie, and James C. McDonald. "A View of Status and Working Conditions: Relations Between Writing Program and Writing Center Directors." *WPA: Writing Program Administration* 24.3 (2001): 59–82. Print.

Bamberg, Betty. "Alternative Models of First-Year Composition: Possibilities and Problems." *WPA: Writing Program Administration* 21.1 (1992): 7–18. Print.

Barnett, Robert W., and Jacob S. Blumner, eds. *Longman Guide to Writing Center Theory and Practice.* New York: Pearson/Longman, 2008. Print.

Bartholomae, David. "Inventing the University." *When a Writer Can't Write: Studies in Writer's Block and Other Composing-Process Problems.* Ed. Mike Rose. New York: Guilford, 1985. 134–65. Print.

Bedore, Pamela, and Deborah F. Rossen-Knill. "Informed Self-Placement: Is a Choice Offered a Choice Received?" *WPA: Writing Program Administration* 28.1–2 (2004): 55–78. Print.

Bergmann, Linda S., and Janet S. Zepernik. "Disciplinarity and Transfer: Students' Perceptions of Learning to Write." *WPA: Writing Program Administration* 31.1/2 (2007): 124–49. Print.

Berlin, James A. *Rhetoric and Reality: Writing Instruction in American Colleges, 1900–1985*. Carbondale: Southern Illinois UP, 1987. Print.

—. *Writing Instruction in Nineteenth-Century American Colleges*. Carbondale: Southern Illinois UP, 1984. Print.

Blakesley, David. "Directed Self-Placement in the University." *WPA: Writing Program Administration* 25.3 (2002): 9–40. Print.

Blair, Catherine Pastore. "Only One of the Voices: Dialogic Writing across the Curriculum." *College English* 50.4 (April 1988): 383–89. Print.

—. "Response [to Gesa Kirsch, De Ann C. Finkel, and Alan W. France]." *College English* 51.1 (1989): 103–106. Print.

—. "Response [to Rebecca M. Howard; David Hess; Margaret F. Darby]." *College English* 51.4 (1989): 435–37. Print.

Blau, Susan, and John Hall, assisted by Sarah Sparks. "Guilt-Free Tutoring: Rethinking How We Tutor Non-Native-English-Speaking Students." *Writing Center Journal* 23.1 (2002): 23–44. Print.

Boehm, Diane. "Traditional Criteria: Solution or Stumbling Block?" *WPA: Writing Program Administration* 20.3 (1997): 17–19. Print.

Bok, Derek. *Our Underachieving Colleges: A Candid Look at How Much Students Learn and Why They Should Be Learning More*. Princeton: Princeton UP, 2005. Print.

Boquet, Elizabeth H. "'Our Little Secret': A History of Writing Centers Pre- to Post-Open Admissions." Barnett and Blumner 41–60. Print.

—. *Writing Centers: History, Theory, and Implications*. Diss. Indiana U., 1995. Ann Arbor: UMI, 1995. Print.

*Bordelon, Suzanne. "The 'Advance' Toward Democratic Administration: Laura Johnson Wylie and Gertrude Buck of Vassar College." *Historical Studies of Writing Program Administration: Individuals, Communities, and the Formation of a Discipline*, Ed. Barbara L'Eplattenier and Lisa Mastrangelo. West Lafayette, Indiana: Parlor Press. 91–116. Print.

*—. *A Feminist Legacy: The Rhetoric and Pedagogy of Gertrude Buck*. Carbondale: Southern Illinois UP, 2007. Print.

Bousquet, Marc, Tony Scott, and Leo Parascondola, eds. *Tenured Bosses and Disposable Teachers: Writing Instruction in the Managed University*. Carbondale: Southern Illinois UP, 2003. Print.

Boyer, Ernest L. *Scholarship Assessed: Evaluation of the Professoriate*. San Francisco: Jossey-Bass, 1997. Print.

—. *Scholarship Reconsidered: Priorities of the Professoriate*. Princeton: Carnegie Foundation, 1990. Print.

Braine, George. "ESL Students in First-Year Writing Courses: ESL versus Mainstream Classes." *Journal of Second Language Writing* 5.2 (1996): 91–107. Print.

Brent, Doug. "Reinventing WAC (Again): The First-Year Seminar and Academic Literacy." *College Composition and Communication* 57.2 (2005): 253–76. Print.

Brereton, John C., ed. *The Origins of Composition Studies in the American College, 1875–1925: A Documentary History*. Pittsburgh: U of Pittsburgh P, 1995. Print.

—, ed. *Traditions of Inquiry*. New York: Oxford UP, 1985. Print.

Broad, Bob. *What We Really Value: Beyond Rubrics in Teaching and Assessing Writing*. Logan: Utah UP, 2003. Print.

Broad, Bob, et al. *Organic Writing Assessment: Dynamic Criteria Mapping in Action*. Logan: Utah State UP, 2009. Print.

*Bromley, Pam, Kara Northway, and Eliana Schonberg. "How Important Is the Local, Really? Cross-Institutional Quantitative Assessment of Typical Writing Center Exit Surveys." *Writing Center Journal* (forthcoming 2012). Manuscript.

Brown, Stuart C., and Theresa Enos, eds. *The Writing Program Administrator's Resource: A Guide to Reflective Institutional Practice*. Mahwah: Lawrence Erlbaum, 2002. Print.

Bruce, Shanti, and Ben Rafoth, eds. *ESL Writers: A Guide for Writing Center Tutors*. 2nd ed. Portsmouth: Boynton/Cook, 2009. Print.

Bruffee, Kenneth A. "Peer Tutoring and the 'Conversation of Mankind.'" *Landmark Essays on Writing Centers*. Ed. Christina Murphy and Joe Law. New York: Routledge, 1995. Print.

*Cady, Frank W. "The Laboratory Method at Middlebury College." *The English Journal* 4.2 (1915): 124–25. Print.

*Campbell, JoAnn. "'A Real Vexation': Student Writing in Mount Holyoke's Culture of Service, 1837–1865." *College English* 59.7 (1997): 767–88. Print.

*—. "Controlling Voices: The Legacy of English A at Radcliffe College 1883–1917." *College Composition and Communication* 43.4 (1992): 472–85. Print.

*—. "Freshman (Sic) English: A 1901 Wellesley College 'Girl' Negotiates Authority." *College Composition and Communication* 15.1 (1996): 110–27. Print.

*—. "Women's Work, Worthy Work: Composition Instruction at Vassar, 1897–1922." *Constructing Rhetorical Education*. Ed. Marie Secor and Davida Charney. Carbondale: Southern Illinois UP, 1992. 26–42. Print.

Carino, Peter. "Early Writing Centers: Toward a History." Barnett and Blumner 10–22. Print.

—. "Writing Centers and Writing Programs." *The Politics of Writing Centers*. Ed. Jane V. Nelson and Kathy Evertz. Portsmouth: Boynton/Cook Heinemann, 2001. 1–14. Print.

—, Lori Floyd, and Marcia Lightle. "Empowering a Writing Center: The Faculty Meets the Tutors." *Writing Lab Newsletter* 16.2 (1991): 1–5. Print.

*Carroll, Shireen, Bruce Pegg, and Stephen Newmann. "Size Matters: Administering a Writing Center in a Small College Setting." *Writing Lab Newsletter* 24.5 (2000): 1–5. Print.

Charlton, Jonikka, and Shirley K Rose. "Twenty More Years in the WPA's Progress." *WPA: Writing Program Administration* 22.1/2 (2009): 114–145. Print.

Cobb, Loretta, and Elaine K. Elledge. "Peer Tutors as a Source of Power for Basic Writers." *Teaching English in the Two-Year College* 9.2 (183): 135–40. Print.

Condon, William. "Accommodating Complexity: WAC Program Evaluation in the Age of Accountability." McLeod, Miraglia, Soven, and Thaiss 28–51. Print.

Conference on College Composition and Communication. *Statement of Principles and Standards for Postsecondary Teaching of Writing*. National Council of Teachers of English. 2007. Web. 1 July 2011.

—. *Statement on Second Language Writing and Writers*. National Council of Teachers of English. 2009. Web. 28 July 2010.

—. *Writing Assessment: A Position Statement*. National Council of Teachers of English, Mar. 2009. Web. 2 June 2010.

Connors, Robert J. "The Abolition Debate in Composition: A Short History." *Composition in the Twenty-First Century: Crisis and Change*. Ed. Lynn Z. Bloom, Donald A. Daiker, and Edward M. White. Carbondale: Southern Illinois UP, 1996. 47–63. Print.

—. *Composition-Rhetoric: Backgrounds, Theory, and Pedagogy*. Pittsburgh: U of Pittsburgh P, 1997. Print.

*Conway, Kathryn M. "Woman Suffrage and the History of Rhetoric at the Seven Sisters Colleges, 1865–1919." *Reclaiming Rhetorica: Women in the Rhetorical Tradition*. Ed. Andrea A. Lunsford. Pittsburgh: U of Pittsburgh P, 1995. 203–27. Print.

*Cornell, Cynthia E., and Robert D. Newton. "The Case of a Small Liberal Arts University: Directed Self-Placement at DePauw." Royer and Gilles 149–78. Print.

Council of Writing Program Administrators (CWPA). "WPA Assessment Gallery: Assessment Models." *WPAcouncil.org*. n.d. Web. 27 July 2010.

—. "Evaluating the Intellectual Work of Writing Program Administrators." *WPAcouncil.org*. 1998. Web. 27 July 2010.

—. "Outcomes Statement for First-Year Composition." *WPAcouncil.org*. 2008. Web. 27 July 2010.

CWPA-NSSE (National Survey of Student Engagement). "Consortium for the Study of Writing in College." CWPA-NSSE. Mar. 2010. Web. 29 July 2010.

Crowley, Sharon. *Composition in the University: Historical and Polemical Essays*. Pittsburgh: U of Pittsburgh P, 1998. Print.

Dartmouth College v. Woodward. 17 U.S. 518. Supreme Court of the US. 1819. *Lexis-Nexis,* n.d. Web. 29 July 2009.

*Deis, Elizabeth J., Lowell T. Frye, and Katherine J. Weese. "Independence Fostering Community: The Benefits of an Independent Writing Program at a Small Liberal Arts College." *A Field of Dreams: Independent Writing Programs and the Future of Composition Studies*. Ed. Peggy O'Neill, Angela Crow, and Larry Burton. Logan: Utah State UP, 2002. 75–89. Print.

Dew, Debra Frank, and Alice Horning. *Untenured Faculty as Writing Program Administrators: Institutional Policies and Practices*. Anderson, SC: Parlor P, 2007. Print.

Dickson, Marcia. "Directing Without Power: Adventures in Constructing a Model of Feminist Writing Program Administration." *Writing Ourselves Into the Story: Unheard Voices from Composition Studies*. Ed. Sheryl I. Fontaine and Susan Hunter. Carbondale: Southern Illinois UP, 1993. 140–53. Print.

"Discipline." *The Oxford English Dictionary*. Online ed. Oxford: Oxford UP, 2010. Web. 14 May 2010.

*Donahue, Patricia. "Disciplinary Histories: A Meditation on Beginnings." Donahue and Moon 220–37. Print.

*—, and Bianca Falbo. "(The Teaching of) Reading and Writing at Lafayette College." Donahue and Moon 38–58. Print.

*—, and Gretchen Flesher Moon, eds. *Local Histories: Reading the Archives of Composition*. Pittsburgh, PA: University of Pittsburgh P, 2007. Print.

Downs, Douglas, and Elizabeth Wardle. "Teaching about Writing, Righting Misconceptions: (Re)Envisioning 'First-Year Composition' as 'Introduction to Writing Studies." *College Composition and Communication* 58.4 (2007): 552–84. Print.

*Dreier, Peter, and Robert Gottlieb. "Occidental's Core Mission of Research with a Problem-Solving Focus Must be the Goal for the Next Generation." *Los Angeles Times* 14 Aug. 1998: 9. Print.

Elbow, Peter. "Writing Assessment in the Twenty-First Century: A Utopian View." *Composition in the Twenty-First Century: Crisis and Change*. Ed. Lynn Z. Bloom, Donald Daiker, and Edward M. White. Carbondale: Southern Illinois UP, 1996. 83–100. Print.

Enos, Theresa, and Shane Borrowman. *The Promise and Perils of Writing Program Administration*. West Lafayette: Parlor P, 2008. Print.

Faigley, Lester. "Writing Centers in Times of Whitewater." *Writing Center Journal* 19.1 (1998): 7–18. Print.

*Falbo, Bianca. "When Teaching is a Private Affair." Hanstedt and Amorose, *Composition in the Small College* 93–109. Print.

*Folsom, Ed. "Degrees of Success, Degrees of Failure: The Changing Dynamics of the English PhD and Small-College Careers." *Profession* (2001): 121–29. Print.

Foucault, Michel. *Discipline and Punish: The Birth of the Prison.* 2nd ed. Trans. Alan Sheridan. New York: Vintage, 1995.

*Fremo, Rebecca Taylor. "Redefining Our Rhetorical Situations: jWPAs in the Small College Context." Dew and Horning 191–219. Print.

Fulwiler, Toby. "How Well Does Writing Across the Curriculum Work?" *College English* 46.2 (1984): 114–20. Print.

Gannett, Cynthia, John C. Brereton, and Katherine E. Tirabassi. "'We All Got History': Process and Product in the History of Composition." Rev. of Donahue and Moon, *Local Histories: Reading the Archives of Composition. Pedagogy* 10.2 (2010): 425–50. Print.

*Garbus, Julie. "Vida Scudder in the Classroom and in the Archives." Donahue and Moon 77–94. Print.

*Genung, John F. "English at Amherst College." Payne 110–15. Print.

*George, D'Ann. "'Replacing Nice, Thin Bryn Mawr Miss Crandall with Fat, Harvard Savage': WPAs at Bryn Mawr College, 1902 to 1923." L'Eplattenier and Mastrangelo 23–36. Print.

George, Diana, ed. *Kitchen Cooks, Plate Twirlers and Troubadours: Writing Program Administrators Tell Their Stories.* Portsmouth: Boynton Cook, 1999. Print.

Gere, Anne Ruggles. "Initial Report on Survey of CCCC Members." Conference on College Composition and Communication. 2009. Web. 13 July 2010.

—. "Kitchen Tables and Rented Rooms: The Extracurriculum of Composition." *College Composition and Communication* 45.1 (1994): 75–92. Print.

Gillespie, Paula, Bradley Hughes, and Harvey Kail. "Nothing Marginal About This Writing Center Experience: Using Research About Peer Tutor Alumni to Educate Others." Macauley and Mauriello 35–52. Print.

—, and Harvey Kail. "Crossing Thresholds: Starting a Peer Tutoring Program." *The Writing Center Director's Resource Book.* Ed. Christina Murphy and Byron L. Stay. Mahwah: Lawrence Erlbaum, 2006. 321–30. Print.

—, and Neal Lerner. *The Allyn and Bacon Guide to Peer Tutoring.* 2nd ed. New York: Pearson/Longman, 2004. Print.

*Gladstein, Jill. "Conducting Research in the Gray Space: How Writing Associates Negotiate Between WAC and WID in an Introductory Biology Course." *Across the Disciplines* 5 (2008): n. pag. Web. 29 July 2010.

*—. "Writing Requirements @ SLACs: What Do the Data Report? A Preliminary Report from a National Survey on Writing at Small Liberal Arts Colleges." Small Liberal Arts College-Writing Program Administrators Conference. Doubletree, Monrovia. 8 Jan. 2010. Presentation.

*—, Lisa Lebduska, and Dara Rossman Regaignon. "Consortia as Sites of Inquiry: Steps toward a National Portrait of Writing Program Administration." *WPA: Writing Program Administration* 32.3 (2009): 13–36. Print.

Glau, Gregory. "The 'Stretch Program': Arizona State University's New Model of University-Level Basic Writing Instruction." *WPA: Writing Program Administration* 20.1/2 (1996): 79–92. Print.

—. "Stretch at 10: Ten Years of Data on Arizona State University's Stretch Program." *Journal of Basic Writing* 26.2 (2007): 30–48. Print.

Greenwood, Davydd J., and Morten Levin. *Introduction to Action Research: Social Research for Social Change.* 2nd ed. Thousand Oaks: Sage, 2006. Print.

Grego, Rhonda, and Nancy Thompson. "Repositioning Remediation: Renegotiating Composition's Work in the Academy." *College Composition and Communication* 47.1 (1996): 62–84. Print.

—. "The Writing Studio Program: Reconfiguring Basic Writing/Freshman Composition." *WPA: Writing Program Administration* 19.1–2 (1995): 66–79. Print.

Griffin, Jo Ann, Daniel Keller, Iswari Pandey, Anne-Marie Pedersen, and Carolyn Skinner. "Local Practices, Institutional Results: Results from the 2003–2004 WCRP National Survey of Writing Centers." WCRP. n.d. Web. 19 July 2010.

Gunner, Jeanne. "Decentering the WPA." *WPA: Writing Program Administration* 18.1/2 (1994): 8–15. Print.

—. "Identity and Location: A Study of WPA Models, Memberships, and Locations." *WPA: Writing Program Administration* 22.3 (1998): 31–54. Print.

—. "Professional Advancement of the WPA: Rhetoric and Politics in Tenure and Promotion." Ward and Carpenter 315–30. Print.

*Haefner, Joel. "Current Assessment efforts at Illinois Wesleyan University." Message to authors. 19 May 2010. Email.

*—. Telephone Interview. 24 May 2010.

Hamp-Lyons, Liz. "What Is Writing? What Is "Scholastic Aptitude"? What Are the Consequences? SAT I Writing—a Trip down Memory Lane." *Assessing Writing* 10.3 (2005): 151–56. Print.

*Hanstedt, Paul. "Service and the Life of the Small-School Academic." *Profession* (2003): 76–84. Print.

*—, and Tom Amorose, eds. *Composition in the Small College.* Spec. issue of *Composition Studies* 32.3 (2004): 9–168. Print.

*—. "The Idea of the Small School: Beginning a Discussion about Composition at Small Colleges and Universities." Hanstedt and Amorose, eds. *Composition in the Small College.* Spec issue of *Composition Studies* 32.3 (2004): 13–31. Print.

Harris, Joseph. "Thinking Like a Program." *Pedagogy* 4.3 (2004): 357–63. Print.

—. "Undisciplined Writing." Yancey 155–68. Print.

Harris, Muriel. "Cultural Conflicts in the Writing Center: Expectations and Assumptions of ESL Students." *St. Martin's Sourcebook for Writing Tutors.* 3rd ed. Ed. Christina Murphy and Byron L. Stay. Boston: Bedford/St. Martin's, 2008. 206–19. Print.

—. "A Writing Center without a WAC Program: The De Facto WAC Center/Writing Center." Barnett and Blumner. 426–42. Print.

—. "Writing Center Administration: Making Local, Institutional Knowledge in Our Writing Centers." *Writing Center Research: Extending the Conversation.* Ed. Paula Gillespie, Alice Gillam, Lady Falls Brown, and Byron L. Stay. Mahwah, NJ: Lawrence Erlbaum, 2002. 75–90. Print.

—, and Tony Silva. "Tutoring ESL Students: Issues and Options." *Teaching Composition: Background Readings.* 3rd ed. Ed. T. R. Johnson. Boston: Bedford/St. Martin's, 2008. 503–18. Print.

Haviland, Carol Peterson, Carmen M. Fye, and Richard Colby. "The Politics of Administrative and Physical Location." *The Politics of Writing Centers.* Ed. Jane Nelson and Kathy Evertz. Portsmouth: Boynton/Cook, 2001. 85–98. Print.

Haviland, Carol Peterson, and Edward M. White. "How Can Physical Space and Administrative Structure Shape Writing Programs, Writing Centers, and WAC Projects." *Administrative Problem-Solving for Writing Programs and Writing Centers: Scenarios in Effective Program Management.* Ed. Linda Myers-Breslin. Urbana, IL: NCTE Press, 1999. 212–222. Print.

Healy, Dave. "Writing Center Directors: An Emerging Portrait of the Profession." *WPA: Writing Program Administration* 18.3 (1995): 26–43. Print.

*Hebb, Judith. "Reenvisioning WPAs in Small Colleges as 'Writing People Advocates.'" *WPA: Writing Program Administration* 29.1–2 (2005): 97–110. Print.

Higher Education Data Sharing Consortium. "HEDS Mission Statement." *E-heds.org.* 2008–10. Web. 27 July 2010.

*Horner, Bruce. "Traditions and Professionalization: Reconceiving Work in Composition." *College Composition and Communication* 51.3 (2000): 366–98. Print.

Horning, Alice. "The Definitive Article on Class Size." *WPA: Writing Program Administration* 31.1/2 (2007): 11–34. Print.

—. "Introduction: What is Wrong with THIS Picture?" Dew and Horning 3–15. Print.

Howard, Rebecca M., David Hess, and Margaret F. Darby. "A Comment on 'Only One of the Voices' and 'Why English Departments Should "House"' Writing Across the Curriculum.'" *College English* 51.4 (1989): 433–35. Print.

Hughes, Brad, and Emily B. Hall. "Guest Editors' Introduction." *Rewriting the Curriculum: Writing Fellows as Agents of Change in WAC.* Spec. issue of *ATD: Across the Disciplines* 5 (2008). Web. 30 May 2009.

Hughes, Bradley, Paula Gillespie, and Harvey Kail. "What They Take with Them: Findings from the Peer Writing Tutors Alumni Research Project." *Writing Center Journal* 30.2 (2010): 12–46. Print.

Huot, Brian. *(Re)Articulating Writing Assessment for Teaching and Learning.* Logan: Utah UP, 2002. Print.

—, and Michael R. Neal. "Writing Assessment: A Techno-History." *Handbook of Writing Research.* Ed. Charles A. MacArthur, Steve Graham, and Jill Fitzgerald. New York: Guilford P, 2005. 417–32. Print.

Hult, Christine, David Joliffe, Kathleen Kelly, Dana Mead, and Charles Schuster. "The Portland Resolution: Guidelines for Writing Program Administrator Positions." *WPAcouncil.org.* 1992. Web. 27 July 2010.

Ianetta, Melissa, Michael McCamley, and Catherine Quick. "Taking Stock: Surveying the Relationship the Writing Center and T.A. Training." *WPA: Writing Program Administration* 31.1/2 (2007): 104–23. Print.

Isaacs, Emily. "What Is Research and Writing?" Enos and Borrowman 175–82. Print.

Jack Kent Cooke Foundation. "Community College Transfer." *Jack Kent Cooke Foundation.* n.d. Web. 3 June 2010.

*Jamieson, Sandra. "Drew University." *DSP*. CompFAQ from CompPile. 20 May 2008. Web. 1 June 2010.

Jarrett, Susan C., Katherine Mack, Alexandra Sartor, and Shevaun E. Watson. "Pedagogical Memory: Writing, Mapping, Translating." *WPA: Writing Program Administration* 33.1/2 (2009): 46–73. Print.

Jaschik, Scott. "Rankings Frenzy '09." *Inside Higher Ed* 20 Aug. 2009: n. pag. Web. 15 May 2010.

—. "Turning Surveys into Reforms." *Inside Higher Ed* 26 Oct. 2009: n. pag. Web. 29 July 2010.

Johnson, R. Burke, and Anthony J. Onwuegbuzie. "Mixed Methods Research: A Research Paradigm Whose Time Has Come." *Educational Researcher* 33.7 (2004): 14–26. Print.

*Jones, Edward A. *A Candle in the Dark: A History of Morehouse College.* Valley Forge: The Judson P, 1967.

*Jones, Libby Falk. "Exploring the Paradoxes of Power in Small College Writing Administration." *Composition Studies* 32.2 (Fall 2004): 75–92. Print.

Kail, Harvey. "Writing Center Work: An Ongoing Challenge." *Writing Center Journal* 20.2 (2000): 25–28. Print.

—, Paula Gillespie, and Brad Hughes. "Welcome!" *The Peer Writing Tutor Alumni Research Project*. n. pag., 2010. Web. 15 July 2010.

Kelly-Riley, Diane, Lisa Johnson-Shull, and William Condon. "Opportunities for Consilience: Toward a Networked-Based Model for Writing Program Administration." *The Writing Program Administrator as Theorist*. Ed. Shirley K. Rose and Irwin Weiser. Portsmouth: Boynton/Cook Heinemann, 2002. 129–43. Print.

Kirsch, Gesa, De Ann C. Finkel, and Alan W. France. "Three Comments on 'Only One of the Voices: Dialogic Writing across the Curriculum." *College English* 51.1 (1989): 99–103. Print.

Kitzhaber, Albert R. *Rhetoric in American Colleges, 1850–1900*. Dallas: Southern Methodist UP, 1990. Print.

—. *Themes, Theories, and Therapy: The Teaching of Writing in College*. New York: McGraw-Hill, 1963. Print.

Knight, Melinda, and Emily Isaacs. "The State of Writing Studies: How Writing Is Done in U.S. Colleges and Universities." Conference on College Composition and Communication. Hyatt Regency, Louisville. 20 Mar. 2010. Address.

Lalicker, William B. "A Basic Introduction to Basic Writing Program Structures: A Baseline and Five Alternatives." *BWe: Basic Writing e-Journal* 1.2 (1999): n. pag. Print.

*Langston, Camille. "A New WPA at a Small Private School with Large Public(ation) Expectations." Enos and Borrowman 182–90. Print.

*Lawrence, LeAnna Michelle. *The Teaching of Rhetoric and Composition in Nineteenth-Century Women's Colleges*. Diss. Duke U, 1990. Ann Arbor: UMI, 1990. Print.

*L'Eplattenier, Barbara. *Investigating Institutional Power: Women Administrators during the Progressive Era, 1890–1920*. Diss. Purdue U, 1999. Ann Arbor: UMI, 1999.

—, ed. *Historical Studies of Writing Program Administration*. West Lafayette, Parlor P, 2004. Print.

—. "WPA's authority/Chair's attitudes." WPA-L: Writing Program Administrators. 5 April 2010. E-list. 27 June 2010.

Lerner, Neal. *The Idea of a Writing Laboratory*. Carbondale: Southern Illinois UP, 2009. Print.

—. "Punishment and Possibility: Representing Writing Centers, 1939–70." *Composition Studies* 31.2 (2003): 53–72. Print.

—. "Rejecting the Remedial Brand: The Rise and Fall of the Dartmouth Writing Clinic." *College Composition and Communication* 59.1 (2007): 13–35.

—. "Time Warp: Historical Representations of Writing Center Directors." Murphy and Stay 3–13. Print.

Lewiecki-Wilson, Cynthia, Jeff Sommers, and John Paul Tassoni. "Rhetoric and the Writer's Profile: Problematizing Directed Self-Placement." *Assessing Writing* 7 (2000): 165–83. Print.

Linton, Patricia, Robert Madigan, and Susan Johnson. "Introducing Students to Disciplinary Genres." *Language and Learning Across the Disciplines* 1.2 (1994): 63–78. Print.

Lucas, Christopher J. *American Higher Education: A History.* New York: St. Martin's P, 1994. Print.

Lunsford, Andrea A., and Patricia A. Sullivan. "Who Are Basic Writers?" *Research in Basic Writing: A Bibliographic Sourcebook.* Ed. Michael G. Moran and Martin J. Jacobi. New York: Greenwood Press, 1990. 17–31. Print.

Macauley, William J., and Nicholas Mauriello, eds. *Marginal Words, Marginal Work? Tutoring the Academy in the Work of Writing Centers.* Cresskill: Hampton P, 2007. Print.

Maid, Barry. "Working Outside of English Departments: Understanding and Negotiating Administrative Reporting Lines." Ward and Carpenter 38–46. Print.

*Maimon, Elaine P. "Beaver College Writing Program." *New Methods in College Writing Programs.* Ed. Paul Connolly and Teresa Vilardi. New York: MLA P, 1986. 12–15. Print.

*—. "It Takes a Campus to Teach a Writer: WAC and the Reform of Undergraduate Education." McLeod and Soven 16–31. Print.

*Marek, Jayne E. "*Scholarship Reconsidered*: Ten Years After and the Small College." *Profession* (2003): 44–54. Print.

*Martinson, Deborah. "Current Assessment Efforts at Occidental College." Message to authors. 21 May 2010. Email.

*—. Telephone interview. 12 June 2010.

*—. "Another sneak peek." Message to authors. 22 June 2011. Email.

MIT/Microsoft iCampus Alliance. *iMOAT: The iCampus/MIT Online Assessment Tool.* iCampus Project, 6 Nov. 2003. Web. 31 May 2010.

*Mastrangelo, Lisa. "Learning from the Past: Rhetoric, Composition, and Debate at Mount Holyoke College." *Rhetoric Review* 18.1 (1999): 46–64. Print.

*—. *Writing a Progressive Past: Women Teaching and Writing in the Progressive Era.* Anderson, SC: Parlor P, 2012. Print.

*Mastrangelo, Lisa, and Barbara L'Eplattenier. "'Is It the Pleasure of This Conference to Have Another?': Women's Colleges Meeting and Talking about Writing in the Progressive Era." L'Eplattenier and Mastrangelo 117–43. Print.

Matsuda, Paul Kei, and Tony Silva. "Cross-Cultural Composition: Mediated Integration of US and International Students." *Composition Studies* 27.1 (1999): 15–30. Print.

McClure, Randall. "An Army of One: The Possibilities and Perils of WPA Work for the Lone Compositionist." Enos and Borrowman 102–108.

*McDonald, Christina Russell. *Converging Histories: Writing Instruction and Women's Education in the Progressive Era, 1890–1920.* Diss. Texas Christian U, 1995. Ann Arbor: UMI, 1995. Print.

McLeod, Susan H. *Writing Program Administration.* West Lafayette: Parlor P, 2007. Print.

McNenny, Gerry, with Sallyanne H. Fitzgerald, eds. *Mainstreaming Basic Writers: Politics and Pedagogies of Access.* Mahwah: Lawrence Erlbaum, 2001. Print.

*Moon, Gretchen Flesher. "First-Year Writing in First-Year Seminars: Writing across the Curriculum from the Start." *WPA: Writing Program Administration* 26.3 (2003): 105–18. Print.

Mullin, Joan, Peter Carino, Jane Nelson, and Kathy Evertz. "Administrative (Chaos) Theory: The Politics and Practices of Writing Center Location." *The Writing Center Director's Resource Book.* Ed. Christina Murphy and Byron L. Stay. Mahwah: Lawrence Erlbaum, 2006. 225–37. Print.

Myers, Sharon A. "Reassessing the 'Proofreading Trap': ESL Tutoring and Writing Instruction." *St. Martin's Sourcebook for Writing Tutors.* 3rd ed. Ed. Christina Murphy and Byron L. Stay. Boston: Bedford/St. Martin's, 2008. 219–37. Print.

NCTE-WPA. White Paper on Writing Assessment in Colleges and Universities. *Council of Writing Program Administrators.* n.d. Web. 14 May 2010.

Neal, Michael R. "Review Essay: Assessment in the Service of Learning." *College Composition and Communication* 61.4 (2010): 746–58. Print.

Neal, Michael R., and Brian Huot. "Responding to Directed Self-Placement." Royer and Gilles 243–55. Print.

Neff, Joyce Magnotto. "Capturing Complexity: Using Grounded Theory to Study Writing Centers." *Writing Center Research: Extending the Conversation.* Ed. Paula Gillespie, Alice Gillam, Lady Falls Brown, and Byron Stay. Mahwah: Lawrence Erlbaum, 2002. 133–49.

*Neff, Julie. "The Writing Center at the University of Puget Sound: The Center of Academic Life." *Writing Centers in Context: Twelve Case Studies.* Urbana, IL: NCTE Press, 1993. 127–44. Print.

Nelms, Gerald, and Ronda Leathers Dively. "Perceived Roadblocks to Transferring Knowledge from First-Year Composition to Writing-Intensive Major Courses: A Pilot Study." *WPA: Writing Program Administration* 31.1/2 (2007): 214–40. Print.

Nelson, Donna Beth. "Writing Laboratories and Basic Writing." *Research in Basic Writing: A Bibliographic Sourcebook.* New York: Greenwood Press, 1990. 191–205. Print.

Nicolay, Theresa Freda. "Placement and Instruction in Context: Situating Writing within a First-Year Program." *WPA: Writing Program Administration* 25.3 (2002): 41–59. Print.

Norris, Dwayne et al. "The College Board SAT Writing Validation Study: An Assessment of Predictive and Incremental Validity." Research Report No. 2006–2. New York: College Board, 2006. Print.

*Oakley, Francis. *Community of Learning: The American College and the Liberal Arts Tradition*. New York: Oxford UP, 1992. Print.

*Occidental College. "By the Numbers." *Oxy.edu*. 2010. Web. 22 May 2010.

Olson, Gary A., and Joseph M. Moxley. "Directing Freshman Composition: The Limits of Authority." *College Composition and Communication* 49.1 (1989): 51–60. Print.

Pak, Michael S. "The Yale Report of 1828: A New Reading and New Implications." *History of Education Quarterly* 48.1 (2008): 30–57.

Payne, William Morton. *English in American Universities*. Boston: D.C. Heath, 1895.

Phelps, Louise Wetherby. "Re: what constitutes a Writing Program?" WPA-L: Writing Program Administrators. 24 Feb. 2009. E-list. 26 Mar. 2010.

—. "Turtles All the Way Down: Educating Academic Leaders." Brown and Enos 3–41. Print.

*Pfnister, Allan O. "The Role of the Liberal Arts College: A Historical Overview of the Debates." *The Liberal Arts College: Managing Adaptation to the 1980s*. Ed. Allan O. Pfnister and Martin J. Finkelstein. *Journal of Higher Education* 55.2 (1984): 145–70. Print.

*Podis, Leonard A., and JoAnne M. Podis, eds. *Working with Student Writers: Essays on Tutoring and Teaching*. New York: Peter Lang, 1999. Print.

The Posse Foundation. "About Posse." *The Posse Foundation*. n.p., 2010. Web. 4 June 2010.

Potts, David B. "Curriculum and Enrollment: Assessing the Popularity of Antebellum Colleges." *The American Colleges in the Nineteenth Century*. Nashville: Vanderbilt UP, 2000. 37–45. Print.

Questbridge. "About Us." *Questbridge*. n.p., 2005. Web. 4 June 2010.

*Read, Florence Matilda. *The Story of Spelman College*. Princeton: Princeton UP, 1961.

Reid, E. Shelley. "Will Administrate for Tenure, or, Be Careful What You Ask For." Enos and Borrowman 203–12. Print.

Ritter, Kelly. "Before Mina Shaughnessy: Basic Writing at Yale, 1920–1960." *College Composition and Communication* 60.1 (2008): 12–45. Print.

—. *Before Shaughnessy: Basic Writing at Yale and Harvard, 1920–1960*. Carbondale: Southern Illinois UP, 2009. Print.

Roen, Duane H. "Writing Administration as Scholarship and Teaching." *Academic Advancement in Composition Studies*. Ed. Richard C. Gebhardt and Barbara Genelle Smith Gebhardt. Mahwah: Lawrence Erlbaum, 1997. 43–56. Print.

—, Barry M. Maid, Gregory R. Glau, John Rampage, and David Schwalm. "Reconsidering and Assessing the Work of Writing Program Administrators." *The Writing Program Administrator as Theorist*. Ed. Shirley K. Rose and Irwin Weiser. Portsmouth: Boynton/Cook Heinemann. 2002. 157–69. Print.

—, Kathleen Blake Yancey, and David Schwalm. "A Prologue and Three Responses." Enos and Borrowman 212–25. Print.

Royer, Daniel J., and Gilles, Roger. "Basic Writing and Directed Self-Placement." *BWe: Basic Writing e-Journal* 2.2 (2000): n. pag. Web.

—. "Directed Self-Placement: An Attitude of Orientation." *College Composition and Communication* 50.1 (1990): 54–70. Print.

—, eds. *Directed Self-Placement: Principles and Practices*. Cresskill: Hampton P, 2003. Print.

*Royster, Jacqueline Jones. "From Practice to Theory: Writing Across the Disciplines at Spelman College." *Writing, Teaching, and Learning in the Disciplines*. Ed. Anne Herrington and Charles Moran. New York: MLA Press, 1992. 119–31. Print.

Rudolph, Frederick. *The American College and University*. New York: Random House, 1962.

*Runciman, Lex. "Ending Composition as We Knew It." *Language and Learning Across the Disciplines* 2.3 (1998): 44–53. Print.

Russell, David R. "Rethinking Genre in School and Society: An Activity Theory Analysis." *Written Communication* 14.4 (1997): 504–54. Print.

—. "Writing across the Curriculum in Historical Perspective: Toward a Social Interpretation." *College English* 52.1 (1990): 52–73. Print.

—. *Writing in the Academic Disciplines: A Curricular History*. 2nd ed. Carbondale: Southern Illinois UP, 2002. Print.

*Rutz, Carol. "Delivering Composition at a Liberal Arts College: Making the Implicit Explicit." Yancey, *Delivering College Composition* 60–71. Print.

*Rutz, Carol, Clara Shaw Hardy, and William Condon. "WAC for the Long Haul: A Tale of Hope." *WAC Journal* 13 (2002): 7–16.

*Rutz, Carol and Jaqulyn Lauer-Glebov. "Assessment and Innovation: One Darn Thing Leads to Another." *Assessing Writing* 10 (2005): 80–99. Print.

Schön, Donald A. *The Reflective Practitioner: How Professionals Think in Action*. New York: Basic Books, 1983. Print.

Schwalm, David. "The Writing Program Administrator in Context: Where Am I, and Can I Still Behave Like a Faculty Member?" Ward and Carpenter 9–22. Print.

Schwartz, Gwen G., et al. "Writing infusion vs. FYC." WPA-L: Writing Program Administrators. 4–6 Mar. 2011. Web. 5 June 2011.

Scott, Fred Newton. "English at the University of Minnesota." Payne 116–23. Print.

Segall, Mary T. "Embracing a Porcupine: Redesigning a Writing Program." *Journal of Basic Writing* 14.2 (1995): 38–47. Print.

*Seery, John E. *America Goes to College: Political Theory for the Liberal Arts.* Albany: SUNY P, 2002. Print.

Severino, Carol, and Megan Knight. "Exploring Writing Center Pedagogy: Writing Fellows Programs as Ambassadors for the Writing Center." Macauley and Mauriello 19–34. Print.

Severino, Carol, and Mary Trachsel. "Theories of Specialized Discourses and Writing Fellows Programs." *Across the Disciplines* 5 (2008): n. pag. Web. 26 Aug. 2009.

*Sharpe, Kenneth. "Why Writing Associates Need Practical Wisdom . . . And How They Learn It." Keynote Address. "Celebrating 25 Years of WAing." Swarthmore College, Swarthmore, PA. 19 Mar. 2011. Address.

Shouse, Claude Fiero. *The Writing Laboratory in Colleges and Universities.* Diss. U Southern California, 1953. Print.

Silva, Tony. "An Examination of Writing Program Administrators' Options for the Placement of ESL Students in First Year Writing Classes." *WPA: Writing Program Administration* 18.1/2 (1994): 37–43. Print.

Simpson, Jeanne H. "What Lies Ahead for Writing Centers: Position Statement on Professional Concerns." *Landmark Essays on Writing Centers.* Ed. Christina Murphy and Joe Law. New York: Routledge, 1995. 57–63. Print.

Skeffington, Jillian, Shane Borrowman, and Theresa Enos. "Living in the Spaces Between: Profiling the Writing Program Administrator." Enos and Borrowman 5–21. Print.

Skipper, Tracy L. "A National Overview of Writing in First-Year Seminars." Conference on College Composition and Communication. Marriott, Louisville. 19 Mar. 2010. Address.

Smit, David R. *The End of Composition Studies.* Carbondale: Southern Illinois UP, 2004. Print.

Smith, Louise Z. "Louise Z. Smith Responds." *College English* 51.4 (1989): 436–7. Print.

—. "Why English Departments Should 'House' Writing Across the Curriculum." *College English* 50.4 (1989): 390–95. Print.

Smoke, Trudy. "Mainstreaming Writing: What Does This Mean for ESL Students?" McNenny and Fitzgerald 193–214. Print.

Soliday, Mary. "From the Margins to the Mainstream: Reconceiving Remediation." *College Composition and Communication* 47.1 (1996): 85–100. Print.

—, and Barbara Gleason. "From Remediation to Enrichment: Evaluating a Mainstreaming Project." *Journal of Basic Writing* 16.1 (1997): 64–79. Print.

Sommers, Nancy. "The Call of Research." *Blurring Boundaries: Developing Writers, Researchers, and Teachers: A Tribute to William L. Smith.* Cresskill: Hampton P, 2007. 9–11. Print.

—, and Laura Saltz. "The Novice as Expert: Writing the Freshman Year." *College Composition and Communication* 56.1 (2004): 124–49. Print.

Soven, Margot. "Curriculum-Based Peer Tutoring Programs: A Survey." *WPA: Writing Program Administration* 17:1–2 (1993): 58–74. Print.

———. "Curriculum-Based Peer Tutors and WAC." *WAC for the New Millennium" Strategies for Continuing Writing-Across-the-Curriculum Programs.* Ed. Susan H. McLeod, Eric Miraglia, Margot Soven, and Christopher Thaiss. Urbana, IL: NCTE, 2001. 200–233. Print.

*SpEL.Folio. "Mission Statement." *Spelman.edu.* 2004. Web. 14 May 2010.

*—. "Writing Portfolio Rubric." *Spelman.edu.* 2004. Web. 14 May 2010.

Spellmeyer, Kurt. "Bigger Than a Discipline?" *A Field of Dreams: Independent Writing Programs and the Future of Composition Studies.* Ed. Peggy O'Neill, Angela Crow, and Larry Burton. Logan: Utah State UP, 2002. 278–94. Print.

Spigelman, Candace, and Laurie Grobman. "Introduction: On Location in Classroom-Based Writing Tutoring." *On Location: Theory and Practice in Classroom-based Writing Tutoring.* Ed. Candace Spigelman and Laurie Grobman. Logan (UT): Utah State UP: 2005. 1–17. Print.

*Spohrer, Erika. "What Margins? The Writing Center at a Small, Liberal Arts College." *Writing Lab Newsletter* 31.4 (2006): 7. Print.

*Spring, Suzanne B. "'Seemingly uncouth forms': Letters at Mount Holyoke Female Seminary." *College Composition and Communication* 59.4 (2008): 633–75. Print.

*Stay, Byron L. "Writing Centers in the Small College." Murphy and Stay 147–53. Print.

Strang, Steven. "Staffing a Writing Center with Professional Tutors." *The Writing Center Director's Resource Book.* Ed. Christina Murphy and Byron L. Stay. Mahwah: Lawrence Erlbaum, 2006. 291–301. Print.

Strauss, Anselm, and Juliet Corbin. *Basics of Qualitative Research: Grounded Theory Procedures and Techniques.* Newbury Park: Sage, 1990. Print.

Stygall, Gail. "Certifying the Knowledge of WPAs." Brown and Enos 71–88. Print.

Sullivan, Patrick, and Howard Tinberg. eds. *What Is "College-Level" Writing?* Urbana, IL: NCTE P, 2006. Print.

*Taylor, Rebecca G. "Preparing WPAs for the Small College Context." *Composition Studies* 32.2 (2004): 53–73. Print.

Tewksbury, Donald G. *The Founding of American Colleges and Universities Before the Civil War: With Particular Reference to the Religious Influences Bearing upon the College Movement*. New York: Teachers College P, 1932.

Thaiss, Chris, and Tara Porter. "The State of WAC/WID in 2010: Methods and Results of the U.S. Survey of the International WAC/WID Mapping Project." *College Composition and Communication* 61.3 (2010): 534–570. Print.

Thaiss, Chris, and Terry Myers Zawacki. *Engaged Writers, Dynamic Disciplines: Research on the Academic Writing Life*. Portsmouth, NH: Boynton/Cook, 2006. Print.

Townsend, Martha A. "Negotiating the Risks and Reaping the Rewards: Reflections and Advice from a Former jWPA." Dew and Horning 72–97. Print.

*—. "Re. WAC SOS." WPA-L: Writing Program Administrators. 29 Sept. 2004. Web. 14 July 2010.

—. "What the Outcomes Statement Could Mean for Writing across the Curriculum." *The Outcomes Book: Debate and Consensus After the WPA Outcomes Statement*. Ed. Susanmarie Harrington, Keith Rhodes, Ruth Fischer, and Rita Malenczyk. Logan: Utah State UP, 2005. 121–127. Print.

—. "Writing Across the Curriculum." Brown and Enos 439–52. Print.

—. "Writing Intensive Courses and WAC." McLeod et al. 233–58. Print.

Trimbur, John. "Peer Tutoring: A Contradiction in Terms?" *Writing Center Journal* 7.2 (1987): 21–29. Print.

Urofsky, Melvin I. "Reforms and Response: The Yale Report of 1828." *History of Educational Quarterly* 5.1 (1965): 53–67. Print.

*Vandenberg, Margaret. "Reinventing Literary History at Barnard College." *Integrating Literature and Writing Instruction: First-Year English, Humanities Core Courses, Seminars*. Ed. Judith Anderson and Christine Farris. New York: MLA P, 2007. 63–81. Print.

*Varnum, Robin. *Fencing with Words: A History of Writing Instruction at Amherst College during the Era of Theodore Baird, 1938–1966*. Urbana: NCTE P, 1996. Print.

Vygotsky, Lev. "Interaction Between Learning and Development." *Mind and Society*. Cambridge: Harvard UP, 1978. 79–91. Print.

Waldo, Mark L. "What Should the Relationship Between the Writing Center and Writing Program Be?" *Writing Center Journal* 11.1 (1990): 73–81. Print.

*Walvoord, Barbara. "Gender and Discipline in Two Early WAC Communities: Lessons for Today." McLeod and Soven 142–56. Print.

Ward, Irene, and William J. Carpenter. *The Allyn and Bacon Sourcebook for Writing Program Administrators*. New York: Longman, 2002. Print.

Wardle, Elizabeth. "'Mutt genres' and the Goal of First-Year Composition: Can We Help Students Write the Genres of the University?" *College Composition and Communication* 60.4 (2009): 765–89. Print.

—. "Understanding 'Transfer' from FYC: Preliminary Results from a Longitudinal Study.' *WPA: Writing Program Administration* 31.1/2 (2007): 65–85. Print.

*Warner, Anne B. "Current Assessment Efforts at Spelman College." Message to authors. 10 May 2010. Email.

*—. Telephone Interview. 24 May 2010.

*Weidner, Heidemarie Z. "A Chair 'Perpetually Filled by a Female Professor': Rhetoric and Composition Instruction at Nineteenth-Century Butler University." Donahue and Moon 58–77. Print.

*Welsch, Kathleen A. "Thinking Like *That*: The Ideal Nineteenth-Century Student Writer." Donahue and Moon 14–38. Print.

White, Edward M. "Re: WPA's authority/Chair's attitudes." WPA-L: Writing Program Administrators. 5 April 2010. E-list. 27 June 2010.

—. *Teaching and Assessing Writing: Recent Advances in Understanding, Evaluating, and Improving Student Performance.* 2nd ed. San Francisco: Jossey-Bass, 1994.

—. "Use It or Lose It: Power and the WPA." Ward and Carpenter 106-15. Print.

Williams, Raymond. *Marxism and Literature.* New York: Oxford UP, 1977. Print.

*Wingate, Molly. "Writing Centers as Sites of Academic Culture." *Writing Center Journal* 21.2 (2001): 7–20. Print.

Witte, Stephen, and Lester A. Faigley. *Evaluating College Writing Programs.* Carbondale: Southern Illinois UP, 1983. Print.

Wright, Elizabethada A., and S. Michael Halloran. "From Rhetoric to Composition: The Teaching of Writing in America to 1900." *A Short History of Writing Instruction: From Ancient Greece to Modern America.* 2nd ed. Ed. James J. Murphy. Mahwah: Erlbaum, 2001. 214–36. Print.

Writing Centers Research Project. "Mission." The Writing Centers Research Project. 2009. Web. 19 July 2010.

Yale College, Committee of the Corporation and the Academical Faculty. *Reports on the Course of Instruction in Yale College.* New Haven, CT: 1828. Print.

Yancey, Kathleen Blake. *Delivering College Composition: The Fifth Canon.* Portsmouth, NH: Boynton/Cook, 2006. Print.

Young, Art, and Toby Fulwiler. "The Enemies of Writing Across the Curriculum." *Programs that Work: Models and Methods for Writing Across the Curriculum.* Ed. Toby Fulwiler and Art Young, Portsmouth: Boynton/Cook. 1990. 287–95. Print.

Young Scholars in Writing. 2011. Web. Curators of U Missouri. 27 June 2011.

Index

accreditation, 190, 194–195
action research, 24, 29, 211
adjunct, 76, 83, 149, 220
administrator, xv, 39, 46, 50, 61–64, 66–67, 69, 91, 144–145, 149, 162–163, 207, 237
agency, 47, 77, 81–82, 84, 106, 182, 207, 236
Alverno College, 190
American Journal of Science and Arts, The, 11
Amherst College, 6, 9, 19, 213, 237–238
Amorose, Thomas, xvi, 15–16, 24, 36, 46–47, 54, 56
Annapolis Group, xvi, 24–25, 228
Anson, Chris M., 23, 114, 139, 241
assessment, x, xi, 25, 27, 31, 40–41, 50, 52–53, 55, 58, 62, 64, 66, 70, 75, 104, 111, 142, 145, 148, 172, 189–202, 205–206, 224–225, 232–234, 242
Atlantic Monthly, The, 12
authority, 33, 46–47, 51, 53, 67–68, 74, 76, 80–84, 86, 89, 91, 117, 209–210, 236
autonomy, faculty, 20–21, 46, 82, 104, 106, 128, 204

Balester, Valerie, 49, 158
basic writer, 171, 185
basic writing, 36, 120, 171, 179, 182–184

Bedore, Pamela, 181–182
Blair, Catherine Pastore, 43, 139, 241
Blakesley, David, xiii, 182, 242
Boehm, Dianne, 67
Borrowman, Shane, xv, 28, 77, 86, 240
Bousquet, Marc, 120
Brent, Doug, 101, 103
Brereton, John C., 9, 12–13, 17, 98, 237- 238
Broad, Bob, 189–191, 196
Bromley, Pam, xiv-xv, 160
Bryn Mawr College, 9, 213
Bushman, Mary Ann, 195, 197

Cady, Frank, 19
Cambridge University, 8–10
capstone writing requirement, x, 87, 96–98, 108–109, 114–117, 189, 208, 218, 221–234, 241
Carleton College, 104, 164, 190–191, 196, 213, 237, 238
Carnegie Foundation, 103, 196–197, 200
Caroll, Shireen, 80, 84, 117
Charlton, Jonikka, xv, 70, 77–78, 80
classical curriculum, 9–10, 12, 14, 17, 19, 107, 136, 238
Colby, Richard, 161–162, 213
College Composition and Communication (CCC), xvi, 7, 31, 77

colleges, historically black, 10, 26;
men's, 26; women's, 9, 26, 238,
252–253
Colorado College, 166, 213
CompFAQ, 183
composition, course, xvii, 12–14,
36, 56, 59–60, 62, 70, 98–101,
103, 117, 120–124, 130, 145,
182, 184, 206, 218–219, 223,
240; history, 12, 17, 19, 120,
237; program, ii, xv, 22, 39, 45,
50, 61, 68, 98, 102, 123, 125–
126, 137, 139, 142, 192, 208; as
requirement, 45, 50, 54, 61–62,
97, 99, 101, 104, 140, 143–144,
199, 205; teachers of, 16, 35–36,
62, 69, 88, 101. *See also* rhetoric
and composition
Composition Studies, xvi, 237
Condon, William, 38, 104, 139,
190–191, 196, 200, 202, 238
Conference on College Composition and Communica-
tion (CCCC), xvi, 31, 77–79,
121–122, 125, 179, 186, 197,
199; *Statement of Principles and
Standards for the Postsecondary
Teaching of Writing*, 121–122;
*Writing Assessment: A Position
Statement*, 179
Connors, Robert, 12, 18, 73,
98–99, 101
Consortium for the Study of Writ-
ing in College, 192
Consortium on Financing Higher
Education, 192
content analysis, 96
Corbin, Julie, 23, 32
core curriculum, 97, 106–107, 199,
201
Council of Writing Program
Administrators (CWPA), xiii, 30,
77, 90, 99–100, 102–103, 111,

190, 192, 198, 241; Portland
Resolution, 70, 85, 90
critical thinking, 100, 102, 171,
173
Crowley, Sharon, 9, 12, 17, 98
current-traditional method, 19
curriculum, x, xvii, 6, 14, 16–19,
21, 24, 46, 51, 53–57, 61, 65–66,
68, 84, 95–96, 104, 107–109,
114–117, 119, 124, 127, 130–
138, 140, 143–144, 146–148,
151, 158, 176, 182, 189, 191,
194–195, 198–199, 202, 206,
208, 218, 221–223; classical,
9–10, 12, 14, 17, 19, 136, 238;
Core, 56, 59, 97, 106–107, 118,
146, 199, 201, 231, 233; development of, 70–75, 216; elective,
13; liberal arts, 195; major, 108,
115–116, 127; standard, 10, 13,
17; vertical, 109, 114–115, 119,
142–143, 206
curriculum-centered domain,
36–37, 40, 44, 51–52, 56–59,
72, 96, 142, 147

Dartmouth College, 6, 237
data analysis, 26, 30, 31
deficit model, 57, 83, 140
departmental culture, 89
departmentalization, 13, 18
developmental model, 50, 140
directed self-placement, 40, 171,
179–183, 186, 209
disciplinary, 13, 62–63, 101–102,
110, 115–117, 120, 129, 132,
134, 144, 148, 164, 175, 198,
203, 220
diversely prepared writers, 27, 40,
171–172
Donahue, Patricia, xvi, 12, 98, 237
Drew University, 179

Eliot, Charles W., 12
embedded requirements, 39,
96–98, 114, 119, 121, 145, 236
Embedded WPA + Explicit WCD,
48, 58, 61, 65, 240
English department, 28, 42, 45,
49–50, 55, 59–60, 62, 68–69,
116, 124, 130–131, 144, 199-
200
English Language Learners, 31, 40,
185–186
enrollment, 11, 14, 26, 105,
122–124, 127, 165, 220, 240
"Evaluating the Intellectual Work of
Writing Program Administrators,"
86, 90
exemption, 39, 73, 98, 121,
123–124, 126, 219
explicit requirements, 41, 96–97,
121, 195, 205
Explicit WPA + Explicit WCD,
48–51, 56, 59, 65, 78, 81, 87,
142, 145–147, 199, 240
Explicit WPA Only, 48, 61, 65
extracurricular writing, 14, 16, 158
extracurriculum, 16, 19

faculty: autonomy, 20–21, 46, 82,
104, 106, 128, 204; development,
x, 27, 41, 49–50, 52–53, 55,
57–58, 60–62, 64, 70–72, 76,
87, 103, 105–108, 111, 113–114,
119, 121, 126–128, 136–138,
142, 145, 162, 191, 196–197,
199–200, 206, 216, 224, 238;
governance, 21, 46, 53, 119, 202;
temporary, 120, 123
Faigley, Lester, 35, 162
Falbo, Bianca, 20, 98, 237
Farris, Christine, 109
first-year composition, 27, 31, 35,
38–40, 45, 48–51, 54, 56–59, 61,
63, 71, 73, 83, 97–99, 101, 103,

105–106, 108, 111, 114–118,
120–128, 130, 137, 139–140,
142–144, 146–147, 170–171,
173, 175, 178–179, 195,
197–198, 205–208, 219–220,
233–234, 240–241
first-year seminar, 96–97, 105, 131
first-year writing, 27, 31, 35,
38–40, 45, 48–51, 54, 56–59,
61, 63, 71, 73, 83, 97–99, 101,
103, 105–106, 108, 114–118,
120–128, 130, 137, 139–140,
142, 144, 170–171, 173, 175,
178–179, 195, 197–198,
205–208, 219–220, 233–234,
240–241. *See also* first-year
composition, first-year writing
seminar
first-year writing seminar, 27,
31, 35, 38–40, 45, 48–51, 54,
56–59, 61, 63, 71, 73, 83, 97–99,
101–106, 108, 111, 114–118,
120–128, 130, 137, 139–140,
142–147, 170–171, 173, 175,
178–179, 195, 197–198, 201,
205–208, 218–220, 233–234,
240–241
focus group, xvi, 27, 30–31, 76, 80,
121, 124, 128, 137–138, 148,
159, 172–175, 177, 204, 234
Folsom, Ed, 239
Foucault, Michel, 12
Fye, Carmen M., 161–162

Gannett, Cynthia, 12–13, 98
genre, 102, 172, 220
Genung, John F., 19
Gere, Ann Ruggles, 16, 77, 122
Gilles, Roger, 73, 181–183
Gillespie, Paula, 166–169, 242
governance, 6, 20, 63, 194, 237
governance, faculty, 21, 46, 53,
119, 202

graduate students, x–xi, 163–164, 166, 239
Grand Valley State University, 182
Grego, Rhonda, 179, 242
grounded theory, xvi, 23–24, 32, 47, 204, 210
Gunner, Jeanne, 42–44, 56, 65–66, 77

Haefner, Joel, 195–197
Hanstedt, Paul, xvi, 15–16, 21, 24, 36, 127, 239
Harris, Joseph, 101, 120, 129
Harvard College, 6, 8, 12–14, 179
Haviland, Carol Peterson, 160–162
Healy, Dave, 49, 80, 158
Higher Education Data Sharing Consortium (HEDS), xvi, 24–25, 239
Historically Black Colleges and Universities, 10, 26; Morehouse College, 10, 214, 238, 251; Spelman College, 10, 104, 191, 195, 199–202, 214, 238
Horning, Alice, 86, 90, 121
Hughes, Bradley, 164, 166–169
Huot, Brian, 183, 189, 201
hybrid, 43, 52–53, 78–81, 83, 85–86, 90, 207
hybridity, 42, 56

Illinois Wesleyan University, 191, 194–197, 201, 213
interdisciplinary, 56, 88–89, 101, 107, 113–114, 127, 129, 144, 148, 220, 222
international students, 170, 181, 186, 195
International Writing Centers Association (IWCA), 70
Isaacs, Emily, xv, 77

Jamieson, Sandra, 179, 184

Johnson, Susan, 101
Johnson-Shull, Lisa, 139

Kail, Harvey, 162, 166–169
Kansas University, 18
Kelly-Riley, Diane, 139
Knight, Melinda, xv, 164, 242

labor, 120–121, 126, 132
laboratory method, 18–19
Lafayette College, 10, 214
Lalicker, William B., 179, 183
Lauer-Glebov, Jacqulyn, 104, 190–191, 202
leadership, xvii, 20–21, 32, 39–40, 43–55, 57–60, 62–67, 72, 74–77, 79–85, 87–89, 91, 95, 98, 108, 114, 119, 124, 139–140, 142–150, 152–153, 167, 169, 192, 197, 199, 205–210, 236, 241
leadership configuration, 40, 43–49, 51–52, 54–55, 60, 64–67, 74–77, 79–80, 83, 85, 87, 91, 98, 119, 124, 140, 142–143, 145–150, 152–153, 192, 197, 199, 205–210, 236, 241
leadership vacuum, 47, 50, 53, 60, 65, 76, 119, 145
lecture, 17
Lerner, Neal, 19, 171, 242
liberal arts, ix, xiv–xvi, 5–7, 9–11, 13–14, 16, 21–23, 25–26, 32–33, 38–41, 48, 67, 69, 95, 111, 115, 117, 124, 130–131, 135–136, 158, 160, 177, 186, 189–192, 195, 197, 203–204, 211, 227, 237–238
Linton, Patricia, 101
literary societies, 16
longitudinal, 117, 189, 192, 196, 198–199, 201
Lunsford, Andrea A., 171

Madigan, Robert, 101
Maid, Barry M., 42
Maimon, Elaine, 238
Marquette University, 166
Martinson, Deborah, xiii, 197–199
Massachusetts Institute of Technology, 164, 179
McDonald, James C., xiii, 49, 158, 237
McLeod, Susan H., xiii, 12, 59, 68–69, 137–138
Middlebury College, 19, 214
mixed methods, xvi, 23, 78, 203
Moon, Gretchen Flesher, xvi, 101, 103, 237
Morehouse College, 10, 214, 238
Morrill Land Grant Act, 9
Mount Holyoke College, 13, 214, 238
Moxley, Joseph M., 68

National Survey of Student Engagement (NSSE), 192, 225
National Writing Centers Association, 80
Neal, Michael, 171, 183, 201
Neff, Joyce Magnotto, 23
Neff, Julie, 157, 167
Nelson, Donna, 185
Newmann, Stephen, 80, 84
No WPA or WCD, 48, 61–62, 65
non-tenure track, 78, 88
Northway, Kara, xv, 160

Occidental College, 191, 195, 197, 214, 231, 234–235
Olson, Gary A., 68
outcomes statement, 99, 102, 196, 208
oversight, 21, 40, 46, 49, 53, 58, 61, 63–64, 70, 72, 144, 146, 152
Oxford University, 9–10

Parascondola, Leo, 120
Payne, John Morton, 19, 120
pedagogy, 12, 15, 17–19, 40, 57, 64, 104, 113, 138, 159, 190, 195, 198, 206, 210; writing center, 18, 61, 162, 164; curriculum-centered, 36–37, 40, 44, 51–52, 56–59, 72, 96, 142, 147; lecture, 17; process-oriented, 110, 206; recitation, 17; WAC-based, 127–128, 164; writing-centered, 57
peer review, 110
peer tutoring, 40, 164, 166–167, 169, 181, 206, 209
Pegg, Bruce, 80, 84
Peterson, Lisa, 77
Phelps, Louise Wetherby, 35, 45, 203
Pomona College, 14, 23, 214
Porter, Tara, xv, 7
portfolio, 52, 58, 77, 80, 91, 96, 103, 137, 152, 178, 184, 196; assessment, 190–192, 201–202; electronic, 200, 202; requirement, 103–104, 123, 190, 200, 218, 225; writing, 199–201
Portland Resolution, 70, 85, 90
pre-tenure, 88–89, 239
Price, Margaret, 200
Princeton University, 9–10
process-oriented pedagogy, 110, 206
program, writing fellows, 37, 45, 51–53, 55, 152, 164–165, 223, 238, 242

qualitative data, 179, 198, 204, 232–233
quantitative data, 40, 77, 160, 189, 196, 204, 232–233

recitation, 17

reflective practice, 168–169
remediation, 159, 161–162, 181
requirements, 21, 38–39, 45–47,
    50, 53–54, 57–59, 62–63, 85,
    87, 89, 95–99, 101, 103–106,
    108–109, 111–112, 114–119,
    121–124, 126–127, 132, 135,
    140, 142–146, 151–152, 178,
    190, 192–193, 196–199, 201,
    205, 207, 218–219, 221, 229
requirements, curricular, 13, 37,
    82, 95–97, 152, 219; embedded,
    39, 96–98, 114, 119, 145, 236;
    explicit, 41, 97, 121, 195, 205;
    mid-level writing, 97, 108–109,
    113–114, 117, 119, 221–222;
    writing across the curriculum, 71,
    121
requirements, writing, 14, 26–27,
    29–32, 37–39, 44, 48, 50,
    52–53, 58–63, 71–72, 85, 87,
    95–99, 101, 103–104, 106–108,
    111–112, 114–119, 121,
    123–124, 130, 137, 139, 140,
    142, 144–145, 147, 150–153,
    184, 193, 195, 197, 206, 218–
    219, 224–225, 228, 233, 236,
    240–241; capstone, x, 87, 96, 98,
    108–109, 114–117, 189, 208,
    218, 221–222; first-year seminar,
    96, 105, 131; portfolio, 103–104,
    123, 190, 200;
research university, German model,
    6, 9, 12, 17; departmentalization,
    13, 18
rhetoric, ix, 6, 10, 12–15, 17–19,
    31, 33, 51, 55–56, 61, 63, 72–73,
    76, 87–89, 98, 106, 120–121,
    126, 128–136, 144, 179, 194,
    203–204; antebellum, 6
rhetoric and composition, 31,
    33, 51, 55–56, 61, 63, 67, 72,
    76, 88–89, 98, 120–121, 126,
    128–129, 132–133, 179, 204
rhetoricals, 16–19, 158
Ritter, Kelly, 170–171, 183
Rose, Shirley, xv, 70, 77–78, 80
Rossen-Knill, Deborah F., 181–182
Royer, Daniel J., 73, 181–183
rubric, 64, 89, 120, 162, 196, 198,
    232–233
Russell, David, 9, 12–13, 17–18,
    101, 147, 238
Rutz, Carol, ix, xiii, xvi, 22, 38,
    104, 138, 190–192, 202, 238

scaffold, 88, 90, 138, 186
Schön, David, 168
Schonberg, Eliana, xv, 160
Schwalm, David, 59, 69, 77
Scott, Fred Newton, 19, 120, 213
Scott, Tony, 120
Severino, Carol, 164, 242
Sharpe, Kenneth, xiii, 157, 169
Sheridan, Harriet, 164, 238
Skeffington, Jillian, xv, 28
Small College Special Interest
    Group, xvi
small college structure of feeling, 5,
    7, 14, 20, 22, 41, 44, 61, 63, 111,
    121, 130, 132, 134, 136–137,
    148, 161, 166–167, 170, 173,
    179, 182–183, 185, 190
Small Liberal Arts College-Writing
    Program Administrators (SLAC-
    WPA), xiii, 25, 27–28, 30, 78,
    211, 228
Smith, Raymond, 109
Solo WPA/WCD, 48, 51–52,
    54–56, 58, 65, 70–75, 78, 124,
    142, 144–150, 152, 193, 197,
    207
Sommers, Nancy, 101, 107, 183
Soven, Margot, xiii, 164

Spelman College, 10, 104, 191, 195, 199–202, 214, 238

Spohrer, Erika, 54, 157, 159

staffing, 37–39, 60, 77, 98–99, 119–128, 158, 163, 165, 206, 217, 241

Strang, Steven, 163–164

Strauss, Anselem, 23, 32

student-centered domain, 37, 49, 52, 55–56, 61, 169

students, ix-x, 8–23, 26, 30, 35, 38–41, 49–54, 56–60, 62–63, 68–69, 72–74, 76, 81, 83, 87, 89, 95–96, 98, 100–118, 121–127, 129–131, 138, 140, 145, 148–149, 151–152, 157–160, 163–167, 169–186, 189–192, 194–202, 205–209, 211, 216, 223–226, 231–234, 236, 238–239, 242; graduate, x-xi, 163–164, 166, 239; international, 170, 181, 186, 195; underprepared, 140, 172, 225, 242

Sullivan, Patricia A., 171, 173

Swarthmore College, xiii, 28, 169, 214

teaching, ix-xi, 9, 11, 19–20, 28, 32, 37–38, 46, 57, 60, 64, 68–72, 76, 80–81, 83–84, 87–89, 100, 102–103, 105–106, 108, 110, 117, 120–122, 125–134, 137–138, 148–149, 159, 162, 164, 166–167, 174–175, 177–178, 185, 190–191, 194, 196, 199, 202, 205–206, 210–211, 220, 222–223, 232, 238–239, 241

temporary faculty, 120, 123

tenure, x, 15, 21, 39, 50, 59–60, 67–68, 77–79, 81–90, 125–126, 149–150, 215–217, 219–220, 239; non-tenure track, 78, 88; pre-tenure, 88–89, 239

tenure track, 85, 125, 149, 220

Tewksbury, Donald G., 8–9, 237

Thaiss, Chris, xv, 7, 29, 117, 240

Thompson, Nancy, 179, 242

Tirabassi, Katherine E., 12–13, 98

Townsend, Martha A., 36, 46, 88, 90, 109, 111, 128, 131

Trachsel, Mary, 164

transfer, 99, 218

triangulation, 32, 96

tutors: development, 62; writing, x, 40, 61–62, 70, 76, 87, 152, 157–158, 160, 162–169, 180, 185–186, 192–193, 200–201, 206, 208–210, 216, 219, 222–224, 242

underprepared students, 140, 172, 225, 242

Union College, 10, 214

United States Supreme Court, 6, 237

University of Calgary, 103

University of Maine, 166

University of Missouri, 111

University of Wisconsin-Madison, 166

Urofsky, Melvin, 11–12, 238

Vassar College, 9, 214, 237–238

Venn diagram, 36–37, 39, 47, 144

Vygotsky, Lev, 168

WAC initiatives, 35, 61, 129

Walvoord, Barbara, 238

Warner, Anne, 199–201

Webster, Daniel, 5–6, 238

Wellesley College, 9, 13, 214, 237–238

White, Edward, 68, 86, 111, 160, 190, 202, 241

Williams, Raymond, 7, 20, 22, 147, 214, 237–238; structure of

feeling, 7, 11, 20, 22, 31, 66, 68,
    81, 84–85, 89, 95, 111, 194–195,
    202, 204, 236
Wingate, Molly, 166
Witte, Stephen P., 35
women's colleges, 9, 26, 238,
    252–253; Bryn Mawr College,
    213; Mount Holyoke College,
    13, 214, 238; Spelman College,
    10, 104, 191, 195, 199–202,
    214, 238; Vassar College, 9, 214,
    237–238; Wellesley College, 9,
    13, 214, 237–238;
workshop, 19, 224
WPA-L, 111, 241
writing: culture of, xvii, 16, 27, 35,
    37–41, 43–46, 49–53, 55–59,
    61–64, 66, 76, 81–83, 89–90, 97,
    101, 106, 111, 131, 146–147,
    149–151, 153, 172, 199, 206,
    209, 226, 236–237; extracurricu-
    lar, 14, 16, 158; instruction, ix,
    xi, xvi-xvii, 16, 18–19, 23, 27, 30,
    33–36, 38–40, 43, 45–46, 50,
    52–53, 56–57, 63, 65–66, 82,
    87, 96–97, 101, 103, 105–109,
    113–114, 116–119, 123, 125,
    128–133, 135–137, 140, 147,
    151–152, 177, 185–186, 189,
    191, 194, 199, 201, 204–210,
    232, 234; process, 100; require-
    ment, 14, 26–27, 29–32, 37–39,
    44, 48, 50, 52–53, 58–63, 71–72,
    85, 87, 95–99, 101, 103–104,
    106–108, 111–112, 114–119,
    121, 123–124, 130, 137,
    139–140, 142, 144–145, 147,
    150–153, 184, 193, 195, 197,
    206, 218–219, 224–225, 228,
    233, 236, 240–241
writing across the curriculum:
    requirements, 71, 121

writing across the curriculum
    (WAC), ix-x, xv, xvii, 7, 19–20,
    27, 31, 35–36, 38–40, 43, 45–46,
    48–52, 54–56, 58–63, 70–71,
    84, 97, 99, 101–103, 108–109,
    111, 114–119, 121, 123–124,
    127–129, 131, 133–134, 136–
    139, 142, 144–145, 149–151,
    159–162, 164–165, 179, 190–
    191, 200–201, 205–206, 208,
    210, 218, 233, 238, 240–241
writing assessment, 31, 64, 66, 70,
    113, 183, 189–195, 198–199,
    201–202, 224, 231, 233–234,
    242; Principles of Effective Writ-
    ing Assessment, 202
writing center, x-xi, xiv-xv, 18–19,
    22–23, 27–29, 31, 33, 35–41,
    45, 47–62, 64–65, 67, 70–72,
    74–76, 77, 79–80, 83–87,
    89–90, 95, 111, 124, 145–146,
    150, 152, 157–170, 178, 181,
    183–186, 192, 195, 197,
    199, 202, 206–208, 215–219,
    222–223, 225–237, 240, 242;
    director, x, xiv, 22, 27–31, 33,
    37, 41, 45, 47–62, 64–65, 67,
    70–81, 83–89, 119, 124, 140,
    142–150, 152, 158–160, 163,
    178, 184, 192–193, 195, 197,
    199, 206–208, 215–216, 219,
    225, 236–237, 240; independent,
    162; pedagogy, 18, 61, 162, 164;
    scholarship, 84, 157, 168, 208;
    studies of, 77; theory, 77
Writing Center Studies, 77
Writing Centers Research Project
    (WCRP), 77–80, 164–165
writing course, 28, 48, 52–54, 70,
    72–73, 76–77, 82, 108, 121, 123,
    126, 142, 178, 184, 192–193,
    198, 216–217, 220, 224–225,

241; mid-level, 108–109,
113–114, 117, 119, 221–222
writing fellows, 37, 45, 51–53, 55,
152, 164–165, 223, 238, 242
writing in the disciplines (WID), ix,
7, 36, 39, 62, 116, 118, 164, 197
writing instruction, ix, xi, xvi-xvii,
16, 18–19, 23, 27, 30, 33–36,
38–40, 43, 45–46, 50, 52–53,
56–57, 63, 65–66, 82, 87, 96–97,
101, 103, 105–109, 113–114,
116–119, 123, 125, 128–133,
135–137, 140, 147, 151–152,
177, 185–186, 189, 191, 194,
199, 201, 204–210, 232, 234;
sites of, xvii, 38, 56, 96, 145, 189,
205, 210
writing intensive, 46, 53, 56, 60,
63–64, 87, 89, 97, 101, 108–109,
112, 151, 164, 221; courses, 60
writing program, ix-xi, xiv-xvii, 13,
21–23, 26–31, 33–36, 38–39,
41–52, 54–67, 69–71, 74–78,
81, 83, 85, 87–90, 95–96,
98–99, 102, 121, 125, 134–135,
138–140, 142, 144, 147–151,
179, 185–186, 189, 194–197,
199, 203–211, 215–219, 223,
225–227, 232, 236–237, 240
Writing Program Administration
Listserv (WPA-L), 111, 241
writing program administrator (WPA), ii, x-xi, 23, 26–31,
33, 36, 38, 41, 43–45, 47–56,
58–59, 61–71, 74, 76–77, 80–83,
85–86, 88–90, 96, 105, 107,
113–114, 116–117, 119, 121,
125, 128–130, 132, 134, 138,
143–145, 148–150, 163, 172,
176–178, 183, 189, 192–195,
197, 203, 205–207, 209–210,
215–216, 219, 225; embedded
WPA, 38, 50–51, 53, 59–60,

62, 74, 76, 86–87, 95, 142–143,
145, 206–207, 236; explicit
WPA, 48–50, 55, 57, 62, 70–72,
74–76, 88, 96, 142–143, 193,
195, 206, 236; literature of, xvii,
36, 43–44, 65, 210; small college
WPA (SLAC-WPA), xiv, 22,
29–30, 33, 39, 41, 43, 47, 52,
54, 67, 70–71, 75–76, 78–80,
131, 137–138, 142, 203, 205,
210–211, 228, 237; work of, xvii,
36–37, 42–46, 69, 72, 137, 184,
210; WPA-L, 35, 68, 111, 241
writing program, development of,
70
writing requirement, 14, 26–27,
29–32, 37–39, 44, 48, 50,
52–53, 58–63, 71–72, 85, 87,
95–99, 101, 103–104, 106–108,
111–112, 114–119, 121,
123–124, 130, 137, 139–140,
142, 144, 145, 147, 150–153,
184, 193, 195, 197, 206,
218–219, 224–225, 228, 233,
236, 240–241; capstone, x, 87,
96, 98, 108–109, 114–117, 189,
208, 218, 221–222
writing rich, 41, 64, 109, 135–136,
190
writing specialist, 62, 83, 127, 131,
233
writing studies, 23, 43, 101, 111,
119, 129, 138, 168
writing-about-literature, 99
writing-about-writing, 99
writing-centered, 57
writing-to-learn, 38, 110
Yale College, 5–6, 9–12, 15, 107,
123, 173, 238; *Yale Report*, 6,
11–12, 15, 107, 123, 173, 238
Yancey, Kathleen Blake, 27, 36, 77
Young Scholars in Writing, 168

About the Authors

Jill M. Gladstein is Associate Professor of English and directs the Writing Associates Program at Swarthmore College, which received a CCCC Writing Program Certificate of Excellence. She is one of the co-founders and the current chair of the Small Liberal Arts College-Writing Program Administrators consortium. As a trained practitioner- researcher in TESOL, Jill explores questions that derive from her experiences in the classroom and as director of a small college writing program.

Photograph of Jill M. Gladstein by Mitchell Gladstein. Used by permission.

She has published on writing centers, writing fellows programs, and writing program administration. Her articles have appeared in *WPA: Writing Program Administration* and *Across the Disciplines*.

Dara Rossman Regaignon is Associate Professor of English and Director of College Writing at Pomona College. She is one of the co-founders of the Small Liberal Arts College-Writing Program Administrators consortium. Originally a Victorianist by training, she has published on nineteenth-century British representations of mothers and paid childcare; writing fellows programs; and writing program administration at small colleges. Her articles have appeared in *Pedagogy*, *WPA: Writing Program Administration*, *WAC Journal*, and *Victorian Literature and Culture*.

Photograph of Dara Rossman Regaignon by John Lucas. Used by permission.

271